AF574603

# Psalms and Slaughter

BOOKS BY
TONY GRAY

NOVELS

*Starting from Tomorrow*
*The Real Professionals*
*Gone the Time*
*Interlude*
(based on an original screenplay by
Lee Langley and Hugh Leonard)
*The Last Laugh*

NON-FICTION

*The Irish Answer*
*The Record Breakers* (with Leo Villa)
*Psalms and Slaughter*

# Psalms and Slaughter

A study in bigotry

Tony Gray

HEINEMANN : LONDON

William Heinemann Ltd
15 Queen Street, Mayfair, London W1X 8BE

LONDON MELBOURNE TORONTO
JOHANNESBURG AUCKLAND
First published 1972

434 30370 4

Printed in Great Britain by
Cox & Wyman Ltd,
London, Fakenham and Reading

For Roland Gant

*'. . . and Cromwell came*
*With psalms and slaughter . . .'*

James Clarence Mangan?
Anon?
Roland Gant?
Any offers?

# Contents

# Contents

# Foreword

There is something of a mystery about the quotation on which the title of this book is based.

A few years ago, when the Rev. Ian Paisley first came into prominence, I mentioned an idea I had about a book on religious bigotry to Roland Gant, Editorial Director of Heinemann. It seemed to me that Ulster was about the last enclave in the civilized world where Christian bigotry of a kind more reminiscent of the seventeenth century than the twentieth still flourished, and I felt that with my own personal background – my mother a Protestant settler from Warrenpoint, Co. Down, with the unmistakably Scottish name of McKee, my father a loyal (to Britain) Dublin Protestant and a survivor of the Dardanelles landing, and myself a poor Protestant with vaguely Republican leanings, brought up in Dublin during the immediate aftermath of the Troubles – I was in a fairly strong position to examine dispassionately this whole question of the delicate relationship between the Prods and the Papishes. After all, the Prods – my people – were the aggressors. Roland was enthusiastic about the idea and came up with a splendid title, *Psalms and Slaughter*. It came, he said, from a James Clarence Mangan poem about Cromwell, which he had picked for the title of a book he himself had at one time been intending to write about Cromwell. He generously made me a present of the title, commissioned me to do this book, and said that we could easily check on the details of the quotation later.

While I was researching the book, it was overtaken by events. I was on holiday in Rapallo in Italy when I heard something about an outbreak of riots in Northern Ireland on Monte Carlo Radio. At the time, what struck me as interesting was that Monte Carlo Radio should lead the news with an item on Ireland, but this I attributed more to the fact that General de Gaulle had recently spent a holiday in Ireland than to any intrinsic importance in the story itself. When, a few days later, I heard another item about Northern Ireland heading the news, this time from an Italian station, I realized that it must be more serious. A copy of the *Daily Mail*, purchased in Laigueglia, had a front page of pictures which might have been taken during the 1916 Rebellion; and I was shaken to the core.

When I got back to England, everybody was talking about the troubles in Ireland, and from the sort of questions I was asked it was quite clear that the book I was working on had suddenly become topical. Unfortunately I had to put it aside for other projects and only now have I been able to return to it; but alas, the subject has lost none of its topicality in the meantime.

When I rang Roland Gant to tell him I was resuming work on the book, he was delighted, but hastily added that he had been unable to find any reference to 'Psalms and Slaughter' in any book by James Clarence Mangan or anyone else, and was beginning to wonder whether it might not in fact be an extract from one of his own early unpublished poems, long since forgotten. Being unable to verify the quotation further, we have left the matter like that, in the hope that using the phrase as a title may spur somebody into recalling how and where it was originally used. It remains a splendid title, wherever it came from.

The questions I had been asked about Ulster on my return from Italy indicated far more than a profound ignorance of what still remains to be settled of the Irish Question; above all they indicated a sheer inability to credit that in this day and age there are still people in the United Kingdom prepared to break one another's heads because they do not, to use the Belfast expression, 'dig with the same foot'.

I hasten to add that I am aware that the troubles in Northern Ireland have social, ethnic, historical, political and, above all, economic origins as well as religious ones. If all of the citizens of Belfast and Derry were as well-heeled as most of the inhabitants of the south-east of England they would find themselves thinking more and more about material possessions and less and less about religion and politics. But there is no doubt that religious bigotry – on the part of the Orange Protestants against the Catholics whom they regard as little better than beasts, for reasons which I hope to explain – was used to fan the flames.

There are people who say that recent events in Northern Ireland were the work of international agitators and were far more a reflection of what had been happening in Paris and Berlin and Chicago than of any aspect either of the religious dispute or of the Irish

Question – and to an extent this could be true. Certainly, the disruptive elements in the fabric of the Ulster society had been there for so long that it would be asking too much to expect anybody to believe that the flash-point occurred when it did, in a year punctuated with carefully manipulated civil disorders, by a purely coincidental process of spontaneous combustion. And Bernadette Devlin has made no secret of the fact that her object is to unite workers – Protestant and Catholic – against their capitalist exploiters, north and south of the border.

But the violence of the feeling aroused had an almost medieval intensity, Torquemada far more than Che Guevara, and this is what made the Northern Ireland disturbances so fascinating. It has, of course, been a feature of religious wars throughout the centuries that men feel morally justified in committing atrocities in the name of religion which they would not dream of committing in the name of economic justice, or for the sake of mere political expediency. I find it curiously fascinating that the essentially non-belligerent Christian message should have been used as an excuse for all the nastier varieties of judicial murder and mayhem by basically well-intentioned men; and this book is a layman's attempt to trace, for other laymen, how all this seems to have come about and how it is that in one small and unimportant corner of what remains of Christendom – unimportant that is, unless you are unlucky enough to live there – the passions which in the past persuaded people to torture, eviscerate and set fire to one another in the name of a faith ostensibly shared by all of them still flourish, fanned by poverty, fear and distrust. To do this, it seemed necessary, initially, to go back to the Reformation, to those disturbances which overtook these islands from the moment when King Henry VIII decided to ignore the Pope and run the English branch of the Church himself. However, as soon as I started work on the book, I discovered that the task was far more complicated than that. I couldn't put Henry VIII's actions into perspective without referring to the events which led to the Reformation in Europe, and I couldn't deal with the Reformation without also going into the circumstances which led up to it. And of course it is impossible to write anything about Ireland unless you are prepared to wade back through the centuries for eight hundred years at least. So I found myself going right back to the beginnings, with the result that the book now includes a brief, but I hope objective, survey of the origin and development of the Christian Church and some of the accretions, innovations, schisms, heresies, reforms and splinter movements which have been such a pronounced feature of the strange history of that remarkable institution.

The remainder of the book attempts to relate what happened after the Reformation in Britain to what has recently been happening in Ulster, though this is in no sense a history of the Ulster Troubles. I am not so much interested in the role of the B Specials, or how many Catholics were rendered homeless, or who threw the first petrol bomb, or whether Bernadette Devlin was really in league with Tariq Ali, as in the fundamental, incredible issue: how did it happen, in the year 1969, the year when Man first set foot on the Moon, that ordinary people in an ordinary society – miniskirts, the Pill, the breathalyser, heart transplants, L.S.D. and all – were still prepared to throw stones and petrol bombs at one another, not for trading with a false God, but for trading with the same one through different channels?

INTRODUCTION

# The Prods and the Papishes

I belong to a generation of people who play golf or clean their cars on Sunday mornings before slipping round to the local, and who believe at best that a man's religion is his own business, or at worst that the whole thing is an outdated bore of no concern to anyone; a generation amused at the slightly comical spectacle of the dignitaries of the main branches of the Christian Church scrambling to repair their differences in order that some at least of them may remain in business; a generation occasionally disturbed perhaps, in the still of the night, at the thought that our children's reluctance to do anything more positive or interesting or purposeful than lurk in the deafening darkness of discotheques and coffee-bars exchanging pills of one sort or another may be due in some slight measure to our own failure or refusal to pass on to them even the faint rudiments of a religious code, but able to convince ourselves, as soon as the sun comes up again, that the whole thing is really the fault of a combination of television, advertising, affluence and various other factors over which we have no control; a generation totally prepossessed with personal possessions and relentlessly preoccupied with the price of things. And to such a generation the fact that as recently as the seventeenth century people were perfectly prepared to be executed, maimed, murdered, mutilated, hanged, burnt and eviscerated for their beliefs (and were) must appear both inexplicable and insane. That these things could have happened in the – relatively – enlightened atmosphere of England a mere three hundred years ago would perhaps be even harder to credit but for our knowledge of the fate of three million Jews at the hands of the German Nazis in our own lifetime. There is not, perhaps, any real parallel, except in the arrogant assumption by a state, or an individual, or a church, that those who do not conform should be either punished or annihilated for their failure, or their inability for racial or any other reasons, to conform. But the fact that this could and did happen in the even more enlightened atmosphere of the twentieth century makes the excesses of the reformers and the counter-reformers seem more credible, if no less monstrous.

But I still found it hard to believe, that morning in Laigueglia, that the Prods and the Papishes were really throwing petrol bombs at each other in Belfast.

In a way it is relatively easy for someone brought up in Ireland in the 1920s and '30s to understand the depth and intensity of the religious bigotry that swept England (and, to a far greater extent, continental Europe) immediately after the Reformation – far easier, anyway, than for somebody reared in the almost aggressively liberal atmosphere of modern Britain, where it is possible to work alongside a man for years without ever discovering his religion, if any.

I was born in Ireland during the Civil War, and went to school at a time when the infant Irish Free State was just beginning to realize that freedom did not in itself provide an instant solution to Ireland's many problems, and that by achieving independence, or at least a measure of it, the Irish Government had merely transferred the Irish Question from England's broad shoulders to its own rather slender ones.

It was a time of continued outbreaks of violence, a time of bitter disillusionment after all the glories of a successful revolution against the greatest Empire the world had ever known, a time when Irish Catholics were particularly thin-skinned and over-sensitive about the few Protestants still left in their midst who, they felt – and rightly, I'm sorry to say, a good deal of the time – were mocking their new state, sneering at their futile attempts to revive the Irish language, and denigrating their feeble efforts to run the country. Of course not all Protestants were so foolish – many of them had been prominent in the literary revival and in the language movement – but it would be idle to deny that there was a hard core of Protestant, pro-British diehards who could see no good in anything Irish. To grow up as a Protestant in this community was to be made acutely aware of religion as a continuing and important facet of everyday life.

I went to a primary school attached to the local branch of the Church of Ireland, St Matthew's, in Irishtown. Irishtown is one of the less salubrious suburbs of Dublin, and it is an interesting reflection on the colonial mentality that Dublin, the capital city of Ireland, should have a district known as Irishtown. Here, in a grisly, grey Victorian building, we studied four Rs – the usual three plus religious instruction – and also, compulsorily, the Irish language. Of the religious instruction we received – it was usually delivered, I remember, by the local rector, whose son was a student at the school – I recall very little beyond a small book with a pale blue cover, called *Roman Claims.* This set out in simple but forceful language the various points on which the teaching of the Church of Rome differed from that of the Church of Ireland (a more democratic, less episcopalian version of the Church of England); and it went on to refute the principal Roman claims, point by point.

I also attended a Sunday-school at which well-intentioned but often fearsomely moustached elderly ladies passed around pictures of the Holy Land, told us garbled versions of stories from the Bible, and continued our indoctrination against our Catholic neighbours, invariably referred to as *Roman* Catholics, or R.C.s. It didn't occur to me then – and it certainly didn't seem to occur to any of those charged with my religious education – that there was anything strange in the fact that this word 'Roman', which for over twenty centuries had represented, in the mind of man, one of the highest peaks ever attained by civilization, should be thus debased and used almost as an insult.

And they would have been horrified if anyone had told them that the survival of the Christian Church during the Dark Ages was due far more to the fact that it was the 'Roman' Church than to any intrinsic indestructibility in the Christian message.

Since, even at this period, the population of the twenty-six counties of the Irish Free State was about 92 per cent Catholic – it is now an almost monolithic 95 per cent – you would not think that there would be much room for schisms within the pathetic 8 per cent remnant of the nation. But in fact the Protestant population of Ireland, and of Dublin particularly, was composed of an astonishing variety of splinter groups. In my own immediate neighbourhood there were both Methodist and Presbyterian churches as well as those of the Church of Ireland; and the relatives to whose homes my family made regular pilgrimages on Sunday afternoons included Quakers, Congregationalists, Unitarians, Plymouth Brethren and Baptists. Also, because the Protestant community was such a small one, and because we were not encouraged by teachers or parents to fraternize with the R.C.s – the vague impression I got as a young child was that they were a light-fingered, unreliable mob much given to cheating and telling lies – we tended to mix with members of the other Protestant sects in a way that rarely happens in England.

When we got a bit older, and the search for fresh supplies of girls took us ever farther afield – though still confining our attentions largely to the Protestant sector of the population – we found ourselves attending Presbyterian and Methodist services as part of the price of seeing some girl home afterwards.

Attendance at the many diverse forms of worship which the courtship of these girls entailed had the effect of destroying any vestige of my own faith which had survived the banalities of the local rector and the inanities of the Sunday-school, with the result that I resolutely refused to be confirmed, soon enlarged the scope of my activities to include Catholics, ultimately married a lapsed Catholic and had two children, neither of whom was even baptized. I confidently expect the same kind of personal immunity from events which occur after my death as I enjoyed – if enjoyed is the word – from all the events which occurred during endless centuries before my birth; and to my mind the greatest mystery of the many surrounding Mother Church is the way in which her employees have conned generations of apparently intelligent men and women into subscribing to all the absurdities and inconsistencies which acceptance of her monstrous dogma entails.

But having said that – and it is necessary, I think, before embarking upon a book of this kind, to state one's own position quite clearly – I must add that I have remained throughout my life fascinated by the effect of this Church on the minds of men. As a reporter on *The Irish Times* during a period when the Catholic hierarchy, far more certain than they now are of the continuing devotion and obedience of the Government and people of Southern Ireland, frequently meddled in political matters, I was in a good position to observe one aspect of this; other aspects emerged from conversations and arguments. What emerged most strongly was that while we Protestants questioned everything until eventually we had succeeded in destroying our own faith, most of the Catholics we met rarely questioned anything. They accepted what went on during the Mass, and what went on in the country as part and parcel of a universal religion which had survived, unchanged and unchanging, throughout the ages, from the time of the Apostles. Although they studied some form of Church history, their ideas on the historical development of the Church were very hazy, as indeed were my own. When I tried to repair the omission by reading up the subject, I soon found that it wasn't all that easy. By their very nature, Church histories tend to be written by men who hold firmly to one version of the faith or another, and are consequently unreliable. Nor was it easy to chart the course of the Church by reading secular histories. Most histories, at any rate until relatively recently, were also written by men who held strong religious views, with the result that they tended to gloss over things discreditable to their own particular branch of the Church, and dwelt at length on things likely to bring discredit on the opposition. Since the Church was intimately involved in almost everything that happened in Europe from the decline of the Roman Empire to the emergence of parliament as a real power in some European countries, all you can do is set one account off against the other, and try to arrive at some conclusion as to what really happened by attempting a synthesis of all the opposing points of view. This I have attempted to do in my summary of the rise and development of the Christian Church in the period between the birth of Christ and the Reformation.

But before delving into the early history of the Church, I want to open the book with a description of Cromwell's activities in Drogheda in 1649, when he rejoiced in the downfall of the Irish in rolling phrases reminiscent of Paisley's first public outpourings. What is interesting about this episode is Cromwell's utter contempt for the Catholic Irish; and I'm sorry to say I do not believe you would have to scratch an Orangeman very hard today to elicit more or less the same reactions.

Cromwell is interesting, too, as a product of the Reformation whose extremely free readings from the Old Testament led him to slaughter Irish peasant men and women in the belief that he was actually exterminating, by the express order of Jehovah, what Hilaire Belloc called 'those unfortunate small tribes with the odd Asiatic names'. Cromwell's attempt to settle the Irish Question once and for all by herding the native Irish into the wild and infertile lands of Connaught, to the west of the River Shannon, and by planting the remainder of the country with loyal and reliable English Protestants, was so disastrous that it must be counted as one of the contributing factors to the current situation.

One widespread belief is that Cromwell's siege of Drogheda represented the ultimate confrontation between, on the one hand, the fined-down, bone-white Puritan, convinced that it was his bounden duty to bring not peace but the sword, and, at his mercy, 3,000 wild, superstitious, priest-ridden Papish wretches, many of them sheltering for sanctuary in the very church where the previous Sunday they had committed what was to him the heinous sin of attending Mass. But it wasn't nearly as simple as that.

For one thing, the 3,000 people whom Cromwell's troops cut down in Drogheda consisted mainly of soldiers of the King – Irish, Anglo-Irish and even English – who had supported the wrong side in the Civil War. It is probably true that they were promised quarter, and that once they had surrendered no quarter was given; and it is also true that there were a number of atrocities involving women and children. But it is altogether wrong to regard it as primarily a religious massacre of civilians. It was a minor engagement in a major war that had already been going on for over a century: the battle for freedom of conscience against both the Divine Right of Kings and the Spiritual Supremacy of the Pope.

Although the popes and the emperors had been struggling with one another for ascendancy ever since that moment in A.D. 800 when Pope Leo III revived the old Roman Empire and hailed Charlemagne as Caesar Augustus, and although the Reformation in England dated from the moment in A.D. 1533 when King Henry VIII decided to ignore the Pope and marry Anne Boleyn without his authority, nevertheless as soon as men started to challenge the authority of the Pope and began to question the Divine Right of Kings it became clear that the kings and the popes (and the bishops) were all really on one and the same side.

Kings and emperors in the past had protected the popes; popes and bishops had instructed their flocks to be obedient to the kings. The kings and the popes and the bishops were alike opposed to such gross presumption on the part of the common man as to dare to judge what was in his own best interests, and they looked with equal anxiety on the development of parliaments which increasingly were taking over the vital business of imposing, collecting and administering taxes, and laying down conditions before advancing money to the monarchy or the Church.

The new man of seventeenth-century England, who was a firm believer in a form of parliamentary democracy, had no time either for pope or for king. He wanted to be free to decide on religious matters according to the dictates of his own conscience, rather than be forced to accept the orthodox dogma of the Church; and he wanted all temporal matters, such as the imposition of taxes, to be removed from the sphere of the kings and the bishops, and placed firmly in the hands of a freely elected assembly of his own peers. This was the great movement in which Cromwell found himself swept along, and over which he contrived to gain control; and the Irish episode was merely a trivial and inconvenient incident, away out of the main stream of events, which occurred partly because the Irish had been agitating, understandably enough, to get their old lands back, and partly because, with their unerring instinct for doing the wrong thing at the wrong time, they had made a treaty with Charles I which was finally concluded only a few days before his execution.

But the depredations of Cromwell had such a profound effect on the racial memory of the Irish Catholics, and the victory in 1690 of King William of Orange over the last Catholic King of England, James II, at the Battle of the Boyne – only a few miles, as it happens, from Drogheda – had such an effect on the Protestants of the north, that this brief period must be taken as sowing the bulk of the seed for the bitter harvest that is now being reaped in Ulster.

After the victory of King William, bigotry steadily diminished and eventually disappeared in England. The present Irish Constitution, while recognizing the special position of the Catholic Church as the religion of the majority, guarantees religious liberty to all and, for the past fifteen years anyway, there has been very little religious bigotry in the Republic – and very little need for it in a population that is so solidly 95 per cent Catholic. But it has persisted through the years in the partitioned-off 'Six Counties' of Northern Ireland (two-thirds Protestant, one-third Catholic, with the Catholics multiplying far faster than the others: a potentially dangerous situation in itself in a province without enough houses or jobs to go round). Most of the time it was kept well under the surface but it used to break through from time to time, particularly in Derry and in Belfast where, throughout what might now be regarded as the peaceable years, the Papishes from the Falls Road and the Prods from the Shankill Road used to fall on one another with solemn regularity every 12 July (the anniversary of the Battle of the Boyne), and where, as I have said, Mr Paisley used to preach the same sort of highly emotive, supercharged, tub-thumping Old Testament sermons so beloved of Oliver Cromwell and his Puritan warriors.

Indeed there is something of the flavour of the old religious tracts of the Cromwellian period in the official toast of the Orange Order, which is still solemnly recited today and which speaks volumes for the antique intransigence and arrogant intolerance of the men of Ulster.

One version of it goes like this:

> To the glorious, pious and immortal memory of King William III who saved us from rogues and roguery, slaves and slavery, knaves and knavery, popes and popery, from brass money and wooden shoes; and whoever denies this toast, may he be slammed, crammed and jammed into the muzzle of the great gun of Athlone, and the gun fired into the Pope's belly, and the Pope into the devil's belly, and the devil into Hell, and the door locked and the key forever in an Orangeman's pocket.

Between my first chapter, which consists of an account of the siege of Drogheda, and the book proper, I have, as already mentioned, interposed a section in which I have attempted to abstract, from a wide variety of standard histories, what seemed to me a reasonably coherent and objective account of the development of the Church from the time of Christ to the time of the Reformation. There is no new material here, and most of my sources are available to anyone in the nearest public library. What I have tried to do is to keep the narrative clear and uncluttered and concerned only with the Church, or with historical movements, such as the Crusades, in which the Church was deeply involved. I have kept all other matters to the irreducible minimum necessary to explain the various economic or military or sociological forces acting on the Church at any given time.

I apologize to readers who feel that I seem to be spelling out facts that are already well known, but it seemed to me to be wiser to skim back over the whole ground – albeit necessarily in a very brief and sketchy way – as a reminder of matters which the average lay reader tends to encounter vary rarely after he leaves school, and sometimes not all that fully at school.

CHAPTER ONE

# The Curse of Cromwell

## 1

They [the Irish] are the very offal of men, dregs of mankind, reproach of Christendom, the bots that crawl on the beast's tail. I wonder Rome itself is not ashamed of them.

I beg upon my hands and knees that the expedition against them may be undertaken whilst the hands and hearts of our soldiery are hot. To whom I will be bold to say briefly: Happy is he who shall reward them as they have served us; and cursed is he who shall do the work of the Lord negligently. Cursed be he that holdeth back his sword from blood; yes, cursed be he that maketh not his sword stark drunk with Irish blood, that maketh them not heaps on heaps, and their country a dwelling place for dragons, an astonishment to nations.

This extract from a political pamphlet published in 1647* gives a fair indication of the frame of mind in which Cromwell and his warriors set sail for Ireland to quell the rebellion there. There is no evidence that this pamphlet or any of the many others in similar vein were distributed among the soldiers of the expeditionary forces before their departure, but there is no doubt that, as they waited to join the ships that were to take them to Ireland, preachers moved among the troops, working on their prejudices, preparing them for this 'crusade' against the godless Irish rebels. Cromwell's troops heard themselves compared to the Israelites proceeding to extirpate the idolatrous inhabitants of Canaan, and described as the chosen instruments by which Heaven was to overthrow the empire of Babylon and establish a new Jerusalem. Cromwell himself more than once reminded his soldiers that no mercy should be shown to the Irish but that they should be dealt with as the Canaanites had been dealt with in the time of Joshua. He had found during the Civil War, in the far more tricky

* *The Simple Cobbler of Aggavam in America* by Theodore de La Guard, London 1647, quoted in O'Connell's *Memories of Ireland* (p. 404) and in Denis Murphy's *Cromwell in Ireland* (p. 44).

matter of inciting English troops to make war on their fellow countrymen, that bloodthirsty sentiments and exhortations to violence were more acceptable to the troops – as they were to Cromwell himself – if allegorically dressed up in the extravagant imagery of the Old Testament.

The preparations for the expedition to Ireland had been going on for several months. Early in 1649, Cromwell was appointed Lord-Lieutenant of Ireland and Commander-in-Chief of the Forces. A squadron of ships was to be at hand, off the Irish coast, and a hospital for sick and maimed soldiers was to be set up in Dublin.

At the very last moment, the departure of the expedition was delayed by a curious outbreak of religious fervour within the ranks of the troops. A sect known as the Levellers had made their first appearance near Cobham, in Surrey, some time earlier; there were about thirty of them, followers of an ex-army man called Everard who called himself their prophet and who foretold that they would shortly number four thousand. They occupied themselves harmlessly enough by digging up the earth and planting it with crops, because Everard had been instructed in a vision, he claimed, to do this; his destiny was to restore creation to its former unspoilt state, in which men everywhere would be able to enjoy the fruits of the earth in peace.

On the night of 26 April a section of the army – not detailed for service in Ireland – became suddenly infected with a fresh outbreak of this strange faith, and refused to accept orders. Cromwell and Fairfax hurried to the scene of the mutiny, arrested and tried fifteen men, sentenced five of them to be shot, but executed only one of them, a young man called Lockyer. As often happens in these cases, his death, so far from squashing the sedition, caused it to spread, with the result that a whole series of mutinies of one sort or another, all loosely connected with the Levellers and Lockyer's death, broke out in several of the regiments destined for Ireland. Parliament left the matter to the Generals to deal with as they thought fit, and Fairfax and Cromwell caught up with the main body of the rebels at Burford, in Oxfordshire. The mutineers defended themselves for a time, but eventually surrendered. Fairfax summoned a court martial which decided that one man in ten out of the four hundred who had surrendered should be shot, but after three of them had been dispatched, the rest were pardoned, restored to their regiments, and marched cheerfully off to serve in Ireland.

The matter is of little importance except to demonstrate what curious cul-de-sacs of Christianity the Reformation had opened up in the ranks of the faithful.

By 5 June 1649, the Council of State had given orders for the regiments to march to their embarkation ports.

Two days earlier, Cromwell had begun his journey to Ireland, by way of Windsor and Bristol. He travelled in a coach drawn by six Flanders mares, accompanied by a number of his officers, also travelling by coach, and escorted by a life-guard of eighty men. By 14 July he had reached Bristol where he spent about a month travelling around, inspecting troops awaiting embarkation, being visited by his wife and family, and showing no great keenness to leave English soil.

The same reluctance to quit Britain had already been shown by some units of his troops. The news from Ireland that the Marquis of Ormonde was approaching Dublin at the head of an army of 30,000 Royalist and rebel troops dampened the ardour of some of the Parliament's soldiers. One regiment refused to embark and disbanded themselves. Another mutinied at Minehead and many of the men deserted. At Bristol a whole battalion refused to embark until Cromwell himself appeared among them and gave them courage.

The news then arrived from Dublin that Colonel Michael Jones, Governor of the City, had routed Ormonde's Royalists at Rathmines, and spirits rose. On Monday, 13 August, Cromwell set sail with the vanguard of his army in thirty-two ships and, after a thoroughly unpleasant crossing, arrived at Ringsend, near Dublin, two days later.

The Division under Colonel Jones, in the Dublin area, and the regiments under General Monk in the north, were also to be under Cromwell's command, which meant that his entire forces would amount to over 17,000 men, most of them well-trained and fighting fit. He had, in addition, several pieces of artillery, ample military stores and a sum of about £200,000 in cash.

Two years earlier, soon after Dublin had been surrendered by Ormonde, Charles's Lord-Lieutenant, to the Parliamentary forces, Jones had ordered all Catholics out of Dublin and had forbidden them to return, under severe penalties. In fact it was quite impossible to enforce such a law in the capital city of a predominantly Catholic country, and, throughout the period, Catholics remained in Dublin. This order was now renewed with a rider stating that any person giving shelter to a priest or a Jesuit, even for a single hour, would forfeit his property.

While he was in Dublin, Cromwell stayed in a house at the corner of Castle Street, and stabled the horses of his troopers in St Patrick's Cathedral, as an indication that he had every bit as much contempt for the episcopalian Church of Ireland and its fripperies as he held for the pomp and panoply of the Papists.

On 1 September, after a few days' rest to recover from the sea voyage, Cromwell set out for Drogheda.

## 2

From the 15,000 men who attended a general muster in Dublin on 31 August, he chose 10,000 'stout, resolute men for the present service', crossed the Liffey at their head, and began the march north, taking the main road through Swords (what is nowadays known as the airport road) and Balbriggan. On the way, his soldiers pulled down an ancient cross and fought off a few scattered attacks by Irish guerrilla forces, while Sir George Ayscue's ships sailed up the coast to attend the army on its march, and then went on ahead to seal off the harbour of Drogheda, to prevent reinforcements from reaching the Royalist garrison by sea.

Drogheda is a walled town on the estuary of the Boyne River, about thirty miles to the north of Dublin. It was held to be vitally important, both as a key garrison on the route between Dublin and northern Ireland and as a seaport convenient to the British coast.

Ormonde, the commander of the Royalist forces, had already decided that it must be defended. He had ordered that its fortifications should be repaired, that provisions and ammunition be laid in for a long siege, if necessary, and that all disaffected and suspect persons be put outside the walls. He had decided not to stay with the garrison himself, as he wanted to be free to move around giving orders to the other Royalist troops. Despite Ormonde's instructions, supplies had been slow to arrive, and the garrison was quite unprepared for a long siege when the attack came. Notably, they were short of armaments.

Drogheda was manned by 2,221 foot-soldiers and 320 horsemen, most of them Irish Catholics, under Sir Arthur Aston, a member of an old Cheshire Catholic family; Aston himself had fought at Edgehill. The city was enclosed within a continuous wall, about a mile and a half around its perimeter; this wall, about twenty feet in height, varied in thickness between four and six feet, and had about nine gates. Sections of the wall are still in existence.

On the night of 2 September the first of Cromwell's horsemen were camping within two miles of the town. By the afternoon of the following day, the main part of the army of 10,000 had appeared and were taking up their positions on all the vantage points around the town. Next they began to move their batteries into position, a task which took some time since many of the heavier guns had been transported to Drogheda by sea, and had first to be unloaded from the ships.

While Cromwell's men were getting the heavy guns into position, the Royalist troops made a few sallies from the city, shots were exchanged, and there were casualties on both sides.

It was Monday, 9 September, before the big guns were ready to begin to batter down the walls of Drogheda. Before opening fire, Cromwell addressed himself to Aston.

> Dear Sir,
>
> Having brought the army belonging to the Parliament of England before this place, to reduce it to obedience, to the end effusion of blood may be prevented, I thought fit to summon you to deliver the same into my hands to their use. If this be refused, you will have no cause to blame me. I expect you to answer, and rest
>
> Your servant,
> O. Cromwell.

As there was no answer to this courteous summons, Cromwell hauled down the white flag that flew over his quarters, ran up the red ensign, and ordered his batteries to open fire. They succeeded in knocking down the steeple of one church, and a tower that stood on the south-eastern angle of the wall, but night fell before further destruction could be achieved.

On the following day, the batteries managed to open a couple of sizeable breaches in the east and south walls of the town, and Cromwell sent in a first wave of about 800 men. The defenders fought gallantly, Cromwell's men were repulsed, and their commander, Captain Castle, was killed.

A second wave went in, to be similarly repulsed, then Cromwell himself led a third wave through one of the breaches, just as it was beginning to get dark. Inspired by Cromwell's leadership the soldiers managed to force Aston back on to his inner lines, demolished these in turn, and before nightfall, had taken the town.

There is some confusion as to whether quarter was offered and, if so, by whom; the general consensus of opinion appears to be that quarter *was* offered to the garrison if they agreed to surrender. According to Ormonde, Cromwell's officers and soldiers promised quarter to all those who laid down their arms, and kept this promise for as long as any of the garrison held out, as an encouragement to the others to surrender. Then as soon as they had the garrison at their mercy, the word 'no quarter' went round and the soldiers were obliged, often against their will, to kill their defenceless prisoners. Ludlow says that Cromwell himself had given positive orders that no quarter was to be given to any soldier. A contemporary author called Cambrensis Eversus says that Cromwell could not take the town until its defenders had received a promise from some persons of high military rank that their lives would be safe if they surrendered. According to Echard's *History of England*, Cromwell issued an order that the life of neither man, woman nor child would be spared, and when one of his officers pleaded for mercy for an unresisting victim, said that 'he would sacrifice their souls to the ghosts of the English they had massacred'.

In any event, whether quarter was promised or not, there doesn't seem to be much doubt that at least 3,000 people were massacred in Drogheda that night and during the following days. Cromwell, in one of his many letters to Parliament, accepts full responsibility: '. . . our men, getting up to them, were ordered by me to put them all to the sword. And indeed, being in the heat of the action, I forbade them to spare any that were in arms in the town; and I think that night they put to the sword about 2,000 men.'

Sir Arthur Aston was among the first who fell – and one of the most gruesome aspects of the whole episode was a dispute which broke out among the soldiers over poor Aston's artificial leg, which was supposed to be full of gold. According to an account of the affair by the Oxford historian, Anthony à Wood, the soldiers wrenched his wooden leg from him as he fell, believing that this was where he hid his gold; but finding nothing in it, they used it to beat out his brains, and then hacked his body to pieces. Ludlow also has an account of this incident and adds that it transpired that Aston carried his gold – some two hundred pieces – in his girdle.

Let Cromwell himself take up the narrative again:

> Divers of the officers and soldiers being fled over the bridge into the other part of the town, where about a hundred of them possessed St Peter's church steeple, some the West Gate, others a strong round tower next to the gate called St Sunday's. These being summoned to yield to mercy, refused, whereupon I ordered the steeple of St Peter's church to be fired, when one of them was heard to say in the midst of the flames, 'God damn me, God confound me, I burn, I burn.'

Those who rushed out of the church to avoid the flames were immediately hacked down. There was only one survivor: a soldier who leaped from the tower and miraculously suffered no more than a broken leg. Cromwell's soldiers, on an impulse, decided to spare his life, 'for the extraordinariness of the thing'.

The next day, two other towers in which a few stragglers were still holding out were summoned, but having seen what had happened to their comrades in arms, the men refused at first to yield. Later, when hunger forced them to submit, 'the officers were knocked on the head, and every tenth man of the soldiers killed, and the rest shipped off for the Barbadoes' (Cromwell's own words again).

## 3

One of the English soldiers who took part in the siege was Thomas, eldest brother of the Oxford historian Anthony à Wood, whom I have quoted above. He had been a captain in Colonel Ingoldsby's troop, and during the winter of 1649, the year of the siege, he returned to Oxford to take up his studies again. While he was there he told his family some of the terrible things he had seen at Drogheda, and these were written down by his brother Anthony, who says that Thomas told them that 'three thousand at least, besides some women and children, were after the assailants had taken part, and afterwards all, the town, put to the sword on the 11th and 12th of September 1649. At which time Sir Arthur Aston, the governor, had his brains beat out, and his body hacked to pieces.' He told them that when the soldiers were to make their way up to the lofts and galleries in the church, and up to the tower where the enemy had fled, some of the assailants would take up a child and use it as a buckler of defence when they ascended the steps, to keep themselves from being shot or brained.

> After they had killed all in the church they went into the vaults underneath, where all the flower and choicest of the women and ladies had hid themselves. One of these, a most handsome virgin, arrayed in gorgeous and costly apparel, kneeled down to Thomas à Wood, with tears and prayers, to save her life; and being struck with a profound pity, he took her under his arm, and went with her out of the church, intending to put her over the works to shift for herself. But a soldier, perceiving his intentions, ran his sword up her fundament. Whereupon, à Wood seeing her gasping, took away her money and jewels, and flung her down over the works.

The fact that Thomas à Wood did not attempt to gloss over his own contemptible behaviour in taking the poor woman's money and jewels before flinging her body over the ramparts might dispose one to accept the remainder of his testimony as truthful, though in all conscience these were tough times, and there was not much point in pretending that he had left the money and the jewels on the corpse for some other soldier to loot. The suggestion that Cromwell's soldiers snatched up young children and used them as shields is familiar atrocity – propaganda material, though it may well have been true, since the Puritan soldiers regarded Catholic children as no better than wild beasts. And the account seems to tally in its general tone with the flavour of Cromwell's own terse dispatches.

On the fate of the miserable wretches caught sheltering in the church, Cromwell had this to say: 'It is remarkable that these people at the first, set up the Mass in some places of the town that had been monasteries, and afterwards grew so insolent, that the last Lord's day before the storm, the Protestants were thrust out of the great church called St Peter's, and they had a public Mass there, and in this very place, nearly 1,000 of them were put to the sword, fleeing thither for their safety.'

He is equally laconic about the fate of those members of the Catholic clergy unlucky enough to be caught inside the walls of Drogheda: 'I believe all their friars were knocked on the head promiscuously but two; the one was Father Peter Taaffe, brother to Lord Taaffe, whom the soldiers took next day and made an end of. The other was taken in the round tower, under the repute of a lieutenant; and when he understood that the officers in that tower had no quarter, he confessed he was a friar, but that did not save him.'

In *Cromwell in Ireland*, a book from which I have drawn heavily for the material in this chapter, Denis Murphy refers to a manuscript history of these events, written at the time by a Jesuit priest employed on the Irish Mission, which is still preserved in the archives of the Irish College in Rome. This gives details of the fate of certain other priests at the hands of the Puritan troops: He writes:

> The blood of the Catholics was mercilessly shed in the street, in the dwelling-houses and in the open fields. To none was mercy shown; not the women, nor to the aged, nor to the young. The property of the citizens became the prey of the Parliamentary troops. Everything in our residence was plundered; the library, the sacred chalices, of which there were many of great value, as well as all the furniture, sacred and profane, were destroyed.

According to this account the Parliamentary troops discovered a Jesuit called John Bathe, and his brother, a secular priest, in the ruins of the city. They were taken to the market place, tied to stakes and shot. An old and ailing priest was, the Jesuit claims, dragged from his sickbed by the soldiers, trailed along the ground, knocking against every obstacle in his way; beaten with clubs and thrown on the side of the road. He was afterwards rescued and concealed by Catholics, but died a few days later.

Two Dominican Fathers were taken outside the walls of Drogheda, and put to death in the presence of the Army. For five days the massacre continued. According to Clarendon, 'the whole army executed all manner of cruelty, and put every man that belonged to the garrison, and all the citizens who were Irish, men, women and child, to the sword'. This doesn't exactly support the suggestion made by the Jesuit that there were still Catholics in Drogheda in a position to offer refuge to the injured priest, but possibly they crept back into the city from the surrounding countryside. According to most accounts of the siege, only about thirty of the inhabitants of Drogheda survived, and they were shipped off to the West Indies to be sold as slaves to the planters.

Cromwell's own losses were trifling – according to one report to Parliament, no more than sixty-four men and two officers – and Cromwell was extremely pleased at the success of his mission.

> I am persuaded [he told Parliament] that this is a righteous judgement of God upon these barbarous wretches, who have imbued their hands in so much innocent blood, and that it will tend to prevent the effusion of blood for the future, which are satisfactory grounds of such actions, which otherwise cannot but work remorse and regret . . . That which caused your men to storm so courageously, it was the spirit of God, who gave your men courage and took it away again; and gave the enemy courage and took it away again; and gave your men courage again, and therewith this happy success. And therefore it is good that God alone have all the glory.

And writing to the President of the Council of State, he said: 'This hath been a marvellous great mercy . . . I wish that all honest hearts may give the glory to God alone, to whom indeed, the praise of this mercy belongs.'

The first of November was observed by order of Parliament as a general day of thanksgiving for the fact that 'it had pleased God to bless the endeavours of the forces of the Commonwealth and their adherents at Drogheda'.

CHAPTER TWO

# The Early Christians and Their Church

## 1

That the Lord of Hosts who, to Cromwell's way of thinking, so gloried in his endeavours at Drogheda, and to whom he gave such fulsome thanks for his victory, was precisely the same God to whom his wretched victims had been praying, after their own fashion, when his soldiers cut them down, probably occurred neither to Cromwell nor to them. And it is highly unlikely that a great many of the people who at that period of time were quite prepared to kill or be killed for their own particular brand of Christianity ever thought very much about how it all started or the circumstances which led to its proliferation in so many and such diverse forms.

For nearly 1,500 years before the birth of Christ, the Jews had been worshipping a single, invisible God with whom they believed Abraham had made a bargain which would ultimately give them predominance on the earth, and from whom, they further believed, Moses had received a list of instructions by which they were to live their lives. Because of this private arrangement with God, the Jewish people, a Semitic race who had escaped out of slavery in Egypt, regarded themselves, despite the many vicissitudes they had already suffered, as God's Chosen People. Many of the rules and regulations which made up their religion were concerned with matters of hygiene, an important consideration for people living a largely nomadic life in a hot climate, but the Ten Commandments which God, they claim, dictated to Moses on Mount Sinai provided the framework for a complete code of conduct and became the basis both for Christianity and for Islam, two religions which between them have comprised the professed belief of almost half of the human race for over a thousand years.

Judaism, as the religion of the Jews was called, was tolerated by the Romans whose formidable Empire had reached the zenith of its powers during the time of Christ and whose legions then dominated western Europe, the Near East and the northern coast of Africa.

Religion in the Roman Empire was a pretty flexible business. The old state religion of Rome had entailed the worship of a wide variety of gods and goddesses, many of them borrowed from the civilizations of Alexandria, Athens and Carthage, and most of them honoured by their own statues, temples and public holidays. These traditional deities were constantly being augmented with fresh gods taken over along with newly conquered tribes. In addition, the Roman emperors might also become gods when they died – and indeed, from the second century onwards, while still alive. In point of fact, only lip-service to the divinity of any of these gods was ever normally required: most Roman citizens enjoyed considerable liberty of conscience, and since things were pretty good for them in this world, they did not worry overmuch about the world to come.

For a people fundamentally rational in their approach, they were, however, curiously superstitious, and religious rites were quite common which were designed to divine the future from an examination of the state of a slaughtered animal's entrails. But in general, the Romans were tolerant enough. And although the Jews, living on the eastern boundary of their Empire, were harassed from time to time, they were usually permitted to practise their faith in peace, despite the fact that their religion prevented them from paying even the customary lip-service to the Roman gods. Their first Commandment ruled out any toleration of the pantheon of mixed gods which the Romans had on offer; and even if a way round this could have been found, these gods almost all clearly involved graven images, so their worship was forbidden under the Jewish second Commandment as well.

So the Jews, who had started to codify their religion in that collection of prophetic, historical, theological and poetic writings we know now as the Old Testament while in captivity in Babylon around 600 B.C., formed a unique community on the fringe of the Roman Empire. They worshipped a God who was just, invisible, universal throughout the earth, and required neither image nor temple. They had been chosen specifically, they believed, to restore Solomon's ancient capital of Jerusalem and make it the capital of the world. But, even from the first, there was an element of mysticism in their religion and it was clear that in certain circumstances Jerusalem might be regarded largely as a nominal capital; and that the real centre and heart of their religion was their book, the Word of God. They also put great store on the teaching of their Prophets, self-licensed interpreters of the laws, and self-appointed preachers of social reform. Another vital feature of their faith was the belief that one day a Messiah, a sort of super-prophet, would come to earth to lead them all to their final inheritance.

The discovery of the Dead Sea Scrolls – a set of documents written by a Jewish sect in the first century A.D. – and the investigations which are still going on at Qumran, Masada, where a whole Hebrew community exterminated itself rather than surrender to the Romans, seem to indicate that the Jewish religion around this period was by no means the solid, settled organization it has since become. On the contrary, it was a seething hotbed of ideas and controversies disputing even such fundamental questions as that of survival after death. One of these sects, the Essenes of Qumran, were awaiting the imminent arrival not of one Messiah but of two – a religious leader and a temporal leader. Some of the sects believed in the concept of angels; others that there was an inherent virtue in celibacy, a point of view directly opposed to traditional Jewish mainstream thought.

In the context of all this turbulence, the origin and development of the Christian Church becomes perhaps a little easier to understand.

## 2

For all the influence that he has had upon the world, very little is known historically about Jesus of Nazareth, known as Jesus Christ. Indeed, throughout history there have always been people who argued that he never existed. There is not, of course, a single word of independent evidence to prove that he did, and the earliest non-Christian reference to the religion, by Tacitus, did not occur until A.D. 64, about thirty years after Christ's execution.

And, to digress for a moment, the Christian writings are not only by their nature suspect, but they are also staggeringly inconsistent, inconsistent to an extent which we – who took it for granted, in childhood, that they all covered broadly the same period of Christ's life and agreed in principle on all the main issues – find it hard to credit.

Only one of the gospels (St John's) specifically mentions the divinity of Christ. Yet although it deals in far more detail than the others with the vital ritual of the Eucharist, it omits mentioning (highly important, surely) that, during the Last Supper, Christ enjoined his disciples to carry on this tradition of taking bread and wine as a symbol of his body and blood. The Virgin Birth is not mentioned at all in Mark and John, and quite inconsistent versions appear in Matthew and Luke (Mary has a visitation in the one, Joseph a dream in the other). Matthew has the Holy Family living in Bethlehem. Luke puts them in Nazareth but, in order to fulfil the Jewish prophecy that the Messiah would be born in Bethlehem, adopts the elaborate and unlikely device of the Census. Unbelievably, the other two Gospels do not mention Christ's birth or childhood, but pick him up in the middle of his ministry. The Gospels are full of similar inconsistencies.

However, whether Christ existed or not, and whether, if he did exist, he ever reappeared to his disciples after his death in any genuinely corporeal form, there is no doubt that his disciples and followers fervently believed that he did. And since the trials and tribulations with which this book is concerned grew out of their teachings and writings, it seems simpler at this stage to accept that the main facts about Jesus of Nazareth are, broadly speaking, those set out in the synoptic gospels.

Thus, he appears to have been a young Jewish teacher, perhaps the son of a carpenter who lived somewhere near Lake Galilee. He began to preach in the synagogues, after the fashion of the prophets of the period, and later, when he had gathered around him a band of followers, he claimed to be the long-awaited Messiah (or Christ – the words are synonymous) of the Jews. He was neither the first – nor indeed the last – to do so, but for some reason, probably not unconnected with the force of his own personality or that of some or all of his twelve disciples, his claim was widely accepted, and the movement he started spread, within a few centuries, all over the known world and set up its headquarters in the city of Rome towards the twilight of the Roman Empire.

When, during a ministry that lasted barely three years, the tenor of Christ's pronouncements began to change from those of a typical Hebrew prophet-reformer to something far more revolutionary and disturbing to traditional Jewish thought, the Jewish authorities in Jerusalem began to watch him very closely. Not only was he claiming to be the Messiah – which was a blasphemy in the eyes of many orthodox Jews, particularly if the claimant appeared unacceptable – but he was also claiming to be the son of God, and in this capacity was offering wholesale entrance to the Kingdom of Heaven on terms which struck at the very roots of the exclusiveness which had previously held the Jews together. They had, as we have seen, always regarded themselves as the Chosen People, privileged in that a covenant on their behalf had been negotiated with God by their forefather, Abraham. Jesus was now preaching that God did not make any bargains, and was welcoming all comers, including heathens and sinners, into the fold. All advantages of privilege, patriotism, family pride, private wealth and personal precedence were being swept away in what amounted to a blanket offer of salvation in return for faith in the divinity of his own person. This, the Jewish religious leaders felt, could not be tolerated.

Jesus was arrested by the Temple guard and taken first to a private house for cross-examination, and finally tried by the Sanhedrin, the supreme court of Jerusalem. There is some confusion in the gospels about the sequence of events, but there doesn't seem to be much doubt that when asked specifically whether he claimed to be the Messiah, Jesus admitted that he did, and was thereupon unanimously sentenced to death for blasphemy.

As the Roman laws did not allow the Jews to carry out capital sentences, the matter had to be referred to the Roman Governor, Pontius Pilate, to whom Jesus Christ was represented as a political agitator trying to set up a new kingdom within the Roman Empire. Pilate seemed satisfied that Jesus constituted no real political danger and did his best to avoid the necessity of executing him; but in the end, to keep the Jews quiet, he ordered his soldiers to carry out the sentence. Jesus was thirty-three years of age when he was crucified on a hill outside Jerusalem.

When, after his death, the word began to spread that he had risen again from the dead and had reappeared to his disciples, they found themselves in a unique missionary position. The religion they preached had all the well-tried common-sense and time-tested logic of Judaism behind it; but because Christ had preached that anyone, regardless of race or former religion, could become a follower of his, Christianity offered a universality and a unity which no other religion until then had enjoyed. The life of Jesus and the simple parables he had preached held an instant appeal for the simple-minded. Much of the additional material he had tacked on to the basic Judaic code – some of it, for all we know, derived from the views of the Essenes and the other Jewish breakaway sects – was exactly the sort of philosophy likely to appeal to oppressed minorities in tough times. He had predicted that the meek would inherit the earth, and time and again had assured his listeners that those who were short on material comforts in this world would, if they tried to live honest and decent lives, get their just rewards in the next. Finally, the disciples had the nucleus of a religion that was based on a personality cult. In place of the cold, remote and invisible Jehovah of the Jews, they were able to offer a warm and human central figure, affectionately remembered by them; a man who was the son of God, but was also God; a Messiah who had come to the earth and had been rejected and killed, but had conquered death and had reappeared briefly as evidence of his future intentions; a Messiah who would return again, this time in glory, to reward the faithful. This event, most of them believed, would occur within their own life-span.

Christ had also, on the night before his execution – which he foretold in accurate if symbolic detail – handed on to his disciples a powerful piece of highly emotive ritual. Taking supper with them for the last time, he spoke of the bread and the wine in terms of his own body and blood and requested them in the future to take bread and wine in remembrance of him and of this occasion. And whether you take this ceremony in a symbolical sense, as the Anglicans do, or in the light of the continuing miracle of transubstantiation, as Catholics do, there is no doubt that it gives the whole religion a highly dramatic focal point.

The twelve disciples, all from the Galilee district (or rather eleven of the original twelve, plus Matthias who was chosen as a replacement for the faithless Judas Iscariot who had betrayed his master) were not left in much doubt as to which of them was to be Christ's successor.

'Thou art Peter,' Christ once said to Peter, according to St Matthew's Gospel (the incident is not referred to in any of the others), 'and upon this rock I will build my church; and the gates of hell shall not prevail against it. And I will give unto thee [Peter] the keys of the kingdom of heaven: and whatever thou shalt bind on earth shall be bound in heaven: and whatsoever thou shalt loose on earth, shall be loosed in heaven.'

If these words are accepted as accurate – and it seems illogical to accept some of the words of the New Testament and balk at others, though many of the details exclusively reported by Matthew are regarded by some scholars as tendentious – there doesn't seem to be much doubt that Jesus was promising heaven's endorsement for whatever Peter might feel it was necessary to do in order to keep the Christian faith alive. Whether this authorization also included an implicit authority to Peter to pass this mandate on to his heirs and successors for ever is far more debatable. Catholics hold that it did, and upon it base their whole argument for papal supremacy and their justification for most of the subsequent accretions to the Christian message. Later, when men learnt to question the Church on matters of dogma, this became a great bone of contention, more especially since in the early days St Peter's successors were elected in the most haphazard fashion and often only after endless disputes which frequently resulted in two or more rival claimants to the Keys of the Kingdom of Heaven.

## 3

Initially the Christian missionaries operated mainly through the synagogues in the Near East, and the first Christians were almost all Jewish. Later, using the roads and shipping lanes provided by the Roman administration, they travelled farther afield, extending the scope of their mission to include an ever-widening cross-section of the population of the Roman Empire and gravitating, as everyone with ideas in those days tended to do, towards Rome itself. It is possible that some of the Roman legionaries posted in the Near East picked up the religion and carried it back with them to Rome; it is certain that not many years after Christ's death, itinerant preachers were spreading the gospel at street corners in Rome, where there was always a ready audience for a novel idea or a new point of view.

Some of the ideas in this new Christian religion were not altogether novel to the Romans either. The idea that there was only one true God, though it seemed poles away from the Roman system of incorporating the gods and goddesses of all the races they had conquered into their own vague faith, had nevertheless a parallel: if, as happened, one god could be known by various different names in his different aspects, then perhaps all the gods might similarly represent merely separate aspects of one basic, universal god. During the periods when conquests of people of similar social and religious habits had been going on – when one Sumerian city-state was being engulfed by another, for example – religious clashes could always be avoided by merging religions and fusing gods; and the priests could be prevailed upon to preach that they were all really the same god, under different names. As it happened, this purely opportunist tactic to some extent prepared men's minds for the Hebrew idea of one, invisible, universal God who embraced all the others.

The idea of immortality was not all that new either. Religious life in ancient Egypt had focused on the desire for immortality, and naturally when Egypt succumbed to foreign conquerors and life in this world became less sweet, the craving for a more satisfactory life in the next one intensified, and the emphasis on this aspect of the Egyptian faith was increasingly stressed.

Even the Christian idea of the Trinity – three persons in the one God: Father, Son and Holy Ghost – was not entirely new to the Romans. When, after the Greek conquest, Alexandria became the centre of the religious life of the Hellenic World, a curious Trinity of gods was worshipped in the Serapeum set up by Ptolemy I. This consisted of Serapis (a rechristened version of the old Egyptian god of the harvest, Osiris, also incorporating another later god, a sacred bull called Apis); the goddess Isis, who bore Osiris a child who in turn became regenerated as Osiris again; and the child in question, who was called Horus. The temples of Serapis were imported from Alexandria to Rome and followed the Roman legions all over the Empire, even as far as Britain, so that although the persons of the Christian Trinity bore no resemblance at all to this curious amalgam of pagan deities, Serapis, Isis and Horus, at least the Romans were accustomed to the idea of a threefold deity.

Other elements which found their way into the Christian faith were already familiar to the Romans, from other, earlier religions. One of these was Mithraism, a faith of Persian origin with a ritual involving a sacred and perpetually bleeding bull, whose blood washed away the sins of the world. Other features of Mithraism included a miraculous birth, a baptismal ceremony, a sacramental meal and Sunday as a day of worship. Mithraism also employed celibate priests and this may have been one source of the fixation with celibacy among certain sections of the Christian Church, though it wasn't until the eleventh century that this became the rule.

It so happened that the birth of Mithras was celebrated at the end of the winter solstice on 25 December, a date which was officially accepted as the date of the birth of Christ from the fourth century. The way in which Easter (ostensibly the anniversary of the crucifixion and resurrection of Christ) wanders all over the spring calendar still puzzles many Christians; but Easter, with its eggs, spring processions, and so on, probably owes more to the Isis/Osiris cult than it does to Christianity. Incidentally, this cult also went in for confessions and absolutions, so that the Romans, who had been exposed to all these influences, were pretty well prepared for the Christian message when it came, and may indeed have adapted it to accommodate some of these already accepted notions.

One of the first Roman citizens to become deeply involved in the new faith was a Greek Jew, Saul of Tarsus. He had never seen Jesus, and in fact had been prominent among the persecutors of the new sect, until one day on the road to Damascus he fell down in an epileptic fit and had a vision, he claimed, of Christ. After that he changed his name to Paul, joined the new Church, and became responsible, more than any other one man, for formulating doctrinal Christianity in its original form. He preached the gospel with all the relentless passion of the convert, and was ultimately beheaded in Rome for treason.

The official tolerance which the Romans had usually shown to the Jews was not at first extended to the Christians, and for a very good reason. The religion of the Jews, being confined to a relatively small and highly selective ethnic group, represented no great threat to Roman law and order. The Christians, on the other hand, welcomed all creeds and nationalities, including Roman citizens, into their new sect; but they had the same reluctance as the Jews to pay even lip-service to the Roman emperor, or the State gods. They publicly declared that their God and their God alone was the true ruler of heaven and earth, and that all other gods, including by implication the Roman emperors, were false. And although it is true that Jesus Christ had instructed his followers to render unto Caesar those things which were Caesar's, nevertheless a great many of his teachings – not to mention the probably far more extravagant sermons of his enthusiastically evangelical first adherents – must have sounded uncommonly like sedition. Also, the cult was beginning to spread among Roman citizens dissatisfied with the excesses of the Roman ruling classes and the shallow emptiness of the Roman religion. Worse still, it held an instant appeal for Roman slaves and freed men who had no reason to feel content with their lot in the imperial capital at this point of time.

The persecution of Christians, which began under Nero in A.D. 64 and continued intermittently for over 200 years, was all that was needed to ensure the spread of the new religion. If a man is prepared to die for his beliefs, then other men are apt to treat his beliefs with respect, and even examine them sympathetically. And as those beliefs appeared to offer something more satisfying than the confused and illogical creeds of the Roman Empire, it is not surprising that every persecution was followed by a fresh wave of conversions to the new faith.

And the early Christians were certainly prepared to die for their faith. In a world in which sudden and violent death was always a distinct possibility anyway, and since martyrdom in the cause of Christianity was about as close as you could get to a guarantee of a place in heaven, without falling into the error of presumption, many Christians appeared almost to welcome martyrdom, and went to their death with a fortitude that must have seemed very impressive to a race of men by no means convinced of the certainty of any kind of after-life.

The first Christians to die for the cause were picked by Nero as scapegoats. He blamed them for causing the great fire of Rome, and by holding the Christians responsible he set a pattern that was frequently followed in the years ahead: whenever anything went wrong in Rome, the Christians were blamed, and another wave of martyrs went to the wall.

St Paul was beheaded and St Peter crucified in A.D. 64. In the same year, many less illustrious of their colleagues were coated in pitch and set alight to illuminate Roman feasts, or cast into the amphitheatre with lions, or shot down with arrows, or buried alive, or drowned, or roasted. Death in ancient Rome took many forms, and every martyrdom gained fresh adherents to the now rapidly growing faith.

By the end of the first century A.D. only one of the original apostles, St John, survived. Most of the people who had known Jesus were dead, but his fame was greater than ever and the faith he had founded was gaining ground everywhere.

Under local administrators – at first called *patres*, or popes, and later, with the exception of the bishop of Rome, known as bishops – Christian communities flourished all over the Roman Empire. The principal centres of the new church were in Rome, Jerusalem, Antioch (in what is now Turkey), and Alexandria.

In addition to the secular clergy who ran the affairs of these communities, Christianity had, from its inception, attracted the attention of ascetics. Originally, these were simply laymen who renounced the world to devote themselves in solitude to the salvation of their souls, but later, in the fourth century, monasticism on the modern pattern began to develop, with celibate communities living according to set regulations – hence the phrase 'regular' clergy.

Irish Christianity, with which we shall be dealing in more detail later, was very quick to adopt the monastic pattern, and the spread of monastic Christianity throughout Britain and Europe was largely the work of Irish missionaries. Theoretically these monastic communities came under the direct authority of St Peter's successors in Rome, but in practice they enjoyed quite a considerable degree of autonomy.

While we are jumping ahead, it might be useful at this stage to refer briefly to another feature of the early Christian Church, the Communion of Saints. The term saint was initially applied – in the Old Testament – to all Israelites as the chosen people of God. St Paul addresses his Epistle to the Philippians 'to all saints in Christ Jesus which are at Philippi'.

However, the practice grew up in the early Church of paying public honour, *as saints*, to particular Christians who had suffered martyrdom rather than deny their faith; Stephen and Polycarp were among the first saints to be honoured in this way. As time passed, devotion to the saints spread and the principle of intercession was adopted; this was a system by which any Christian could address his prayers to a saint, requesting the saint to augment them with some prayers of his own and otherwise to use his influence with the Almighty on behalf of the postulant. Most of the early Christian saints were martyrs, and the relics of the saints which even today have to be sealed into the altar of every Catholic Church must include the relics of one martyr.

One of the great strengths of Christianity in its early days lay in its attitude to women. Until then, although goddesses and virgins had featured in some of the religious ceremonies in Greece and Rome, and priestesses were not uncommon in the pagan world, most religious messages had been addressed primarily to the menfolk.

St Paul made the point that women, too, have souls to save, and many of the early Christian martyrs were women. Since women, either in the capacity of housewives or of slaves or servants, are frequently in a position to influence any young children left in their care, here was another practical way in which Christ's gospel could be spread.

The first fissures now began to appear in the fabric of the Church. About A.D. 100 a cult called Docetism gained some adherents; according to this cult Jesus did not exist at all in fact, but was merely a spirit or ghost. In the second century, Marcian, a wealthy ship-owner, repudiated the Old Testament, claimed, like the Docetists, that Jesus had existed only as a spirit and not in fact, and argued that the God of the Jews was a totally different and altogether inferior deity to the God of the Christians. For a time, Marcianism enjoyed quite a following and had its own churches and even bishops.

A century later a complex religious movement known as Gnosticism began to gather supporters in the ranks of the Christian Church. The Gnostics within the Christian Church also argued that Christ had not really been born, nor did he in fact actually live or die, or rise again from the dead; and that the events described in the gospels were symbolically rather than historically true. They also repudiated certain bloodthirsty and carnal elements in the Old Testament. Both of these heresies were successfully scotched by the vigorous young Church.

Nor were the Christians yet safe from attacks from without the faith. Roman persecution was intermittent but at times violent. The Christians had been permitted to build their own burial vaults around Rome, and when the going was tough they used to hold their meetings in the vast catacombs they had carved out of the living rock there. At least one of the early popes was surprised in the act of celebrating Mass and executed on the spot; and there is evidence that some Christians were walled up alive in sections of the catacombs.

In A.D. 258 the Emperor Valerian ordered the catacombs to be closed, proscribed the Christian religion and called for the arrest and execution of all the clergy. But by this time, according to some estimates, nearly a quarter of the entire population of the Empire had taken up this new religion. There were legions in the Roman Army which were Christian to a man, and Christian missionaries had already started on the task of converting the wild Teuton tribes which by then were beginning to seep in across the northern frontiers of the Empire. The clergy merely went into hiding for a while and the Christian movement as a whole went underground until the danger was past.

The final wave of persecutions at the hands of the Romans came at the beginning of the fourth century, with the Emperor Diocletian. Christians who refused to acknowledge the Roman gods had their right eyes gouged out – and sometimes the tendons in their legs severed – and were sold into slavery. But by this time the Christian religion had penetrated right into the very heart of Imperial Rome; one of the martyrs to suffer death at Diocletian's hands was St Sebastian, who had been a captain in the Emperor's own bodyguard. The Diocletian reign of terror pursued the Christians to the farthest limits of the Roman Empire, and the first British martyr, St Alban, was among its victims.

It was from Britain that one of the next Roman emperors set out for Rome. Constantine, illegitimate son of the Emperor Constantius, was proclaimed Emperor by the legions of York, and as he marched towards the imperial city to stake his claim, he had, according to legend, a vision of a fiery cross in the sky and heard voices exhorting him to conquer in the sign of the cross. Although he was not instantly converted, he did take the precaution of removing the imperial eagles from his standards and replacing them with Christian symbols. And when he succeeded in defeating his rival Maxentius the next day, he promised to repay his debt to the Christian God. The following year he issued an edict which guaranteed freedom of conscience to all religious faiths and installed the bishop of Rome in one of his residences, the Lateran Palace, which remained the headquarters of the Christian Church until the Avignon adventure. Within a few years, Christianity had become the official religion of the Roman Empire.

Although he was not baptized until shortly before his death, Constantine took a great interest in Christianity throughout his life and his mother, St Helena, was tireless in her search for relics and sites associated with Christ and the original disciples. It was Constantine who called the famous Council of Nicaea (in modern Turkey) – the first ecumenical meeting of all the heads of the Christian Church – to settle yet another argument which had now broken out within the ranks of the faithful.

Arius, a priest of Alexandria, had begun to teach that there were not in the beginning three distinct and separate personages, God the Father, God the Son, and God the Holy Ghost; but only one, God the Father, and that therefore God the Son must at some subsequent point in time have been created by God the Father. The two hundred bishops from all over the Roman world who met to discuss the matter agreed on a formula: God the Son was held to be 'consubstantial' with God the Father.

About thirty years later, some Arian bishops began to preach that the Holy Spirit was less than divine. They were condemned at a second great Council of the Church which reaffirmed the Nicene Creed, defined the divinity of the Holy Spirit as proceeding both from the Father and from the Son, and inserted the term *filioque* ('and from the son') in the Creed to shore up this point and at the same time underline the consubstantial divinity of God the Son, still under fire in certain quarters. The Nicene Creed, still recited today from time to time in all Catholic churches and in some branches of the Protestant Church, dates from these early Church councils.

Another survival from this period are the vestments worn by a Catholic priest when he celebrates Mass. In an excellent article on early Christianity published in *The Observer* colour supplement in April 1967, Colin Cross pointed out that while strictly speaking there were no sacred vestments as such in the early Church, it became customary to keep a special set of smart clothes on one side for the saying of Mass. These started out as ordinary Sunday-best clothes of the period but, as fashions changed, remained basically the same, though later they became stylized and more highly ornamented.

> Modern Mass vestments [he wrote] are basically the best suit of a low-class citizen of the Roman Empire. The main vestment, the chasuble, was the topcoat of the poor man not entitled to wear the upper-class toga. The priest of 1967, in his second-century garments, whispering his commemoration of Felicitas and Perpetua [two early Christian martyrs, a rich girl and her slave, who died in an arena in North Africa: they were put to the sword after they had been painfully, but not fatally, gored by an angry cow] represents a unique continuity.

CHAPTER THREE

# The Death and Rebirth of the Roman Empire

## 1

After the first Council of Nicaea, Constantine decided to move his imperial headquarters from Rome to a centre closer to the main focus of the Empire's trade, from which he would also be better placed to repulse enemies from the East. He chose a small seaport town on the narrow straits between the Black Sea and the Sea of Marmara, known as the Bosporus. The town was called Byzantium, after a Greek adventurer, and now was renamed Constantinople.

For a thousand years this city was the centre of one of the most splendid civilizations the world has ever known, though inevitably it soon grew away from Rome and developed stronger ties with Greece and the Near East. From Byzantium, a new wave of missionaries set out to convert Russia and spread Christianity – in the form now known as the Greek Orthodox Church – throughout the Balkans and the Near East.

Meanwhile, in the other principal Christian centres – Rome, Antioch, Alexandria and Jerusalem – the Church was slowly building up an elaborate organization and amassing a vast reservoir of literature, interpreting and formulating its policy, its doctrine and its liturgy.

From time to time, further heretics cropped up and had to be dealt with. There was Nestorius, a Syrian monk who tried to assail the position of Mary as Mother of God; and Pelagius a lay monk, born in England, who claimed that man could save himself by his own efforts without supernatural Grace. These heresies were duly disposed of and the mountain of interpretative literature continued to grow apace.

In the seventh century an Arab camel-drover called Mohammed started to preach a new religion which soon spread like wildfire throughout the Arab world. Mohammed seems to have been an epileptic, or subject at any rate to seizures of one sort or another. He claimed that he had visions of the Archangel Gabriel who dictated to him a mass of material which later became the Koran. He was plainly much influenced by what he had heard of the Jewish and Christian religions, and behaved very like one of the early Hebrew prophets, talking first to his wife and to those around him about the One True God, and later preaching the new faith in the streets. Like Christianity, it was largely based on the sound and well-tried tenets of the Jews. The creed which Mohammed himself taught was, like Christ's message, extremely simple: his disciples had only to love Allah the one true God, honour and obey their parents, be honest with their neighbours, and live humble, charitable and temperate lives. The new religion was to have no priests, and its mosques were merely large assembly halls where the members of the faith could gather to discuss the Koran and pray together, turning to face Mecca.

The instinct which led the early Christian martyrs to die in the Roman arena with such fortitude in the hope of place in Heaven was even more marked among the Moslem missionaries, because the sin of presumption was unknown to the followers of Mohammed. For he had preached, as a matter of doctrine, that all those who died fighting the enemy would be *certain* of a place in heaven. Since most of Mohammed's followers were forced to eke out a pretty grim existence in this world, this fact may explain why they made, both at that time and throughout history, such persistent and formidable adversaries.

By the eighth century, Mohammed's followers, fired by his ideas and vying with one another for all those promised places in heaven, had launched themselves on the Mediterranean world with such ferocity that they had soon won North Africa, Egypt, Palestine and Syria from the Constantinople-based section of the Roman Empire. The apostolic headquarters at Jerusalem, Antioch and Alexandria were now all lost to Christianity, and the religion was reduced to two Principal Sees, one in Rome and one in Constantinople.

It was inevitable that sooner or later there would be a clash between them.

The first trouble arose over the use of images in divine worship. This was not a straight fight between Rome and Constantinople; opinions even in Constantinople were divided on the subject. Under pressure from Islam, and to a lesser extent from the quite powerful Manicheans – they were followers of Mani, a Persian teacher who claimed to have had a vision of an angel who had imparted a new revelation which was to supersede the Christian one – some of the bishops and priests in Constantinople began to oppose the use of images in worship. One of their reasons for doing this was that the use of icons constituted a grave obstacle to the conversion of Moslems and Jews, both of whom were expressly forbidden by the terms of their commandments to bow down to any graven image. Indeed one of the more mysterious achievements of the early Christian Church – as the latter-day reformers were soon to discover when they went back to the scriptures to check the sources of some of the Church's sacred precepts and rituals – was that while Christ's teachings were clearly based on the Old Testament of the Jews, and Christianity's basic code of conduct derived from the Ten Commandments given to Moses by God, the Church had somehow or another contrived to lose the Second Commandment of the Jews, forbidding the worship of graven images, while nevertheless retaining the original total of ten commandments.

The second Council of Nicaea, in 787, settled the matter on dogmatic grounds – since the Word had been made flesh, images would be permitted, though they were not in fact worshipped for their own sake – but it is significant that this was the last council accepted by the Eastern Church.

## 2

Explanations of the final break between the two remaining headquarters of Christ's Church on earth vary according to the sources consulted, but there is no doubt that it owed as much to history, geography, politics, and even economics, as it did to theology.

In Rome, the Church and its bishop had survived all the invasions and upheavals which had led to the final dissolution of the Roman Empire and the disappearance of the legions and their emperor. For twelve generations, Rome had been overrun by tribes of barbarians, pushed down into the old territories of the Empire by the invasion of Europe by the Huns. These barbarians plundered the palaces, wrecked the roads and bridges, burned down the public buildings and reduced the centre of civilization to a benighted wilderness where war, murder, rape, arson and plunder were daily occurrences, and only the Roman Church could claim any sort of continuity with the past, until the whole institution was ended in A.D. 476 by an announcement to Constantinople to that effect, made by Odoacer, chief of the barbarian troops, who reported that there was no longer an emperor in the West.

When Theodoric's Gothic-Roman kingdom – itself founded on no basis more valid or secure than a murder – collapsed in the sixth century, the Goths were succeeded by weaker and more backward tribes like the Lombards. Under these circumstances, it became possible for the more politically sophisticated bishops of Rome to strengthen and maintain the independence of what they now looked upon as their own city-state, and in time a few pathetic remnants of the old Empire, scattered through the peninsula of Italy, came to accept the bishops of Rome as their political as well as their spiritual rulers. For although the Roman Empire was clearly at an end, the concept of an Empire based on Rome remained fixed in men's minds – it was, after all, the only order they had known in a world growing increasingly disorderly – and in the absence of any other candidate with any claim to continuity, the Church of Rome was accepted as a temporal power in the area as well as the supreme spiritual one, and the bishops of Rome adopted the title of Pontifex Maximus, the most ancient of all the titles the Roman emperors had enjoyed.

With the exception of the Anglo-Saxons who took over from the Roman colonial provincials in Britain and continued to govern themselves as they had done previously in their own lands, the Germanic invaders did not impose their own political institutions on the remains of the Roman Empire, but lived alongside the old Roman population in conditions more or less the same as before the Empire collapsed, though now it was the Church which effectively ran the remnants of the Empire. The invaders did, however, import their hereditary kingships.

It was also very largely due to the Church's influence that, except in Germany and in Britain, the Germanic tribes which settled in former Roman territory in Europe adopted variants of the Latin tongue in place of their own Germanic languages: French, Italian, Spanish, Portuguese and the other 'Romance' languages like Provençal and Romansh were all based on the Latin, the writing of which, in this period, was kept alive mainly by the Church. The Church also provided the only schools then in existence and preserved such learning as there was; it is no coincidence that the words for clerk and cleric are similar in many European languages.

Under a bishop called Gregory – who was a descendant of the ruling class of ancient Rome – the Christians of western Europe officially recognized the bishop of Rome, now known as the Pope, as the head of the entire Church of Christ on Earth. With the first taste of power was born the desire to strengthen it and put it on a firmer basis.

Although many of the barbaric tribes which had invaded the Roman Empire had been long since converted to Christianity and professed, and even showed, great respect for the bishop of Rome, the popes of this period were well aware that the situation could easily change with the arrival of fresh sets of invaders from north of the Alps, and they set about trying to find an ally powerful enough to defend their city-state if the need should ever arise.

The Franks, a Germanic race who had occupied north-western Europe, seemed the most promising prospect, and before long Rome was making overtures to Pepin, the son of the famous Charles Martel who had defeated the Moslems, not very far from Paris, in their attempt to conquer Europe via Morocco and Spain, and had pushed them back behind the Pyrenees.

Pepin, as Mayor of the Palace, was the *de facto* king of the Franks, but he wanted to be king *de jure* also and felt that the Pope's *imprimatur* would take a good deal of the harm out of the *coup d'état* he was planning. Emissaries were sent to Rome to inquire whether the royal title should not in fact go to him who exercised the supreme authority, rather than be held by one who enjoyed only the appearance of authority. The Pope gave his assent to this rather dubious opportunist argument and Pepin deposed the last degenerate descendant of the line of Clovis. The Pope endorsed his coronation by anointing him, by allowing the words *dei gratia* (by the grace of God) to be inserted in the coronation ceremony, and by conferring on him the title of Roman patrician. Pepin repaid the debt by capturing Ravenna and a few other scattered cities and adding them to what had now become the Papal States.

A generation later, Pepin's son Charlemagne got involved in a contract with the Pope which altered the whole course of European history and resulted in the revival of the Roman Empire in a very curious form.

Charlemagne – who already probably entertained ideas of his own of becoming overlord of the area formerly known as the Roman Empire of the West – went to Rome to quell a riot, and while attending Mass in the ancient basilica of the Lateran Palace on Christmas Day A.D. 800, was suddenly and unexpectedly crowned by Leo III and hailed with the title of Caesar Augustus. There is some evidence that Charlemagne was a bit taken aback by the way in which this honour was bestowed upon him by a man whom he regarded as *his* protégé. Perhaps he felt, and perhaps he was right, that the Pope did it in this way so that he could ever afterwards claim that as the title of Emperor of the Roman Empire had been bestowed on Charlemagne by him, without prior discussion, it could equally well be withheld, or taken back, or presented elsewhere. Be that as it may, the Pope, by his action, had created a new Roman Empire of the West and had placed it in the hands of a German tribal chieftain who could barely read and certainly could not write.

The event had immediate repercussions in the old Roman Empire of the East. Over the years, Constantinople had been drawing ever farther away from its Roman origins and turning towards Greece and the East. And in the eyes of the still highly civilized Byzantine Greeks, the Pope was guilty of a grave insult to the East by crowning a barbarian like Charlemagne as Emperor of the Roman Empire of the West. The Emperor of the Roman Empire of the East was obliged to recognize his imperial opposite number in Rome, and did in fact write to congratulate him, but resentment against the Roman pope continued to grow in Constantinople, while Rome, for her part, resented the refusal of the Church in Constantinople to accept without question the Roman claim to supremacy.

Matters between the two branches of the Church went from bad to worse during the Crusades. But before dealing with these, it is necessary to consider what had been happening in Europe in the meantime.

## 3

Not long after Charlemagne's death in 814 there had been a dispute among his grandsons over the succession, and the crown of the Holy Roman Emperor had passed from hand to unworthy hand for a number of years until in 962 the Pope crowned the German King,

Otto I, who was reckoned the most formidable of the various rulers in western Europe at this period. Otto was duly crowned Emperor of the Holy Roman Empire of the German Nation by Pope John XII, and the title of Emperor of the Romans passed into the highly unlikely hands of a north German tribal chieftain and remained in the hands of his successors until 1806 when the title was voluntarily relinquished. But very shortly before that (in 1804) an upstart Corsican general, Napoleon Bonaparte, had summoned the Pope to Paris to crown him as Emperor of the French, he proclaimed himself heir to the tradition of Charlemagne, and added the imperial eagle of ancient Rome to his escutcheons. With some interval, Napoleon's line finally ended about seventy years later.

The tokens of the Roman Empire of the East survived a little longer. The imperial double eagle which was the standard of Constantine's Eastern Roman Empire found its way to Russia by marriage when Constantinople was overrun by the Turks in the fifteenth century. Constantine's insignia was finally eclipsed by the hammer and sickle when Tsar Nicholas II and other members of the Romanov family were murdered by the Bolsheviks in a cellar at Ekaterinburg on 16 July 1918.

Charlemagne's Holy Roman Empire ran into trouble right from its inception. For a start, it was under constant attack from three sides. To the south, in Spain and Africa, lived the highly warlike and dangerous Moslems. The eastern frontier was liable to be invaded at any moment by hordes of savage Magyars, Slavs and Tartars. The western coast was continuously ravaged by expeditions of Norsemen in search of loot and women. The demand for strong leadership to protect these frontiers gave rise to the feudal system by which the Empire soon became partitioned off into a multitude of principalities, organized as fighting units and ruled by dukes, counts, barons and even, in some cases, bishops. These local lords assumed most of the rights and privileges of the Emperor over their own subjects in return for a promise of protection in times of trouble.

At the head of this shaky Empire, which soon consisted of no more than Germany and part of what is now Italy, there were now two figureheads, the pope and the emperor, and while in theory there should not have been any dispute between them since the pope's province was confined – at any rate in the emperor's view – to purely spiritual matters, situations were bound to arise in which the authority of emperor and pope would overlap if not actually conflict.

There was one way by which an emperor could avoid an open confrontation between himself and the Church. Up to this time, the system of appointing popes had remained rather haphazard and the emperor could often ensure that a candidate likely to favour his own ambitions was elected to the Holy See. In fact the Holy Roman Emperor frequently went to Rome whenever the Papacy fell vacant, to make certain that the Keys of Heaven fell into the right hands.

But this system didn't always work. No sooner had Pope John XII placed the crown on Otto's head than he began to intrigue against an emperor who looked like threatening his overlordship of Rome; Otto replied by returning to Rome, whence he convoked a synod which deposed John and put Leo VIII in his place. But Otto had hardly left Rome before Leo was pushed from the throne and John restored; and after John's death, without consulting the Emperor, the Church elected Benedict V as Pope. Otto besieged Rome, exiled Benedict V and restored Leo VIII. It was an undignified business, which did the image of the Papacy no good at all.

In the middle of the eleventh century the Church removed this source of danger by arranging that future popes would be elected by a secret ballot of prominent churchmen known as the College of Cardinals. One of the first popes elected under this new system in 1073 was Gregory VII, a man of enormous determination, who regarded himself not only as absolute head of the now very powerful Christian Church, but also as the ultimate authority on all secular matters. In a way, given that the initial premise was valid, the argument of the popes was unassailable: kings and emperors were crowned by the Church, *dei gratia*, and since the Pope represented Christ on earth, God's grace could be withdrawn or withheld at any time. Furthermore, the Pope regarded himself as being responsible for the behaviour of Christ's entire flock and in the eyes of the Lord and of his viceroy, the Pope, the king or emperor was merely one member of that flock.

Gregory now set about reforming the Church in a number of ways. He introduced clerical celibacy – as we have seen, there had been for some time a growing tendency within the Roman Church towards celibacy; now it became a rule – and he attacked the lay investiture of bishops and introduced regulations which made it difficult for the Emperor to control or even influence the appointment of bishops.

To the Emperor this was a matter of prime importance, since the foundation of his power lay in the bishops, invested with the crozier and ring by him and therefore holding their power from him and acknowledging obedience to him in a way that he could no longer count on the powerful feudal barons to do.

The Emperor at that period, Henry IV, replied by instructing his own bishops to repudiate the Pope and declare him unworthy of office. Gregory thereupon excommunicated two German archbishops plus the Emperor himself, and absolved Henry's subjects from all allegiance to him. This was the first recorded deposition of a civil monarch by the Church.

The powerful German barons and princes, anxious for their own reasons to be shut of Henry, were quite happy at this development and invited the Pope to come to Augsburg to help them elect a new emperor in his place.

Gregory left Rome, and travelled north towards Germany. Henry, realizing the weakness of his position, met him *en route* at the castle of Canossa near Reggio nell'Emilia, between Parma and Modena, and sought an audience to make his submission. After keeping the Emperor waiting for three days in the snow outside his castle, to ram home the point, Gregory graciously allowed him to enter and granted him absolution.

Although the Pope didn't get away with this in the last analysis, the very fact that he would dare to keep a powerful emperor waiting in the snow illustrates how far the Church had by now progressed from the harassed groups of ill-clad missionaries who had arrived in Rome from the Holy Land in the first and second centuries to preach the new gospel, only to find themselves in the arena facing the wild beasts.

What happened in this case was that as soon as he regained power, Henry renewed his opposition to the Pope and was once again deposed and excommunicated. This time Duke Rudolf of Suabia was nominated by the Pope as his successor. Instead of accepting this, Henry marched on Italy, seized Rome and set up a rival Pope, Clement III. Gregory was forced to retire to Salerno, and not for the first nor for the last time was the Christian Church embarrassed by the presence on earth of two claimants to the succession.

This was the opening skirmish in a long series of disputes between pope and emperor, which never really settled anything but slowly eroded away men's faith in the idea that the Bishop and Church of Rome were above and beyond the shabby business of power politics.

CHAPTER FOUR

# The Crusades and the Fall of Byzantium

## 1

After their great push westwards following the death of Mohammed, the eastern Moslems learned to live more or less at peace with their Christian neighbours. They had captured and occupied the Holy Land, but because they regarded Jesus Christ as a prophet, though a lesser one than Mohammed, they rarely molested pilgrims who wished to visit the various shrines there connected with the events of his life.

However, early in the eleventh century, a Tartar tribe from the wilds of Asia, known as the Seljuk Turks began to dominate the Moslem states in western Asia. By 1071 they had captured almost all the territories still held in Asia Minor by the Roman emperors of Constantinople. They now began to threaten Constantinople itself, and make life unpleasant for any Christians who crossed their path.

It is quite possible that the stories of the atrocities which these 'infidels' had inflicted upon pilgrims to the Holy Land were grossly exaggerated by vested interests such as the Italian city-states that had established highly profitable trading colonies along the coast of Asia Minor and Palestine, which they now felt were in danger, but there is no doubt that the Seljuk Turks had no great love for the Christians.

The Byzantine Emperor, Michael VII, was naturally rather nervous about the fate of Constantinople, and despite differences with Rome he appealed to Rome for assistance.

At the Council of Clermont in 1095, Pope Urban II, a Frenchman, launched the Crusades. He probably had a good many motives: the existence of a new common enemy gave the Pope a chance to unite Christendom and call for a truce among Christians. Also he probably reckoned that an exercise like a crusade against the Turks would absorb a good deal of the excess fighting-energy of the warlike barons of Frankish, Norman and German origin who had lately been growing increasingly independent of both Pope and Emperor. Furthermore, Europe was in a bad way. Primitive agricultural methods which had not changed greatly since Roman times had resulted in frequent food shortages, whereas the Near East was known to be a rich and verdant land capable of feeding many millions of mouths.

In any event, and however mixed his motives, Pope Urban called on French knights in particular and Christians in general to go out to the Holy Land and reclaim the Holy Sepulchre from the Turks.

A man called Peter the Hermit immediately took up the cause and travelled through France and Germany, barefoot, clothed in rags, and riding a donkey; he carried a cross and called for volunteers in the streets and market places. The result was a wave of crusading hysteria which swept the Continent. Men walked away from their work in the fields and cities and towns and headed east with no more precise plan than to set upon the first Turks they encountered. Most of them had no money and were forced to beg or steal to support themselves. Some of them were killed by the angry country people on whose lands they trespassed on the way. Few of them ever got near Jerusalem.

Two great mobs of the first 'People's Crusade' barged their way into Hungary, assumed that the recently converted Magyars were the infidels they had been enjoined to destroy, immediately set about attacking them and were, in their turn, massacred. A third wave, after murdering all the Jews they met *en route*, also reached Hungary and were destroyed. Two other contingents, led by Peter the Hermit himself, succeeded in reaching Constantinople crossed the Bosporus and were almost immediately wiped out by the Turks. The episode was a total disaster on all counts, though it did demonstrate that, very largely because of the effect of the Christian religion upon man's conscience, the plain people of Europe could be aroused and swept along, even at the risk of their own lives, in a great popular movement.

The next crusade – usually referred to as the First Crusade, since it was the first official one – was a more highly organized affair. A year was spent training and equipping an army of 200,000 men, largely under Norman leadership, and this expedition, which set out in 1096 and spent a full year on the siege of Antioch, eventually reached the Holy Land in 1099, captured Jerusalem after a month's siege and very considerable slaughter, and fought its way, foot by bloody foot, into the Church of the Holy Sepulchre.

With the crusaders holding Jerusalem, plus the city of Antioch and a few small principalities in the area, of which Edessa in Syria was the main one, the Byzantine Empire now began to take back some of the territories it had lost to the Turks. This put the Crusaders in the unenviable position of acting as a buffer State between the Turks and the Greeks of the Byzantine Empire, for whom they felt no great liking. In fact the Greek Orthodox Patriarch of Jerusalem found that things were not much better under the Christian crusaders than they had been under the infidels, and when they are stripped of all their romantic elements, the Crusades begin to look very much like a mass exploitation of the remnants of the Roman Empire of the East by the remnants of the Roman Empire of the West, though it must be added that the Crusaders believed that the Greeks despised and cheated them, and all over Europe there was a deep conviction that the failure of the Crusades was due partly at least to the treachery of the Eastern Church. On the whole, the Crusaders had far more respect for the Turks, who proved to be fair and generous enemies, than they had for their allies; while the Greeks, with every reason as it turned out, feared and mistrusted the barbarous crusaders.

In 1144 Edessa fell to the Moslems, and this led to a second organized Crusade, which failed to retake Edessa but probably prevented Antioch from succumbing to the Turks.

In 1169 the forces of Islam found a new leader in Saladin, who followed the example of Pope Urban and preached a Holy War against the Christians. By 1187, Jerusalem was back in Moslem hands and a Third Crusade was being mounted. This failed to retake Jerusalem, and a Fourth Crusade, which set out in 1202, made no pretence at all of pushing on to the Holy Land, but fell instead on the Byzantine Empire, sacked Constantinople, set up a 'Latin' Emperor, Baldwin, in place of the Byzantine Emperor, and carted most of the treasures of the capital back to Europe. The city of Venice owes much of its splendour to the spoliation of Constantinople, and indeed the Doge of Venice was one of the prime instigators of this adventure. It came about in this way.

The first waves of crusaders had discovered to their cost that the overland route to the Holy Land was both too long and too dangerous; subsequent expeditions travelled overland as far as Italy, and the remainder of the way by sea. A good deal of this very considerable traffic in men, materials and weapons of war was handled by the city-state of Venice, which had made quite a profitable business out of it, both by lending money – as many of the other medieval cities *en route* also did – to the propertied knights, in return for mortgages of one sort or another on their possessions, and by getting the remainder to pay for their passage in kind. Since the only service which the crusaders would offer was war, they were obliged to pay the owners of the vessels by doing a bit of fighting on their behalf on the way out east. By this means, Venice greatly increased her territories along the Adriatic coast, in Greece and in the Aegean. And when the knights and warriors of the Fourth Crusade were ordered by the Doge to turn on Constantinople, and in all conscience it didn't take much persuasion, Venice recovered the cost of transporting this Crusade by annexing part of the coastline and some of the islands of the Byzantine Empire, as well as by shipping back tons of marbles and mosaics to grace the Doge's palace and other buildings in Venice. In fairness, it must be said that Pope Innocent III, so far from endorsing the crusaders in their decision to attack Constantinople, had gone to the lengths of excommunicating the Venetians for their part in the affair.

This was the final, irreparable breach between the two principal branches of Christ's Church on earth. And although after the 'Latin' Emperor had been installed, the Roman and Greek Churches were declared reunited, this was a makeshift business with no real prospect of success. Sixty years later the Greeks got rid of their Roman overlord and reverted to their old Orthodox ways.

There was to be one last-minute, desperate attempt to heal the breach. In the fifteenth century, when it became quite clear that the city could not hold out much longer against the Ottoman Turks, the Byzantine Emperor and Patriarch went together to Europe to seek help, accepted once more the reunion of the Greek and Roman Churches, and returned to Constantinople with a vague promise of help, which never came.

The people of Constantinople, in any case, were not prepared to make the concessions that unity with Rome required. They would prefer to retain their Orthodox rites and take their chances with the Turk, whose onslaught could not be much longer delayed.

In 1453 the Turks attacked by land and sea, even carrying their ships overland to the enclosed waters of the Golden Horn, so the city was soon surrounded on all sides. After a siege that lasted for more than six weeks, Constantinople fell. The Emperor Constantine Palaeologus perished in the ruins of his capital – since the bodies were all decapitated, his remains were never identified – the once resplendent churches were turned into mosques, and Constantinople became the Turkish city now known as Istanbul.

Some years after the fall of Constantinople, Zoë, daughter of the Emperor's brother Thomas, married Ivan III of Russia, which explains how the Grand Dukes of Moscow acquired the standard of the Emperor Constantine, and why the imperial crown worn by the tsars of Russia carried the double eagle of the old Roman Empire of the East.

## 2

However disastrous their effect on the unfortunate Eastern branch of the Church, and ultimately and indirectly on the Western branch, the Crusades had a highly beneficial effect on Europe. After the Crusades, things in Europe were never again quite so hopeless and gloomy as they had been during the Dark Ages.

The business of transporting the crusaders and revictualling their bases led to the development of Italian maritime commerce, which in turn had the effect of opening up Europe again to the more varied and sophisticated commodities which the East had to offer. Also, the crusaders themselves brought back new manners, new customs, new tastes, and a profound discontent with the dreary life afforded by the feudal unit. As Hendrik Van Loon remarks in his *The Story of Mankind*, 'the Crusades, which had begun as a punitive expedition against the Heathen became a course of general instruction for millions of young Europeans'.

But it was some considerable time before these benefits broke through to the surface; and in the meantime the battle for supremacy continued between the popes and the emperors.

For a period, at the beginning of the thirteenth century, when the short-lived union between the Eastern and Western headquarters of the Christian Church had been achieved, with Constantinople under a 'Latin' Emperor, and again for another spell at the end of that century, when an outbreak of political rivalry prevented agreement being reached on an emperor for nearly fifty years, a united Christendom under the rule of the pope seemed a distinct possibility. From the barren, rocky coast of Ireland in the west, to Bulgaria (and, for the first sixty years of the period, still farther afield to the now somewhat dimmed but still effulgent splendour of Constantinople) in the east; and from the remote and splendid fjords of Norway in the north to that tiny archipelago in the Mediterranean, only about fifty miles off the Libyan coast, where St Paul had been shipwrecked on Malta on his way to Rome for trial, the pope's rule was supreme. There had been scandals, it is true – wicked, worldly popes like the two Johns, XI and XII, in the tenth century and Benedict IX in the eleventh, who had been driven from Rome accused, between them, of a formidable total of crimes including murder and incest, had shaken the edifice a bit – but the Church had survived, as it had survived the first, tentative brushes with the emperors and the kings. It seemed, for the moment, in an unassailable position.

Yet, from this period, the power of the popes of Rome, both in the temporal sense and, even more so, over the minds of man, began to decline, imperceptibly at first, but soon unmistakably and, within three hundred years, disastrously, in the avalanche known as the Reformation.

For convenience, I dealt with the Crusades consecutively; it is now necessary to go back a bit in time to take up again the story of the struggles between pope and emperor.

The next significant round was fought between Frederick Barbarossa and the Popes Adrian IV and Alexander III. This was lost in advance by the Emperor, for the simple reason that the Empire no longer comprised, as it had done in Charlemagne's time, all the Christians in Europe. Most Englishmen and Frenchmen, being Christians, were still prepared to acknowledge the authority of the Pope; but being Englishmen and Frenchmen, could not recognize the authority of a Holy Roman Emperor who was effective ruler only of a relatively weak collection of feudal German states and a section of what is now Italy.

Nevertheless Frederick Barbarossa held the view that he was the successor not only to Charlemagne, but also to the ancient Roman emperors, and since they had existed before Christ, he refused to recognize the authority of the Pope over his Empire. On the contrary, he believed that the Pope was, in the last analysis, merely one of his subjects. He marched on Italy and became involved in a series of exhausting struggles with the urban communities of the Lombardy Plain – rich, independent municipal republics with no great regard for the rights of the Emperor. In the end, with his imperial army cut to pieces by the Milanese and their allies, he submitted to Pope

Alexander III in Venice, where, having cast aside the trappings of the Emperor, he prostrated himself and abjectly kissed the pontiff's feet.

His grandson, Frederick II, carried on the struggle to far more effect. When he was only four years old, Frederick had inherited the Kingdom of Sicily, which a century before had been won from the Arabs by a party of Norman knights returning from a pilgrimage to the Holy Land. Frederick was raised in an atmosphere that was at least half Oriental and was thus able to view the Christian Church with some detachment. As a result, he grew up without respect for any religious faith, and made no secret of this fact, a remarkable thing at that period, all the more so since he had been made a ward of the then Pope, Innocent III.

Innocent III was a firm believer in total religious conformity. When, in the south of France, a rich merchant called Waldo began to preach a return to the simple life and faith of Jesus Christ, and had the Bible translated into Provençal so that people could read it for themselves, Innocent III supported a crusade against Waldo and his followers. The Waldenses were repressed with terrible cruelty, many of them being burnt alive by the soldiers of the king of France.

Innocent III also mounted a crusade against another heretical sect, the Albigenses – called after the town of Albi, in Provence – who maintained that all material things belonged to the realm of Satan and that the path of salvation lay in the repression of all natural instincts, particularly sexual ones. This was a self-defeating heresy, in that, carried to its logical conclusion, its principal tenet held that universal continence would end the domination of matter by the extinction of the human race. Before they had an opportunity to put their theories into effect, the Albigenses were exterminated by a crusade under Simon de Montfort at the beginning of the thirteenth century.

Innocent III was also responsible for encouraging and assisting St Dominic to set up an organization known as the Inquisition, an instrument for the tracking down and punishing of heresy, and, in effect, for trammelling free thought. It was an organization so fundamentally opposed to the new spirit which was just beginning to stir in Europe around this time, that it could not but lead to wars and revolutions.

When it fell to Frederick's lot to become Emperor of what was left of the Holy Roman Empire, the Pope laid down certain conditions. Before he would approve the succession, Frederick would have to acknowledge that Sicily was a fief of the Holy See, free the German priests from taxation, make war on German heretics with the same ferocity with which the French king had been prevailed upon to put down the unfortunate Waldenses and Albigenses, and mount another crusade to recover Jerusalem.

Frederick promised to do all of these things, without any real intention of keeping his promises, and simply stayed on in Sicily. Innocent III died without finding a solution to the problem, and so did his successor, Honorius III, who crowned Frederick Emperor in 1220 in the belief that he still sincerely intended to keep his promises.

In 1227, Gregory IX became Pope and decided to have it out with Frederick. He renewed the order to Frederick to set out on another crusade, and when Frederick prevaricated, he excommunicated him. In a predominantly Christian state, within easy reach, for supervisory purposes, of the Holy See, excommunication could be a very powerful weapon. If the Pope put a whole nation under an interdict, most of the functions of the priesthood had to stop: the priests were forbidden to say Mass, or perform marriages, or bury the dead, though the business of baptizing babies continued unabated. In the very largely Arab atmosphere of Sicily, on the other hand, excommunication did not inconvenience Frederick unduly.

Next the Pope addressed an open letter to Frederick, listing all his vices and heresies. Frederick replied with an open letter to the princes of Europe, drawing their attention to the vast wealth of the popes, and to their growing temporal demands, and calling on the princes to unite against any further usurpation of their rights by the Church.

Having fired off this salvo, Frederick, who by now had acquired the nickname 'Wonder of the World', suddenly departed on his long-promised crusade. But instead of marching an army on the Holy Land, and setting on the Saracens, as all the previous Crusaders had done, he met the Sultan, discussed the whole thing in a civilized manner, and arranged for the return of Jerusalem by private treaty.

On his return to Europe, Frederick resumed his struggle with the Pope. In 1239 he was again excommunicated – primarily for failing to free the Sicilian Church from secular control – and the struggle dragged on after Gregory's death and into the reign of Pope Innocent IV, when Frederick wrote a second open letter denouncing the pride and arrogance of the clergy, drawing attention once again to the inordinate wealth of the Church, and hinting that it might be in the best interests of all, including the Church herself, if some of her lands were to be confiscated.

This latter suggestion held an immediate appeal for the lay princes of Europe who, for some time past, had been troubled by the amount of land which was in the hands of the Church. Quite apart from the lands which had been transferred to the Church by Constantine and his successors – who had also transferred to the Church all the immense wealth of Rome's pagan temples – it had long been the practice of penitent Christians who died childless to leave all or part of their lands to the Church; indeed they were encouraged to do so by the clergy. And since, as H. G. Wells tartly points out in his *Short History of the World*, 'men are always dying and the church never dies', its possessions continued to grow over the centuries until they now amounted, in some European countries, to almost a quarter of the total. Land held by the Church was largely wasted land so far as the local knights and barons were concerned. Self-supporting abbeys and monasteries peopled by communities of monks and nuns gave little employment and produced neither wealth nor fighting men; furthermore, they were effectively controlled from Rome, and if they paid any taxes at all, paid them to Rome. As a final indignity, the Church had, from the time of Charlemagne, claimed tithes, that is to say, the right to levy tax up to one-tenth of the property of all laymen, in addition to whatever taxes they paid to their local overlords. Since most quarrels, in the last analysis, are really about money, Frederick's suggestion that some of these lands should be confiscated gave the princes and kings of Europe food for serious thought.

But before any of the temporal rulers got around to seizing any of the Church property, the Papacy made yet another attempt to put them firmly in their places.

## 3

Although the Church made regulations regarding such matters as the payment of taxes by the clergy, these regulations were not always observed by the Christian princes and kings. In the late thirteenth century, the then King of France, Philip IV, known as Philip the Fair, who reckoned that he derived his authority from Charlemagne, and disliked admitting any principle of subordination to the pope in secular matters, slapped a heavy tax on French priests without consulting Rome. Edward I of England also imposed heavy taxes on Church estates.

Pope Boniface VIII, an Italian with no great love for the French, and an almost fanatical determination to restore the Papacy to the position of political domination it had enjoyed in the time of Innocent III, replied with a series of bulls. One of these, *Clericis laicos*, issued in 1296, strictly prohibited laymen from imposing any taxes on the clergy without the consent of the Pope, and threatened excommunication on all lay princes who failed to obey this instruction.

But while in the time of Innocent III Christendom was a unified entity which could be organized – as, for example, during the Crusades – national identities had now begun to emerge. In particular, both France and England had developed strong feelings of nationality, and in England this had already led to representatives of the nation as a whole taking a hand in the running of things.

The Great Charter, which the barons, bishops and burghers had forced King John to sign in 1215 at Runnymede near Windsor, was the first declaration of rights of the English nation; and it stipulated, very categorically, the principle that all taxes should be voted by the nation or its representatives. Less than fifty years later a national assembly known as Parliament was meeting regularly in England, with representatives of the burghers sitting beside the nobles and the bishops, and associating with the sovereign in the task of administering the country. The Statute of Mortmain, passed in 1279, prohibited lands from falling into the hands of the Church.

In England, Edward ignored the Bull and continued to levy the taxes. In France, Philip went further and prohibited the export of money and letters of credit, a move which deprived the Pope of all the revenues he drew from France. The Pope was forced to modify the Bull, and it has been argued that the canonization of St Louis in 1297 was another gesture designed to mollify France and encourage her to open her financial frontiers again.

In 1300 a great jubilee of the Christian faith was held, and vast numbers of pilgrims thronged Rome – the total has been put as high as 200,000 – to pay homage to the Pope and obtain indulgences extended to those who paid visits to the tombs of the Apostles.

Indulgences were a practice which went back to the Crusades. Anyone who agreed to go on a crusade was granted an indulgence by the bishop which remitted a previously imposed penance. The theory behind indulgences was an ingenious one. Since the saints had all lived perfect lives on earth, there was a considerable balance of virtue in the heavenly bank – far more than the saints themselves needed for their own salvation – and this could be dispensed, by the bishops, to Christians in need of some assistance in that direction. There was no danger that this bank balance of superfluous credits – known as the *thesaurus meritorum sanctorum* – could ever be exhausted, since it also included the bottomless balance of virtue accumulated by Jesus Christ while on this earth.

In time, indulgences were issued not merely to those who took part in the Crusades, but also to those who stayed at home but helped to finance them. From this the step to the 'sale' of indulgences in return for support of one sort or another, or for financial assistance towards the construction of a cathedral or a church, was a very short one. By the fifteenth century the popes were claiming the authority to remit penalties in purgatory as well as on earth, and while these indulgences were not openly sold, the granting of a pardon was usually timed, as Roland H. Bainton puts it in his book, *The History of Christianity*, 'to coincide with the contribution of money by a sinner'.

Pope Boniface, a bit carried away by the devotion of so many pious Christians, now accused Edward, King of England, of violence and injustice against the Scots. The English King convoked Parliament and invited it to decide on the legality of the papal claims; prelates, barons, knights and burghers were all united in their indignant rejection of the Pope's interference.

By the time news of this defeat reached him, the Pope was deep in yet another controversy with the French King, Philip, over the arrest of a papal legate called Saisset. He demanded Saisset's immediate liberation, revived the prohibition on taxing Church property, and addressed the French King in another Bull, *Ausculta fili*, in which he reminded him that St Peter's successors in the Vatican were above princes and states.

At this stage France had no parliament, but following Edward's example, Philip of France convoked the first meeting of the States-General to decide on the question of the King's sovereignty. In 1302, delegates representing the clergy, the nobility and the burghers met in the Cathedral of Notre Dame and again decided in favour of the Crown against the Pope.

The Pope replied with yet another Bull, the famous *Unam Sanctam* Bull of 1302, which incidentally has never been retracted by the Holy

See and therefore still stands as a specific statement of the papal position in relation to secular power.

> We are taught by the words of the Gospel [the document runs] that in this Church there are two swords, namely a spiritual and a temporal. It is necessary that one sword should be under the other and that temporal authority be subjected to the spiritual. For, truth bearing witness, the spiritual power should instruct the temporal power and judge it, if it be not good. Hence we declare, affirm, and define and pronounce that it is altogether necessary for the salvation of every creature to be subject to the Roman Pontiff.

Later, after further arguments with Philip's advisers, he defined the papal position further: 'We declare that in no way do we wish to usurp the jurisdiction of the king. And yet neither the king nor anyone else of the faithful can deny that he is subject to us, where a question of sin is involved.' The final Latin phrase is *ratione peccati*.

And this phrase *ratione peccati* is, of course, the crux of the whole problem. The Church had indicated that she considered herself justified in intervening in secular matters 'when an otherwise temporal affair (like civil legislation) affects the religious interests of the faithful by putting an unfair burden on their conscience, exposing them to sin, or otherwise conflicting with that spiritual welfare over which the Church believes she alone has ultimate jurisdiction by the mandate of her Founder'. The paraphrase I have used is not my own; it is taken from *Religions of the World* by John A. Hardon, S.J., Associate Professor of Comparative Religion at the Western Michigan University.

But the point is that the only authority competent to decide whether the religious interests of the faithful are involved in an otherwise purely temporal matter is, of course, the Church herself.

It was under this general principle that the Church insisted on having its own law courts which operated independently of the civilian courts. The Church believed that all cases involving priests, monks, students and crusaders, as well as all matters affecting wills, and oaths or marriages, should be dealt with in these special Church courts, which also claimed the right to try all cases of witchcraft, sorcery and, of course, heresy. Laymen who felt the need to have recourse to the law to redress a grievance against a priest naturally found it irksome not to be able to bring the priest before the ordinary courts of law, but to be obliged to go before a court biased, in the nature of things, on the side of the cleric.

These clerical courts were often used to reinforce doctrinal conformity and this, perhaps, was where the Church erred most gravely in failing to appreciate the temper of the times. The thinking man, from the fourteenth century on, and increasingly afterwards, when the Renaissance had opened up again the glories and freedoms of the past, and the arrival of cheap paper and the printing press enabled him to check the scriptural references for himself instead of having them interpreted to him from a book which he would not have been allowed to possess even if it had been freely available – the thinking man grew less and less willing to accept the Church's dictation on matters of dogma, though he was still prepared to go along with it on moral issues.

But before the great battle between the reformers and the traditionalists took place, the Church was to suffer yet another severe blow to its power and prestige: the Great Schism towards the end of the fourteenth century when rival popes ruled at Rome and Avignon, each excommunicated by the other, while the whole of Christendom lay under the interdict of one pope or another.

CHAPTER FIVE

# The Great Schism—— and the Reformation

## 1

The *Unam Sanctam* Bull which was designed to establish the supremacy of the pope over all kings, princes and heads of state for all time could do nothing of the sort; the papal claim to supremacy had already been roundly rejected by the three estates – clergy, nobility and commons – in both France and England.

Previously the popes had normally been dealing with one man, the emperor; in the fourteenth century they found themselves confronting entire nations.

King Philip of France, a very formidable adversary, now began to question the validity of Pope Boniface VIII's election, and indeed there were strong grounds for questioning it, inasmuch as his predecessor had abdicated in slightly suspicious circumstances. In 1303, a second assembly of the States-General approved King Philip's announced intention to refer the matter to a general council of the Church.

In the meantime, Philip sent an agent called Guillaume de Nogaret to Italy to seize the Pope and, if possible, force him to abdicate. De Nogaret actually got into the Pope's bedroom and made him prisoner in his own ancestral palace at Agnani; he was rescued after a few days by the townspeople of Agnani and returned to Rome but died shortly afterwards.

That this rough treatment of the pontiff did not arouse any storm of protest in Italy, England or even in the remains of the Holy Roman Empire, shows how much the temper of the times had altered.

Boniface's successor, Benedict XI, reigned for only a year, and in 1305 was succeeded by Clement V, a Frenchman, and King Philip's own candidate for the post. Clement set up his court in the town of Avignon on the Rhône, and never went near Rome. There his successors remained until 1377, demonstrating to the world that the Papacy had sunk to the rank of a mere instrument of the French king.

In 1377 Pope Gregory XI returned to Rome from Avignon, but unfortunately for the Church, the cardinals were now divided in their loyalties. As a result, when, in 1378, Gregory XI died, and an Italian Pope, Urban VI, was elected to replace him, the French cardinals, whose sympathies still lay in Avignon, declared the election invalid and elected another Pope, Clement VII, in his place.

This was the beginning of the Great Schism. Thereafter, for a period of over thirty years, a succession of popes remained on in Rome, enjoying the loyalty of all the people in Europe who were anti-French in feeling – the English, the Germans, the Poles and most of the people in the north of Europe. Another succession of popes – known as anti-popes by the Roman-based branch of the Church – continued to rule at Avignon, enjoying the support of France, Scotland, Spain, Portugal and a few German princes. Both popes freely excommunicated each other and their adherents and inevitably people began to think about religion for themselves.

Now began to appear the first precursors of the Reformation. In 1342 Marsilius of Padua had written a tract known as the *Defensor Pacis* which, translated into both French and Italian, attacked the Papacy as incompatible with the Holy Scriptures, defined the Church as the community of those who believe in Jesus Christ, and stated that the pope was merely a bishop like any other, who should confine his activities to preaching the faith and administering the sacraments and held that the supreme authority in the Church should rest, not with the pope, but with a Church council.

John Wycliffe, born in England in 1320, became a priest and, relatively late in life, began to attack the corruption of the clergy. England had continued to progress along the path which led away from Rome. The English Parliament had already begun to campaign against the system by which taxes on Church property went to Rome, and in 1376 Parliament had demanded the expulsion of the Curia's collectors and had pressed for legislation forbidding the export of money. The Emperor Frederick II's suggestion that some of the Church lands should be confiscated and secularized had cropped up on more than one occasion in the English Parliament.

John Wycliffe taught that the head of the Church was Christ and not the pope. The Word of God, as written in the Bible, was the basis of his teaching, and he pointed out that there was nothing in the

Bible to justify the rich and powerful organization that the Church had now become. He preached poverty; he held that there was no essential difference between priest and layman, and that the priests should be answerable to the secular laws. In order that people could study the Word of God, he sponsored a translation of the Bible into English. He also held that England was independent of the pope, since the power of the king was derived from God. He organized a number of poor priests, the Wycliffites, to spread his ideas; and finally, as his influence increased and his fame spread, he grew bolder and denied that transubstantiation actually took place during the Mass. Although accused of heresy and attacked by many prominent Churchmen, he had sufficient supporters among the burghers – who liked his doctrines for their political implications as much as for their religious content – to evade persecution and died peacefully in his bed at Lutterworth at the age of sixty-four.

After Wycliffe's death, Henry IV of England, at war with France and anxious for his own purposes to gain the support of the Pope, turned on Wycliffe's supporters – who became known to their enemies as the sect of the Lollards: the word refers to a noxious weed – and introduced a law condemning heretics to be burnt at the stake in England. He also forbade the translation of the Bible into English, and his successor Henry V sent Lord Cobham, one of Wycliffe's followers in the House of Lords, to the stake.

In Europe the Great Schism was then at its height and Christendom was divided into two factions, an eventuality which had financial as well as religious repercussions inasmuch as the two papal courts worked out about twice as expensive to run as one, and had to be financed out of the same grand total of Christians.

Strenuous efforts were made to heal the Schism, but the two rival popes remained adamant, and neither would step down sufficiently to allow the other to call the Ecumenical General Council that would be needed to settle the matter. However, the cardinals in the end got together, and took the unprecedented step of convoking a General Council in Pisa in 1409 over the heads of both popes.

The two popes, Gregory XII in Rome and Benedict XIII in Avignon, protested equally bitterly, but the Council went bravely ahead with its work, declared them both heretics, deposed the two of them, and put a new pope, Alexander V, in their place. The only short-term result of this was that there were now three rival popes all claiming to be the direct successor of St Peter on earth.

However, having elected Alexander V, the cardinals could not immediately depose him, and he was in turn succeeded in 1410 by John XXIII.* A council which met for the first time in Constance in 1414 deliberated for three years while finding a solution to the problem. It deposed John XXIII, persuaded Gregory XII to step down, and condemned Benedict XIII, who refused to give up his claim, as a heretic. Towards the end of 1417, the unity of the Church was restored by the election of Pope Martin V. There was a widespread feeling in the Church itself, as well as among the laity, that its organization was due for overhaul.

At this time in Bohemia, John Huss, greatly influenced by Wycliffe's teaching, adapted his message to the political needs of Czech nationalism, and preached a return to the simple faith of the Bible. He insisted, among other things, on the right of laymen to take wine from the chalice during Mass. This right had been removed not long before by the Church, fearful lest any drop of the 'blood of God' should be spilled. Huss argued that Christ had exhorted his followers: 'Drink it, all of you.' The Church's reply to this was that Christ's exhortation was addressed to the Apostles, all of whom were priests. Huss was also against the use of indulgences as a means of raising money for the Church.

Huss had been invited to attend the Council of Constance to discuss his ideas on reform with the Church leaders, and had been promised safe conduct by the Holy Roman Emperor, Sigismund. He went to the Council in the hope of converting some of the prominent churchmen of his day to his way of thinking; instead, and despite the safe conduct promised to him by the Emperor, he was seized, tried for heresy and burnt at the stake. This action had precisely the same effect as the persecution of the first Christians centuries earlier in Rome. It made him a martyr for the cause, fanned the faith of the Hussites and led to an insurrection, the first of a series of religious wars that plagued Europe for nearly two centuries.

Pope Martin V, the new head of the reunited Christian community, preached a crusade against the Hussites and, in all, five attempts were made to conquer the tough Czech nationalists who now sacked their clergy, confiscated all Church property, and went back to the Bible as the only valid source of instruction. Unfortunately, as subsequent reformers were soon to discover, free interpretation of the scriptures

* Actually John XXII, since owing to a mistake in the numbering there never was a John XX; this was later rectified.

inevitably leads to an endless diversity of small splinter groups of the faith; and this began to happen, even at this stage, among the Hussites, now known also as Taborites after a new holy city of Tabor, built on the site of the castle of Kozihradek where Huss had once lived. One sect, the Adamites, returned to life as they believed it to have been lived in the Garden of Eden, casting off their clothes and living on an island in the middle of a river, an impractical arrangement which was doomed to failure in the inclement climate of Bohemia.

In 1436 an agreement was patched up between the Hussites and a new council of the Church at Basle, which acknowledged some of the objections to the practices of the Roman Church. In fact, for a time around this period, it looked as if the Roman Church was going to avert the Reformation by reforming itself from within. Many of the cardinals were in favour of altering the whole autocratic structure of the Church and turning the Papacy into something more closely approaching a constitutional monarchy, under the Council, but unfortunately no general agreement on this point could be reached, and after yet another split, a Council meeting at Basle deposed Eugenius IV and appointed Felix V, the last of the Avignon-based popes, in his place, deliberated the matter intermittently for a further ten years, and finally dissolved itself in utter despair in 1449.

Once again, it looked as if the pope was the victor. The monarchical structure of the Papacy was retained intact and the pope remained supreme within his Church; but the Church, in the process, had lost much of its power over the minds of monarchs and of men. As a result of the long dispute between the popes and the councils, the kings – whom both parties to the dispute had been keen, at various periods, to woo – were able to regain some measure of control over the appointment and conduct of the bishops in their kingdoms, and the Papacy exercised very little political power outside Italy. Furthermore, after Adrian VI (1522–23), the popes, now installed in their new headquarters in the Vatican City, were exclusively elected from the ranks of the Italian cardinals. This prevented any repetition of the Avignon incident, but at the expense of the universal status which the Papacy had formerly enjoyed. Also, it made it that much easier for kings like Henry VIII of England to defy what he could now claim had become a purely foreign institution.

## 2

The Renaissance need not concern us here except for the effect it had on the minds of men, and to the extent that the temptations it put in the way of the already far too worldly popes and bishops of the Church to add to the splendours of their new headquarters in Rome, contributed to the final schism which ripped apart the now fragile fabric of Western Christendom, led to over a century of bitter religious warfare, violent persecutions and revolutionary upheavals, and left a legacy of bigotry and intolerance which flared up again in Belfast towards the end of 1968.

The first links between modern Europe and the old civilizations of Greece and Persia (and, indeed, farther east to the ancient wisdom of China) were forged, not by the cultured Christians, but by the hated and despised infidel. When the Moslem empire forced its way right across North Africa and the Straits of Gibraltar to Spain in the west, and through Persia to Turkistan in the east, pushing ever eastwards until it encountered the Indians and the Chinese, the intellectual stimulus which resulted affected all mankind and changed the whole course of civilization. In Persia the Arabs came in contact with scientific Greek literature, both in the original Greek and in Syrian translations. In Egypt, too, they encountered much long-forgotten Greek learning. In central Asia they met with Buddhism and were introduced to some of the material achievements of the Chinese civilization, among them the manufacture of paper which made printed books a possibility. In India they were exposed to Indian mathematics and philosophy.

The effect of all this cross-fertilization of ideas was an intellectual rebirth which considerably antedated and prepared the way for the European Renaissance of the fourteenth century. The systematic accumulation and criticism of observed facts which had been begun by the Greeks, and had been abandoned for nearly one thousand years, was now resumed by the Arabs. Considerable advances were made in medicine, the physical sciences and above all in mathematics. The inflexible Roman numerals were replaced by the Arabic figures still used today, and the zero sign was introduced. The very words algebra and chemistry are both Arabic.

The European Renaissance is generally taken to date from the fourteenth century, though there were signs that men were starting to think for themselves from the twelfth century onwards. There were many reasons for this, some of which have already been discussed. They included the higher standards of living which followed the Crusades; the stimulation of men's minds caused by their experiences during the Crusades; the growth of the semi-independent city states, all trading centres with travellers constantly coming and going, stimulating one another and exchanging ideas; and the fact that the Greek scholars, fleeing from Constantinople after the fall of the Byzantine Empire, brought immense cargoes of classical manuscripts to Europe with them.

Probably the greatest single factor, at any rate so far as the ordinary public was concerned, was the manufacture of paper. Chinese paper-makers had been among the prisoners captured by the Moslems in Samarkand in the eighth century, and Arab paper manuscripts dating from the ninth century still exist, but it wasn't until the fourteenth century that paper was sufficiently plentiful and cheap enough for printed books to become a practical possibility.

One immediate result of the development of the printed book – which profoundly affected the Church at a time when it was at its most vulnerable – was the appearance of large numbers of copies of the Bible, so that people were able for the first time to read the Word of God and interpret it for themselves. At the same time many school books and textbooks of one sort or another were printed, and a knowledge of reading (and, through it, a knowledge of all sorts of other subjects) began to spread rapidly among the ordinary people.

The domination of the Latin Church was now nearing an end, and the intellectual and material leadership was passing into the hands of the new Europeans.

## 3

It was unfortunate, if understandable, that the throne of St Peter should have been occupied, at this juncture, by as worldly a collection of rogues as ever darkened the doorway of the Vatican. Rome was now a flourishing city state, of course, and the popes of this period had most of the sordid vices as well as some of the towering talents of such purely secular ruling dynasties as the Visconti, the Sforza, and the Medici.

Sixtus IV, who built the Sistine Chapel, had been engaged in a conspiracy to overthrow the Medici, in the course of which Giuliano de' Medici was assassinated by a priest at Mass in Florence cathedral.

Alexander VI had four illegitimate children, among them Cesare Borgia and his notorious sister Lucrezia, and held orgies in the Vatican itself.

Pope Julius II (the patron of Michelangelo) donned armour and led his own troops into battle, scaling the walls of Bologna at the head of his army, an action which shocked many people who felt that the Viceroy of the Prince of Peace had no business waging war.

Leo X, a member of the Medici family – who was Pope when Martin Luther made his famous attack on the Church at Wittenberg – much preferred his hunting lodge to the Vatican and is reported to have said: 'The Papacy is ours. Let us enjoy it.'

To finance such excesses, the Papacy was drawn increasingly into extravagant dealings with the bankers, despite the traditional Christian condemnation of usury, and was obliged to lean heavily upon its supporters all over Europe in order to raise money to repay those bankers.

By the early years of the sixteenth century the complaints against the Church had crystallized into three main grievances: corruption and immorality among the clergy; intolerable financial demands upon the Christian communities outside Rome; and neglect of the parishes everywhere. The enforcement of clerical celibacy had merely produced a rash of concubines: complaints about the general behaviour of the clergy were rife throughout the whole of Europe, and the popes of Rome were among the worst offenders in this matter.

The papal taxes had long been causing resentment in many European countries, more especially as the money collected was often used by the popes to conduct their own private wars, very often contrary to the best interests of the countries from which the taxes had been extorted. The sales of offices within the Church was a widespread scandal and the traffic in indulgences had reached the proportions of another major scandal. People resented the payment of tithes when non-payment meant excommunication – particularly if those tithes were being used for the further adornment of the Vatican palace in Rome, when the parish church contributing the cash badly needed a new roof to keep out the rain. In some areas, so much money was taken from local parish-church funds for the support of the Church's headquarters in Rome, that priests were unable to live on the revenue of one single parish and had to combine several, a practice known as 'pluralism' which led local parishioners to believe, quite rightly, that their interests were being neglected in the interests of Rome.

## 4

The next formidable attacks on the Church came from a Dutch scholar called Erasmus. He had been brought up in the tradition of the Brethren of the Common Life, a loose, mystical breakaway movement which had originated in the Netherlands. Their principal belief was in the importance of following in the footsteps of Christ, and they rejected indulgences on the ground that a prodigal son needs no indulgence to secure his father's forgiveness.

While he was the guest of Thomas More in London, Erasmus wrote a book called *The Praise of Folly* (*Moriae encomium*) which was a shattering indictment of corruption within the Church. He was against monasticism because of the system's insistence on celibacy and its withdrawal from society. He rejected the cult of relics; and he believed in reducing dogma to those tenets simple enough to be universally understood, holding that God could not possibly punish men for not believing some piece of sophistry which their minds could not grasp. He considered the doctrine of transubstantiation as an unwarranted accretion, and interpreted the presence of Christ in the sacrament in a purely symbolical sense. The essence of his reform was a return to the Bible.

But the reformer who was to change radically the whole pattern of Christianity was a Catholic monk initially interested only in reforming himself, an introspective and tortured individual whose soul-searchings led him eventually to question the authority of the Church on all major matters. Martin Luther entered the Augustinian monastery at Erfurt, in Germany, at the age of twenty-two. Assigned to the chair of biblical studies at Wittenberg university, he took the degree of Doctor of Theology and soon reached the conclusion that the interpretation of the scriptures could and should be undertaken by all Christians of good faith, under the guidance from the Holy Spirit, and should not be left solely to the clergy.

If his post at Wittenberg had not required him also to carry out the ordinary duties of a parish priest, it is possible that the reforms he advocated would have gone no further than an effort to confine theological education to a study of the scriptures. However, his duties as parish priest brought him up against one of the worst examples of the misuse of indulgences. Albert, Archbishop of Magdeburg and Bishop of Halberstadt – and a member of the house of Hohenzollern – wished for political reasons to be made Archbishop of Mainz and Primate of Germany. The normal fee to the Pope for appointment to the See of Mainz was exorbitant enough, but a special price was struck for Albert, who borrowed ten thousand ducats from the banking house of Fugger in Augsburg and paid this money over to the Pope, to ensure his appointment. To enable Albert to repay the loan, the Pope allowed indulgences to be 'preached' throughout his territories for eight years, half of the proceeds going to repay the bankers and the other half going towards a basilica which he was erecting over what were believed to be relics of St Peter and St Paul in Rome. Extravagant claims were made for these indulgences: not only would they remit penalties imposed, but also the sins themselves, and in some cases they would even remit sins not yet committed.

Galled by such overt cynicism, Martin Luther decided to act. On the eve of All Saints Day, 31 October 1517, he posted a series of points for debate on the door of the castle church at Wittenberg; known as the Ninety-five Theses, they were soon being hotly discussed all over Germany. Among them Luther claimed that the pope had no power over Purgatory, but that if he had, he should empty the place for nothing and not charge for the privilege. More important, he condemned as damned all who try to bargain with God to escape damnation, and by implication rejected the whole concept of the treasury of virtue on which the doctrine of indulgences had been based.

In arguments which followed, he began to switch his attack to the Church's authority. For the infallibility of the pope and the Church councils, he substituted the infallibility of the scriptures, failing to realize, perhaps, what divergences there could be in the interpretation of these scriptures.

Luther was not to be excommunicated for nearly four years because the popes of the period were too busy trying to manipulate the election of the next Holy Roman Emperor: they did not want to see any additional power falling into the hands of those already powerful monarchs, Francis I of France and Charles I of Spain. The Papacy's choice, Frederick the Wise of Saxony, a minor prince, was a lucky one for Luther. Frederick, who had founded the University of Wittenberg and had already secured a first hearing for Luther on German soil rather than at Rome, was a supporter of Luther's. While the Papacy dithered about taking action against him, Luther proceeded to turn out a whole series of telling tracts printed in German and addressed not to scholars but to ordinary people.

Pope Leo finally issued a papal bull – from his hunting lodge, needless to say – calling on Luther to recant, but there was a further considerable delay in delivering this bull to Luther, which he occupied in publishing yet more tracts rejecting a number of Roman sacraments and doctrines and laying the foundation of what was to become the Protestant faith.

Guaranteed a safe conduct by Frederick the Wise – which would probably have been worth as little as the safe conduct earlier guaranteed to Huss, if in the meantime the printing press had not changed things and if Luther had not had many influential friends among the German princes – he attended a conference known as the Diet of Worms, and restated his position: he could not accept the authority of popes and councils because they had in the past patently contradicted each other. Luther was banned as an excommunicated heretic, but was allowed to hide for nearly a year in a castle called the Wartburg where he spent his time translating the New Testament into German.

In 1522 Luther returned to Wittenberg, where he lived unmolested for another twenty-five years and formulated what was originally known as the Lutheran faith. By 1524, the saying of Mass had been abolished in the city, and within the next few years the Lutheran faith had spread through Germany, to the Netherlands, Denmark, Norway and Sweden.

Right from the outset, the new religion ran into difficulties inherent in its very freedom from fixed dogma. One of Luther's colleagues, Carlstadt – a co-founder of Lutheranism – interpreted the doctrine of the priesthood of all believers to mean that ministers should be laymen without special titles, qualifications, or dress, and should support themselves by manual labour. He also wanted to reject church music and all religious images, but these Luther insisted on retaining, even going to the lengths of publishing two hymn-books for the new religion, writing the words for many of the hymns himself and collaborating with an organist on the tunes.

Two other innovations of Luther's were the abolition of

monasticism and celibacy of the clergy, and he himself married a nun from the convent at Wittenberg, which had been dissolved.

By 1530, Lutheranism had consolidated its hold over large areas of Europe and was expanding rapidly; Catholic minorities were allowed to continue to practise their religion in predominantly Lutheran areas, but the same liberty was not extended to Lutheran minorities in Catholic areas. This is probably an over-simplification but it was basically because they protested against this situation that Lutherans were given the name Protestants.

While Lutheranism was expanding in Germany, another variety of Protestantism developed in German Switzerland, originally under the Swiss humanist, Zwingli; and later under the French theologian, John Calvin. Known as Calvinism, this breakaway movement developed into a number of diverse forms of Nonconformist Protestantism, among them Presbyterianism and Methodism. As a result of the Calvinist belief that to labour industriously is highly acceptable in the eyes of God – an idea which contrasted sharply with the medieval notion that it was blessed to be poor and that usury was wicked – Calvinism held an immediate appeal for the new middle-class merchants. While the Calvinists and their successors shunned luxury and held thrift to be a virtue, nevertheless their teachings implied that financial soundness was a mark of God's favour. In this way, Calvinism became closely related to the rise of capitalism, in a curious mixture of both cause and effect.

Calvinism very quickly also became international in outlook; the Calvinists did not accept the territorial principle but spread their religion wherever they could get a foothold – in France, in the Netherlands, in New England, Lithuania, Poland, Hungary, and, of course, in England and Scotland. We shall be dealing in more detail with the effects of the Reformation in the British Isles in the next chapter; in the meantime, it is perhaps worth adding that even at this comparatively early stage in the history of the Reformed Church, it had produced splinter groups and movements acceptable neither to the Lutherans, the Catholics nor the Calvinists. To take one example, the Anabaptists – who believed in adult baptism – were burned by the Catholics and drowned by the Protestants.

But despite all these and other teething pains, the Reformation had taken firm roots throughout Europe. Unlike the earlier reformers, Luther came on the scene at exactly the right time, at a period when economic individualism and the forces of nationalism guaranteed support for his ideas and ideals. Initially, he was supported primarily by the German peasants, who were genuinely shocked at the abuses he had revealed in the management of the Church, but soon he was enjoying the support of the noblemen who saw in his new religion a way of breaking the domination of the pope. Also, his condemnation of monasticism found supporters all over Europe among rulers and noblemen who, for years, as we have seen, had been looking with growing envy at vast tracts of land owned by the Church, and who saw, in the new Lutheran doctrines, a possible justification for getting their hands on some of this property.

Whatever the minor differences within the ranks of the Protestants, the big schism was now between Catholics on the one hand and Protestants on the other. Catholicism naturally reacted by mounting a Counter-Reformation. In 1540, a group of dedicated Catholics who had originally planned a missionary expedition to Palestine – the group included Ignatius of Loyola and Francis Xavier – obtained a bull from Pope Paul III authorizing the formation of the Society of Jesus, or the Jesuits as they are more commonly called.

Their organization was military and autocratic, and they enjoyed many privileges as the *corps d'élite* of the armies of the Counter-Reformation. They paid no taxes, acknowledged no secular authority and were exempt from the jurisdiction of all prelates save their own. Their prime job was to preach and teach – above all teach, since children are more susceptible than adults – and for centuries the Jesuit schools and colleges all over the world were the most influential instruments for spreading Catholic faith and propaganda.

CHAPTER SIX

# The British Isles and the Papacy

## 1

The existence of the British Isles was known to the Romans before the third century B.C. Pytheas of Marseilles had circumnavigated them in the fourth century B.C. and had proclaimed the existence of two large islands which he called Albion and Ierne. In 55 B.C. and again in the following year, Julius Caesar had led exploratory expeditions to Britain – he got as far as Brentford and was victorious to the extent that he was able to bring a party of British hostages back to trail at the heel of one of his triumphal processions through the streets of Rome. But it was another century – a century which saw the birth and death of Christ, and the foundation of the Christian Church – before the Romans returned to invade and subjugate Britannia, as they now called the larger of the two islands.

At this period of history, Britain was populated by a race of Celts, not unlike the inhabitants of Gaul in their appearance or their way of life, and Scotland by the more primitive Picts. Their principal religion was Druidism; in fact, Britain was the headquarters of the Druidical religion, about which relatively little is known except that the Druids worshipped in sacred oak groves and many of their rites were related to the sun, the planets and other natural phenomena, and some of them were extremely cruel, often involving human sacrifice.

In A.D. 43, almost a century after Caesar's exploratory landings in Britain, an army of 20,000 Roman soldiers conquered the country after a fierce and cruel campaign. The more recalcitrant Celts were pushed away into the damp, dark fastnesses of Wales, or behind Hadrian's Wall in the north of England; the others settled down under Roman rule and for almost four centuries – roughly as long as the period which separates the reign of Queen Elizabeth I from that of Queen Elizabeth II – lived happy and prosperous lives in what had become a province of the Roman Empire. The province was eventually policed by an army of occupation of 40,000 men – after a few generations recruited locally and mostly of British birth. The wealthier Britons in this period probably lived better lives, from a material point of view, than at any period since, until the present century. They had hot baths and central heating and enjoyed a freedom of movement throughout the Empire – at that period amounting to the known world – which has only come about again within our own generation.

The Romans wiped out Druidism within a few years of their conquest of Britain, though it persisted for several centuries in Ireland, a country which the Romans, for some reason, did not bother to invade, though they did some trading with the Irish Celts. This failure of the Romans to colonize Ireland may well have contributed something to what later became the Irish Question. For it is probable that 400 years of exposure to orderly Roman rule might have turned the Celts into a tractable, law-abiding, peace-loving people, accustomed to the idea of colonization and centralized control by another race; and it is certain that a system of long, straight Roman roads would have made the country far easier to administer and control, both from a military and civil point of view.

Very little is known about the arrival of Christianity in Britain, but some time after the Roman invasion the first Christian communities appeared and there were British bishops at the first great council of the Church. But towards the end of the third century, when the barbarians began to make inroads into the Roman Empire in Europe, Britain was assailed by Picts and Celts from beyond Hadrian's Wall, as well as by Saxons who rowed in long-boats across the North Sea. Again and again the Picts and Scots broke through the wall, while ruthless Saxon invaders destroyed villas and homesteads, cities and fortresses. For a century, the Romans made valiant efforts to protect the province, but Rome herself was being more and more heavily pressed by the barbarians at this period, and eventually the legions were withdrawn and Britain was left to fend for herself.

Up to this point the Christian communities survived. It is on record that the Bishop of Auxerre, later St Germanus, came to Britain to disabuse the British clergy of the Pelagian heresy to which they had succumbed – this was a doctrine which assigned what was in the Church's official view, an undue importance to free will.

But this was merely a brief respite. Soon the mass invasions of Saxons, Angles and Jutes from north Germany began, and an impenetrable darkness closed in over England's history – a darkness during which Christianity went underground or perhaps disappeared altogether.

And it was from Ireland that Christianity was reintroduced into England. In the last days of the Roman rule, a band of Irish pirates made a raid on the Severn valley and captured, among others, a young Roman-Briton, the son of a Christian deacon, called Patrick. The young Patrick was carried off and sold into slavery in Ireland. For six years he herded sheep on the slopes of a mountain in County Antrim. Eventually he escaped to the Continent, studied for the priesthood and returned to Ireland in A.D. 432 as a bishop, determined to bring Christianity to the savage pagans among whom he had spent his youth.

St Patrick's mission was an instant and resounding success. The Celts seemed to take very readily to the Christian message. Patrick organized such Christianity as was already in existence and converted whole kingdoms which were still pagan.

In the dark ages of Europe, the tiny island now became an ecclesiastical centre of learning that was known throughout the Continent. Irish monks and priests were in great demand as scribes, teachers and translators all over Europe, and students flocked to Ireland to study. And it was from Ireland that the Christian message was carried to the north of England where the first attempts were now made to convert the Picts. Columba and other Irish monks born after Patrick's death, but imbued with his ideals, founded a monastery at Iona and sent out missionaries all over Britain – and, in effect, the Irish missionaries reconverted England to Christianity.

There was, however, a profound difference between the form of Christianity which was spread by St Patrick and St Columba and that which was practised throughout the Christian countries of Europe. The former was monastic in its pattern and tended to be autonomous, and rather too independent of Rome for Rome's liking, a circumstance which became a contributing factor in England's domination over Ireland centuries later.

In the meantime the popes in Rome watched the activities of St Patrick and St Columba with interest, but also with a certain amount of alarm inasmuch as these new branches of the Christian Church, while undoubtedly gratifyingly ardent in their faith, also seemed to be alarmingly independent of Rome. Accordingly, towards the end of the sixth century, Pope Gregory decided to send an emissary to

Britain to bring about a closer liaison between the British Church and the Papacy. A cultured monk called Augustine was chosen for the task, and he attempted (though without any marked success) to establish British Christianity along the European hierarchical pattern, with headquarters at Canterbury. Ireland, for some reason, he left to its own devices. Some years later another Roman envoy, Paulinus, came to England and achieved the conversion of further heathen tribes, until by the middle of the seventh century all of Anglo-Saxon England had been converted to Christianity. There remained only a considerable difference of opinion as to whether the Roman or the Celtic approach to Christianity should prevail.

An attempt was made, at the Synod of Whitby in 663, to settle this question once and for all, and about five-sixths of the island went over to the Roman system, so that for the first time there was a unity of faith, morals and Church government prevailing throughout the greater part of Britain.

Then the Danes came, and for a time ruled over the greater part of England. During the reign of King Canute, Britain was part of a Danish confederation. The Normans, a hardy race of Nordic adventurers – the Romans called them Normani – who found the fertile farmlands of northern France far more to their liking than their own harsh northern shores and had already settled there, conquered England in 1066 and added it to their domains. The Normans were good Christians and they built many fine churches and cathedrals in the north of France and in England and further strengthened England's ties with Rome.

And it was during the early years of the Norman rule in Britain that the first military and diplomatic contacts with the Irish were made. England's Norman barons, looking for fresh estates and raw material for their armies, had already been casting envious eyes at the relatively unknown and undeveloped land not far across the water, but it was one of a series of endless disputes between the Irish kings which led directly to Norman intervention in Irish affairs. Dermot MacMurrough, King of Leinster, one of the Irish provinces, defeated and banished by the then High King of Ireland, Rory O'Connor, went to England and sought permission from Henry II to raise an army of auxiliaries in south Wales to recapture his kingdom. Travelling to Bristol, he brought his beautiful daughter Eva with him, offering her hand in marriage to any Norman baron prepared to lead an expeditionary force against Ireland; Dermot's own plan was to take over the High Kingship of Ireland himself, with the support of Norman troops.

Permission was granted and a Norman expeditionary force landed at Waterford in 1170, under the command of the Earl of Pembroke, known as Strongbow. He had been brought up in Wales but, like most of the Norman barons, still spoke French. He conquered Waterford and Dublin and was just settling in, preparatory perhaps to breaking away from England and setting up his own independent Norman kingdom in Ireland, when Henry II arrived with an army of knights to ensure that Ireland became part of his own personal kingdom. Ignoring the High King and the whole Irish monarchical structure, he parcelled Ireland up between various of his Norman barons and a few native kings who agreed to pay annual tribute to him for the privilege of being permitted to continue to rule in their own country. To be fair to Henry, he did not do this without authority of a sort. Pope Adrian IV – the only English pope, Nicholas Brakespeare – had issued a bull bestowing the island on the Norman rulers of England. He had several reasons for doing this. As we have seen, the Papacy had been increasingly alarmed by Ireland's divergence from the Roman pattern of Christianity, and Pope Adrian IV felt that under strong Norman rule it would be easier to bring the Irish Church back into line. Furthermore Ireland alone of all the countries of Christendom had taken no part in the Crusades and was in bad need of a skelp of the crozier on that score alone.

The struggle between the popes and the emperors, discussed earlier, took place in England in microcosm during the reign of Henry II, and although Thomas à Becket was murdered by Henry's knights, the final victory went to the Church which retained the system of clerical courts independent of the royal authority and the right to appeal to Rome over the head of the king in cases of differences of opinion between bishop and king, the two major points upon which Becket had defied the king.

We have already seen that England was among the first of the European countries to take a stand against the Papacy on such matters as legacies of land to the Church. Right from the earliest Anglo-Saxon times, the English had inclined to the theory of kingship to which the Elizabethan reformers later returned. There was a widespread belief that the monarch was appointed by God, not only to rule the State, but also to protect the Church.

On this issue, matters reached a head during the reign of King

John. The death of the Archbishop of Canterbury, Hubert Walter, his most trusted statesman, reopened the unsettled question as to whether king or pope should elect the Primate of England.

The pope at this period was Innocent III, one of the greatest of the medieval popes, and one who was determined to increase the temporal power of the Church. Rejecting both the candidate chosen by the clergy of Canterbury and King John's own candidate, the Pope selected Stephen Langton for the position. Langton was an English cardinal of impeccable character and qualifications, but John refused to accept him and began to wage a bloodless war on the Church. When he started to persecute the clergy and seize Church lands, the Pope retaliated by laying the whole of England under an interdict. Church bells were silent, church doors were closed to the faithful, and the dead had to be buried in unhallowed ground without the solace of extreme unction.

King John, as obstinate as the Pope, redoubled his attacks on Church property. Then in 1209, the Pope took the ultimate step of excommunication. John replied by seizing still more ecclesiastical property, until the Exchequer overflowed with the spoils. Innocent's reaction to this was to form an alliance with the king of France which might have resulted in a French invasion of England, if John had not turned the tables by offering to make England a fief of the Papacy. Innocent jumped at the prospect of this valuable addition to his temporal possessions, accepted the sovereignty of England from John and returned it to the English King as his vassal, and John now had the Pope as an ally.

Edward I, as we have already seen (p. 52), also ran into trouble with the Church and made it very clear that he did not appreciate the Pope's interference in secular matters within his realm.

Two other events in Edward's reign are worth mentioning in passing. One is that he was the first monarch to summon what amounted to a House of Commons, calling knights of the shire and borough members as well as the King's Great Council to assist him in running the country, though initially they sat separately in three chambers.

The second is the expulsion of the Jews. This came about because land, at this period of history, was beginning to change from a feudal possession with moral rights and duties, to a saleable commodity. The Jews, then as now in the forefront of the finance business, had installed themselves in the social fabric of thirteenth-century England

and were quick with mortgage offers to financially embarrassed knights and barons, with the result that a sizeable portion of the ancient soil of England was passing into Jewish hands. Small landowners who were being pressed for heavy repayments on their mortgages, and feckless knights unable to meet their commitments were loud in their complaints against the heartless money-lenders. Atrocity stories began to circulate – Little Hugh, buried in Lincoln Cathedral, was said to have been the victim of a ritual murder by the Jews – and Edward took the easy way out: he expelled all Jews from his realm. The ban persisted for four centuries, until Cromwell's time.

The next round in the battle between the kings of England and the Papacy occurred during the reign of Richard II and concerned the question of the jurisdiction of royal courts as against the Church courts. Richard passed a series of Statutes of Praemunire which provided that anyone who obtained a transfer of a case to Rome, or who obtained processes, sentences of excommunication, bulls, instruments or in 'any other things whatsoever which touch the King, against him, his crown and regality, or his realm, should lose the royal protection and forfeit all his goods to the King' (I quote from Churchill's *A History of the English-speaking Peoples*).

These statutes became a favourite instrument of Cardinal Wolsey's for exacting money for the King, and did much to pave the way for Thomas Cromwell's subsequent diversion of the wealth of the monasteries into the Exchequer and into the pockets of the English landed gentry.

The stage was now set for the final break between England and Rome, though it did not come until the reign of Henry VIII.

But before moving on to Henry VIII and the pattern of the Reformation in England, it is necessary to glance at some of the effects of the aftermath of the Norman invasion of Ireland.

For a time the Norman conquerors had to fight to hold on to the lands that were assigned to them by Henry II, but gradually they spread their power piecemeal, reproducing in Ireland the whole feudal structure of manors and abbeys, castles and fortresses. And eventually their presence came to be accepted by many of the Celtic Irish while the Normans, in their turn, began to adopt Irish habits and customs and in some cases even learned to speak the Irish language.

Second and third generation Anglo-Norman lords, born and brought up in Ireland, started to think of themselves not as Anglo-

Norman, but as Anglo-Irish or Norman-Irish, a situation which did not appeal to the English monarchs who feared an eventual line-up between these Anglo-Irish barons and the native Irish kings and chieftains. So, every effort was made to drive a wedge between them.

The first Parliament of Ireland was convoked towards the end of the thirteenth century. It consisted of ecclesiastical and lay peers plus knights and burgesses from 'the colonies'; no native Irish were invited to attend and all business was conducted in French and English. One of the first actions of this Parliament was to condemn colonists who persisted in wearing Irish hair-styles or clothes.

Subsequent parliaments set about creating a situation which would prevent any effective collusion between the Norman colonizers and the native Irish. It was made illegal for the settlers to intermarry with the Irish, or dress in the Irish style, or sponsor Irish children, or recognize any of the ancient Irish laws, or maintain Irish poets, bards or minstrels; and any Anglo-Norman subject caught speaking Gaelic was liable to have his lands confiscated. Thus the settlers were forced – against their will in many cases – into the position of a foreign colony, set among a people with whom they were forbidden to fraternize: a state of affairs which could not but lead to bitterness and strife. And it needed only the Reformation to add the highly explosive ingredient of religious bigotry to an already highly inflammable situation.

## 2

Henry VIII was a devout Catholic. In fact, until the death of his elder brother, Prince Arthur, he had been intended for the Church. From the Pope he had earned the title 'Defender of the Faith' – which is still, illogically, part of the official title of the English monarch – as a consequence of a tract he wrote attacking Luther.

Henry VIII's quarrel with Rome was not over doctrine, nor even finance, but on a matter of politics: royal marriages came under the heading of politics, inasmuch as the succession to the throne was involved. At the time of his quarrel with the Papacy, Henry VIII had been married for sixteen years to Catherine of Aragon, who was eight years his senior, and who had given him, in all those years, only one child, a daughter Mary. He desperately wanted a son, and he also desperately wanted to marry Anne Boleyn, a niece of the Duke of Norfolk.

Catherine had previously been married to Henry's elder brother, Arthur, for several months, so that technically Henry's marriage to Catherine was prohibited by the laws of the Church, though a papal dispensation had been granted on the grounds that Catherine's marriage to Arthur had never been consummated. Catherine herself stoutly maintained that her marriage to Arthur had *not* been consummated, but nobody believed her. The question of the legality of the marriage was put first to a number of English bishops, who held that once the papal dispensation had been granted, the marriage was perfectly legal. But Henry next sent an ambassador to Pope Clement VII, requesting not only an annulment of the marriage but also a dispensation to marry Anne Boleyn at once. In all probability the Pope could have found some formula which would have enabled him to oblige Henry in this matter were it not for the fact that he was at this juncture virtually a prisoner of Charles V, both Holy Roman Emperor and King of Spain, and nephew of Henry VIII's wife, Catherine. In fact, Charles's troops had just sacked Rome, in 1527, as a protest against the fact that they had not been paid.

Cranmer, a young university lecturer in Divinity, now suggested that the question as to whether Henry's marriage to Catherine was legal should be taken away from the bishops and submitted to the universities of Europe. In the main – and including some within the Papal States – they held that the King was within his rights and that the Pope could not legally set aside so fundamental a law.

King Henry VIII now began to pass a whole series of minor measures undermining Rome's authority, as much perhaps to test the reactions of the English public as for any other reason. Yet he remained a Catholic in all matters of doctrine.

The break with Rome occurred gradually, over a period of years. In 1530 the whole body of the clergy in England were charged with breaking the Statutes of Praemunire (see p. 74), and, in return for a pardon, were forced to pay over vast sums to the King; the province of Canterbury alone contributed £100,000 to the Exchequer. In February 1531, the clergy were obliged to acknowledge the King as 'their special Protector, one and supreme Lord, and, as far as the Church allows, even supreme head'.

Through all this wrangling, and despite the fact that Henry was spending a great deal of his time with Anne Boleyn, Catherine and her daughter Mary remained at Court. In 1531 they were banished, whereupon Rome threatened excommunication or an interdict if Henry did not get rid of his concubine Anne Boleyn within fifteen days. Henry replied with the Annates Bill: if Rome attempted to excommunicate England or put the country under an interdict, the sacraments and divine services would continue to be administered, and the interdict would not be executed. Bishops nominated by the King would become bishops with or without Rome's approval, and as a final stroke, in the region of finance, where it hurt most, the Annates – principal source of the papal finances – would be restricted to five per cent of their former amount.

By May 1532, Henry had become, in effect, spiritual head of the Church in England, and later that year he openly flouted the Pope by offering the Archbishopric of Canterbury to Cranmer, a man who had married twice: the second time *after* his ordination, and to the niece of a well-known Lutheran.

In January 1533, Henry married Anne Boleyn without any further communication with the Pope on the subject.

The final and irreparable break with Rome came with the Act of Appeals, a bill which vested in the Archbishop of Canterbury the power, formerly possessed by the Pope, to decide on all appeals from ecclesiastical courts in England. The judgements of English courts would no longer be affected by papal verdicts or by excommunication, and any priest who refused to celebrate the divine service or to administer the sacraments would be liable to imprisonment. In a letter, written at this period, Henry described himself as 'King and Sovereign, recognizing no superior in earth but only God, and not subject to the laws of any earthly creature'.

When Catherine refused to renounce her title of Queen of England voluntarily, Cranmer held a court at Dunstable which pronounced that she had been married to Henry in fact, but not in law, and Anne Boleyn was crowned Queen in June 1533. That September the future Queen Elizabeth was born, but already King Henry was paying court to Jane Seymour.

Nevertheless, he had an Act of Supremacy passed to ensure that Elizabeth, and not Mary, would succeed to the throne, and every person of legal age was forced to swear allegiance to this Act, which also confirmed Henry's position as Supreme Head of the Church. A prayer was prescribed for use in all churches containing the words: 'Henry VIII being immediately next unto God, the only and supreme head of this Catholic Church of England, and Anne his wife, and Elizabeth daughter and heir to them both, our Princess.' To suggest that the King was a heretic or a tyrant was regarded as high treason and many hundreds of people were hanged, drawn and quartered for their inability or their refusal to accept this sudden change in the pattern of a religion which they had regarded as permanent and changeless. Shortly afterwards Henry was excommunicated by the Pope and technically deprived of his throne, though by this time what the Pope did or said was hardly even of academic interest to Henry.

In January 1536, Queen Catherine died. In May of the same year Anne Boleyn was beheaded on a variety of charges including infidelity to the King and incest with her brother. Ten days later the King married Jane Seymour with whom he seems to have been relatively happy for eighteen months, until her death in 1537, immediately after the birth of a child, the future King Edward VI.

## 3

Henry now turned his attention to the dissolution of the monasteries.

This work had already begun in a small way in Cardinal Wolsey's time, and in fact it was an ancestor of Oliver Cromwell's who had been largely responsible. Thomas Cromwell was the son of a Putney publican and had spent some years on the Continent as a mercenary and then a money-lender before returning to England with enough capital to set up in business. Cardinal Wolsey heard of the man and offered him the job of managing his business affairs. One aspect of these business affairs involved the takeover of some small monasteries whose revenues the Pope had permitted Wolsey to use for the foundation of a new college at Oxford.

Now, with King Henry as Supreme Head of the Church in England, there seemed to be no good reason why the remainder of the monasteries should not be 'investigated'. The Germans had already led the way in this enterprise: since the Reformation many merchants and nobles had grown rich on the spoils of the monasteries. As Henry's chief minister, Cromwell was in a very strong position to urge the King to examine the monasteries, not indeed that the King needed much persuasion, since he was yet again running short of revenue.

The dissolution of the monasteries held an instant appeal for the landed gentry who were able to acquire all kinds of fine estates on extremely favourable terms. In the main, the displaced monks were not too unhappy either, since they were granted substantial pensions; some even married and transformed themselves into the new parish clergy of the Reformed Church of England.

By 1540 most of the monasteries had gone, and both Henry VIII and Thomas Cromwell were a good deal the richer. Their dues from land and stock – perhaps a fifth of all British plough and pasture, as Hilaire Belloc puts it in his biography of Cromwell – went to the Crown, along with their beasts, and the money made on the sale of their furniture plus the fittings, books, gold and silver and even buildings. The agents, with Cromwell at their head, took a percentage. One result of the dissolution of the monasteries was to commit the landed gentry and the merchants firmly to the Reformation. The working classes, particularly in the north where there was considerable unemployment, were by no means so firmly behind it; they had always counted to some extent on the monasteries for succour when times were hard and found their new landlords far less anxious to aid them.

Although Henry's own religious beliefs remained unaltered except in relation to Rome's authority, many of his ministers, notably Cranmer, now inclined heavily towards the Lutheran outlook. Complete printed Bibles, translated into English by Tyndale and Coverdale, appeared in 1535, and the clergy were encouraged to give readings from them. In 1538 this English Bible, revised yet again by Cranmer, was ordered to be placed in all churches; and later the Creed, the Ten Commandments, the Lord's Prayer and some Canticles were also translated from Latin into English. Henry's attitude seemed strangely ambivalent: in a sense he had reached the sort of inconclusive conclusion reached by today's ecumenical reformers in Rome who have agreed that the business of the Church should be conducted everywhere in the vernacular but are half-fearful that the effect of this decision may be to undermine the Church's authority.

## 4

It is now necessary to look again at events in Ireland.

The Reformation had no immediate effect whatever upon the native Irish. At this period the everyday language of the ordinary

Irish people was still Irish (Gaelic), and no serious attempt was ever made to convert the Catholic masses to Protestantism because the bishops of the reformed Church and the Tudor officials who accompanied them were cut off from the only language through which this conversion might have been achieved.

The Reformation was heralded in Ireland – as it was in England – by the suppression of the monasteries, abbeys, convents and all the other institutions which might have been used as a base for attempts to spread the Reformed religion.

The Reformation did, however, add to the Crown's problems with the degenerate English, or Anglo-Irish, for it had the effect of making many of the English settlers, who objected to the religious change, side with the native Irish.

Fully aware of this danger, and aware too that he could no longer claim the country under an ancient papal grant when he had so signally refused to recognize the pope's authority on other matters, Henry VIII had the title 'King of Ireland' conferred on him by edict of the Irish Parliament in the presence of many of the Irish and Anglo-Irish chieftains. At the same time he tried out a new policy in an effort to make the ruling classes more dependent on him. He made the Irish and the 'degenerate' Anglo-Irish chieftains surrender their lands to him and receive them back, to be held by knight-service. Some of these Irish chieftains were given English-style titles, which explains how families like the O'Neills of Ulster – descendants of an ancient High King of Ireland – came to hold such English-sounding titles as Earl of Tyrone.

Religion was now becoming more and more a key element in power politics. It is easy to overlook, and cannot be too strongly stressed, that despite his quarrels with the Pope, Henry was, and remained to his death, a Catholic. The older nobility, too, although more than content with the political revolution – that is, the break with Roman supremacy and the suppression of the monasteries – wanted the Reformation to stop there, and opposed all the Lutheran doctrinal changes favoured by Cranmer and his following. In 1539, Henry issued, through Parliament, a Statute of Six Articles of Roman doctrine and practice to deny which counted as heresy; these articles reaffirmed the essentially Catholic (as opposed to Lutheran) nature of Henry's independent religion.

The Duke of Norfolk headed the faction which was opposed to any change in the Catholic doctrine and practice, with Stephen

Gardiner, Bishop of Winchester (later Queen Mary's adviser), as his chief counsellor. The other faction was headed by Edward Seymour, Earl of Hertford, who later became Duke of Somerset.

An alliance between the Emperor Charles V and the French made it imperative for Henry to seek allies on the mainland of Europe. The Duke of Cleves to some extent shared Henry's own attitude to religion – a dislike of papal interference combined with a very lukewarm attitude to extreme Lutheranism – and when Cromwell suggested that Henry should marry Anne of Cleves, the King agreed, and did marry her, though he found her so unattractive that the marriage was never consummated and was shortly afterwards annulled. This provided Cromwell's enemies with the excuse they had been waiting for, and Cromwell went the way of others of Henry's advisers.

After Cromwell's execution, the Duke of Norfolk attempted to strengthen his position by marrying another of his nieces, Catherine Howard, to Henry (she thus became wife number five) but the now ageing Henry was incapable of satisfying her sexually and within two years she was found guilty of misconduct and executed on precisely the same spot where Anne Boleyn had been beheaded.

Henry wanted his nephew James V, King of Scotland, to marry his eldest daughter Mary. James, however, preferred the French alliance and married Mary of Guise, a formidable member of a powerful French house. Shortly before he died, in 1542, a daughter was born to him, also called Mary, and later known as Mary Queen of Scots.

At this period Scotland, like England, was divided on the religious question: in many areas the Calvinist Reformers were making headway among the middle and merchant classes, but the French alliance tended to shore up the Catholic faith, particularly among the ruling classes.

Henry now made yet another attempt at an alliance with Scotland through marriage (his thoughts never strayed very far away from the marriage bed as the soundest foundation for military alliances) by suggesting that the boy Prince Edward should be betrothed to the child Mary Queen of Scots. The Scottish Parliament would have been quite happy to accept this arrangement, but Mary of Guise, a French Catholic, would have none of it.

Henry was now married to his sixth and final wife, Catherine Parr, a widow and a Protestant, who outlived him. She ran into a certain amount of trouble with the Catholic Bishop Gardiner and one of her ladies was burnt at the stake; but her own influence over Henry saved her. Henry had been allowed by Parliament to nominate his heirs: he left the kingdom first to Prince Edward (Jane Seymour's son and a Protestant) and his heirs; next to Mary (Catherine of Aragon's daughter and a Catholic); and then to Elizabeth (Anne Boleyn's daughter and a Protestant, though with leanings similar to Henry's own); and fourthly to the heirs of his younger sister Mary, now dead. In doing so, he passed over the claim of Mary Stuart (Mary Queen of Scots), granddaughter of his elder sister Margaret, presumably because her mother had refused to allow her to be betrothed to his son, Prince Edward.

One question dominated the final months of Henry's reign; his successor, Prince Edward, was a sickly boy of nine, and what everybody wanted to know was who was going to be the real power behind the throne when Henry, now fifty-five and in poor health, died. Would it be the Catholic Norfolk or the Protestant Hertford? Would England retain that singular form of independent Catholicism which Henry had devised, or would the Lutherans prevail? Without warning, Hertford accused Norfolk of plotting with the French; and Norfolk and his son, Surrey, were imprisoned in the Tower.

The Earl of Hertford, later Duke of Somerset,* was pacing up and down in the corridor, planning his next moves, outside the room in which Cranmer was attending to the dying king. The question had been answered: for the moment, at any rate, the Reformers were in the ascendancy in England.

* One of the more confusing features of the study of English history is the way in which the chief protagonists keep changing their titles: it is difficult to remember that Seymour, Hertford and Somerset are all one and the same person. Soon we are going to run into problems with Warwick, who became Northumberland; and Wentworth, who became Strafford.

CHAPTER SEVEN

# The Pendulum Years

## 1

Edward VI was only a little over nine years of age when he came to the throne of a country which had grown grimly accustomed to executions. Not merely had his father sent to the scaffold two of his queens, two of his chief ministers, one bishop, and countless abbots, monks and ordinary people of all denominations (because it was a curious feature of Henry VIII's particular brand of Christianity that 'Roman' Catholics were hanged for treason while Lutherans, with equal impartiality, were burnt at the stake for heresy). Henceforward, although English people who wished to avoid persecution had to be prepared to change sides on the religious front pretty smartly, the issue was a clear-cut one in the sense that at any given moment either the Protestants or the Catholics were in control.

And now, for the present, with Somerset installed as the King's Protector and adviser, the Protestants had the upper hand. One of Somerset's first acts was to renew the attempt made by Henry to have young King Edward betrothed to Mary Stuart, the young Scottish Queen. As the Reformers were steadily gaining ground in Scotland despite the French alliance, this might have succeeded if Somerset had not attempted to force the issue by arms; for although the Scots were defeated, Mary of Guise persuaded the Scottish Parliament to send Queen Mary to France where she was betrothed instead to the Dauphin Francis, heir to the French throne.

Somerset then summoned a Parliament which, as was normal in those days, proved obedient to the ruling power, and at his bidding abolished Henry's Statute of Six Articles preserving the Catholic rites and doctrines. This Parliament also ordered a complete English prayer-book, forbade the use of images in churches, and deprived the Church of yet more property.

Cranmer brought out the Prayer Book in 1549 and an Act of Uniformity was passed compelling its use. That an entire nation should conform to the religious beliefs of its ruler was taken as axiomatic in those days. There was even a word for the practice – Erastianism.

The new English Prayer Book did not, however, go far enough for the Calvinists; and three years later Cranmer brought out a second one, still further purified of Roman taints, to meet their demands.

Cranmer and Somerset now had started on the task of turning Henry's political reformation into a religious one. Foreign scholars from Europe were brought in to educate the British clergy in the bleaker variants of the Protestant faith. The law against images provided an excuse for wanton destruction in the churches and many ancient schools were destroyed during the confiscations of church property. Most of the confiscated property went – according to the custom of the times – to Somerset and his friends and successors, but some of it was used to endow a series of new schools which are still in existence and are known as the King Edward the Sixth Grammar Schools.

The enforcement of the new Prayer Book on the highly conservative peasants caused a rising in the west. At the same time there was a rising in the eastern counties about land: the landlords who had taken over the confiscated monasteries there had been a bit too grasping and had also enclosed a great deal of 'common' land – land on which the peasants had formerly had the right to graze their beasts. Both risings were abortive, but Somerset had lost face and was succeeded as Protector by the Earl of Warwick, who put down the revolts with considerable cruelty: in his first engagement 3,500 men were killed – and there were no wounded.

Warwick now became Duke of Northumberland, married his son to Lady Jane Grey, granddaughter of King Henry VIII's sister Mary, and persuaded Edward to leave the throne to her rather than to the Catholic Princess Mary, so as to prevent England from becoming Catholic again. By this action – which naturally had the approval of Archbishop Cranmer – he almost certainly sealed the fate of Lady Jane Grey.

During the centuries of Norman rule, Irish Christianity had remained largely monastical in pattern. The ordinary people showed no particular religious fervour. When in Europe the Reformation produced the Counter-Reformation an attempt was made in 1542 to stir up some religious zeal in Ireland. A Jesuit mission proved singularly unsuccessful and departed in six weeks, deeply disappointed that the heirs of St Patrick and St Columba turned out to be so lukewarm about the faith of their fathers. However, the Irish being the Irish, what persuasion failed to do, proscription brilliantly succeeded in achieving, and when a simple order in the name of the boy King Edward VI was issued forbidding the celebration of Mass they rallied to the Catholic Church, and brought to their religious duties a pitch of fervour scarcely matched even in the Vatican itself. Since very few of the Protestant clergymen sent over by the English made any effort to teach the new doctrines to the native Irish, and those few who might have done so couldn't because they spoke no Gaelic, the native Irish retained their Catholic faith and, what was more dangerous, began to equate Catholicism with Irish nationalism and regard all Protestants *ipso facto* as anti-Irish.

Edward died in July 1553, not yet sixteen years old. The proclamation of Lady Jane as Queen was received in sullen silence by the people of London; Northumberland (formerly Warwick) was now bitterly hated throughout the land for the cruel way he had put down the revolts of the peasants. The common people flocked to Mary's support and the Council allowed the tide to carry them along. Ten days later, Mary entered London with Elizabeth at her side, and Lady Jane Grey and her husband were imprisoned in the Tower. After less than seven years of Lutheranism the people of England were now going to have to re-embrace the Catholic faith – and not the relatively easy-going, individualistic Henry VIII version of it either, but the genuine Roman variety, right down to a form of inquisition.

This fact was not made immediately apparent to the people of England, who welcomed Mary's accession because the religious changes made by Cranmer had gone too far and too rapidly, and there was a general desire to return to Henry VIII's religion (Catholic in all respects other than submission to Rome).

But Mary, now middle-aged, weak in health, and soured by the treatment meted out to her mother by Henry VIII, was resolved to revenge herself on all Reformers by restoring the Pope's full authority in England and seditiously rooting out all heretics.

Her first objective, however, was to marry her Spanish cousin Philip, son of the Emperor Charles V, who was willing to marry her to gain England as an ally against France. As soon as Mary announced her intentions in this matter, there was a strong upsurge of feeling against the match throughout the country and the Commons protested to the Queen. It was one thing to bring back the Mass, but an alliance with Spain, the land of the Inquisition and so closely linked with the Holy Roman Empire, was another matter altogether.

So, for the moment, Mary contented herself with restoring the Roman communion. She had Cranmer's new prayer-book banned by Act of Parliament. The Catholic Archbishop Gardiner, who had been the brains behind the Norfolk pro-Catholic party in the closing days of King Henry VIII's reign, now became Chancellor, and Cranmer and a number of Protestant bishops were imprisoned for their share in Northumberland's plot to make Lady Jane Grey Queen of England.

One thing Mary could not do, however, was to restore to the Church the monastery lands and possessions which had been parcelled out to the Tudor gentry: the Tudor gentry were prepared to go to Mass instead of Matins but they were not prepared to sacrifice any of their material possessions. And it seems likely that Mary misjudged the temper of the ordinary people, particularly in London, who were now beginning to couple Roman Catholicism with foreign influence. Some of the Protestant leaders fled to Switzerland and Germany; and those who remained on in England inevitably began to plot against the Queen. And it was natural, since Lady Jane Grey had been rejected by the people, that these plots should now centre around Princess Elizabeth, by this time aged twenty, a Protestant, committed to her father's version of the Reformed faith and without a drop of foreign blood in her veins.

When Mary again raised the matter of her intention to marry Philip of Spain, despite the protest from the Commons, Sir Thomas Wyatt hatched a plot to prevent the marriage by force, and a rebellion broke out in southern England. Wyatt and his men marched on London, but were cut down by the Queen's soldiers. Wyatt was executed; so, too, were Lady Jane Grey and her husband. Next the Spaniards tried to make it a condition of the marriage that Mary would first dispose of Elizabeth. Elizabeth was imprisoned for some time in the Tower and fully expected to be executed, but Mary could not bring herself to order this. After a time Elizabeth was released and lived in what amounted to close captivity at Woodstock, awaiting the next turn of events.

In the summer of 1554, Philip of Spain travelled to England. Mary journeyed to Winchester to meet her bridegroom, where she was married according to the rites of the Catholic Church. Parliament sanctioned the marriage and allowed Philip the title of King though he was not to be allowed to exercise any real authority.

Now Mary began to show her true colours. A third Parliament accepted the restoration of the pope's authority over England, and the heresy laws were re-enacted. Then, in 1555, the persecutions began, against the better judgement of Mary's husband Philip, who knew that they would damage both himself and Spain in the eyes of the English people. In any event, as he had no great love for his elderly wife, he soon returned to Spain where he became King on the abdication of Charles V, and thought little more about England for the moment.

This desertion by her husband was a cruel blow to Mary, already bitterly disappointed by the fact that she had been unable to have a child. Convinced that she was being punished by heaven for insufficient ardour in her pursuit of the faithless, she redoubled her efforts. Bishop Hooper had been one of the first to go to the stake; he was now followed by Cranmer, Ridley and Latimer.

H. A. L. Fisher writes in his *A History of Europe*:

> The number of Protestants condemned to the stake for their beliefs under Queen Mary did not probably exceed three hundred, but in this number, small as it was in comparison with continental standards, were included the chieftains of the reforming party, and the men most eminent for virtue and talent in the country. The fires that kindled round Cranmer and Latimer and Ridley were not soon extinguished. In the Martyrology of John Foxe, in which the lives and deaths of the victims of the Marian zeal are vividly recounted, the Protestant world obtained a record, deemed only less sacred than the Bible itself, of the high spirit which animated the fathers of their faith, and of the courage with which, rather than betray their convictions, they faced the fiery torments of the stake. Nothing so greatly served to purify and deepen the Protestant religion in England or to implant in the minds of the common people a horror of Rome against these ill-judged severities undertaken against the prudent judgement of Charles V, on the initiative of a solitary and miserable woman.

In other words, the Marian persecutions did for the Protestant faith in England precisely what the Roman persecutions had done for the early Christian religion in Rome.

As Foxe's *Book of Martyrs* is not perhaps as assiduously studied in British schools these days as it used to be, it might be worth including here a couple of excerpts, just to give readers an idea of the flavour of the work, and, indeed, of the attitudes which lay behind the persecutions.

For example, during Mary's reign, information was given against a common woman called Margaret Polley, to Maurice, Bishop of Rochester, who questioned her as follows:

> ROCHESTER: Are not those heretics, who maintain and hold other opinions than our holy mother and Catholic Church doth?
> MARGARET POLLEY: They are, indeed, heretics and grossly deceived, who hold and maintain doctrines contrary to the Word of God, which I sincerely believe was written by holy men taught by the Holy Ghost.
> ROCHESTER: Do you hold and maintain that in the sacrament of the altar, under the form of bread and wine, there is not the very body and blood of Christ and that the said body is verily in heaven only, and not in the sacrament?
> MARGARET POLLEY: What I have learned from the Holy Scriptures I steadfastly maintain, viz. that the very body was crucified for the sins of all true believers, ascended into heaven, is there at the right hand of the Majesty on high; that such body has ever since remained there, and cannot, according to my belief, be in the sacrament of the altar. I believe the bread and wine in the sacrament are to be received as symbols and representatives of the body and blood of Christ, but not as his body real and substantially. I think, in my weak judgement, that it is not in the power of any man, by pronouncing words over the elements of bread and wine, to change them into the real body and blood of Christ.

She was burned at the stake in 1555.

In the same year, John Hooper, Bishop of Gloucester and Worcester was also burned at the stake, in the presence of about seven thousand. Here is Foxe's account of his final sufferings:

> When he had risen from his last devotions in this world, he prepared himself for the stake. He put off his host's gown, and delivered it to the sheriffs requiring them to see it restored to its owner, and put off the rest of his apparel, down to his doublet and hose, wherein he would have been burned. But the sheriffs would not permit that, unto whose pleasure he very obediently submitted himself. And his doublet, hose and waistcoat were taken off. Thus, being in his shirt, he took a point from his hose himself, and trussed his shirt between his legs, where he had a pound of gunpowder in a bladder, and under each arm the like quantity, delivered him by the guard.

> Command was now given that the fire should be kindled. But because there were not fewer green faggots than two horses could carry, it did not kindle speedily, but was some time before it took the reeds upon the faggots. At length it burned about him, but the wind having full strength in that place, and it being a lowering cold morning, it blew the flame from him so that he was in a manner little more than touched by the fire. Endeavours were then made to increase the flames, and then the bladders of gunpowder exploded, but did him little good, being so placed and the wind having such power. In this fire, he prayed with a loud voice, 'Lord Jesus, have mercy on me! Lord Jesus, have mercy on me! Lord Jesus, receive my spirit!' And these were the last words he was heard to utter. Yet he struck his breast with his hands, until by the renewing of the fire his strength was gone, and his hands stuck fast in striking the iron upon his breast. So immediately bowing forward, he yielded up his spirit. Thus lingering were his last sufferings. He was nearly three-quarters of an hour or more in the fire, as a lamb, patiently bearing the extremity thereof, neither moving forward, backward, nor to any side; but he died as quietly as a child in his bed.

Cranmer, an old friend and a frail man, was so badly treated in prison that he signed a recantation, which he immediately regretted, and when the time came for his execution, in 1556, he resolved that he would first consign to the flames his right hand – the hand that signed the recantation. Let Foxe take up the narrative:

> There was an iron chain tied about Cranmer, and they commanded the fire to be set unto him. When the wood was kindled, and the fire began to burn near him, he stretched forth his right hand which had signed his recantation, into the flames, and there held it so that the people might see it burnt to a coal before his body was touched. In short, he was so patient and constant in the midst of his tortures, that he seemed to move no more than the stake to which he was bound; his eyes were lifted up to heaven, and often he said, so long as his voice would suffer him, 'This unworthy right hand!' and often using the words of Stephen, 'Lord Jesus receive my spirit', till the fury of the flames putting him to silence, he gave up the ghost.

The martyrs themselves knew that their deaths were not in vain. Latimer and Ridley were burned together and as the flames crackled around them Latimer said: 'Be of good comfort, Master Ridley and play the man, we shall this day light such a candle, by God's grace, in England as I trust shall never be put out.'

## 2

Queen Mary's reign had no effect – from the religious point of view at any rate – on the Celtic Irish. No native Irish Protestants were persecuted for the reason that there were none to persecute, and she was no more able to restore the confiscated land to the monasteries in Ireland than she had been in England.

She did, however, introduce a policy which was to cause untold trouble in Ireland in the years ahead. In the time of Edward VI, English forces had driven two rebellious chiefs, the O'Mores of Leix and the O'Connors of Offaly, from their lands and had posted military garrisons there to control the population. Mary now proposed to clear all the Irish out of these two counties and to 'plant' them with English settlers. Speculators undertook to pay rent for the counties and repopulate them with colonies of English farmers, who would be armed in order to be able to keep off the former owners of the farms. As the O'Mores and the O'Connors were among the Irish chieftains who had voluntarily handed over their possessions to Henry VIII to be regranted them in return for knight-service (see page 80) this was a rank injustice. There is also a curious anomaly in the fact that such a vehemently Catholic Queen should clear Catholics off the land and replace them with English farmers, many of them Protestants. However, justice was never one of Mary's more marked features and it is probable that she mistrusted Irish Catholics even more than she disliked English Protestants. The Catholic Irish inhabitants of the two counties moved out with all their belongings to make a new life where they could – or stayed on, to work as labourers for the English.

In 1558 Mary died, having named Elizabeth as her successor.

## 3

When Queen Elizabeth succeeded to the throne of England, at the age of twenty-five, her subjects, understandably, were in a pretty confused state of mind in regard to their attitude to religion. In her father's day it had been equally perilous to be either a Roman Catholic or a Lutheran. During the few years of the boy King Edward's reign, it was highly dangerous to be a Catholic, while in the five years between his death and Elizabeth's arrival on the scene it was even more unhealthy to be a Protestant.

Elizabeth had been brought up as a Protestant and would probably have liked a return to some sort of compromise between her father's version of Christianity and the Protestantism of Cranmer, but Mary's excesses had made this impossible. There was the added problem that, as the daughter of Anne Boleyn, she could not be recognized by Rome, who regarded Mary Queen of Scots as the rightful heir to the English throne. Indeed, Elizabeth could find only one bishop in all England prepared to crown her. The nation was looking to her to resolve the religious confusion. And there were military matters to add to her problems. England was still at war with France and during the last two reigns the fleet had not been maintained. Finally, there was the question of her own marriage: Parliament was anxious to know along what lines she was thinking in that respect.

She probably decided right from the beginning not to marry; certainly, to marry a foreign prince would have meant taking a definite decision on the religious question, which she was anxious to avoid, or at any rate postpone.

Then, at a tournament in 1559, the King of France, Henry II, was accidentally killed and was succeeded by Francis II, husband of Mary Queen of Scots. This put Elizabeth in an extremely awkward situation. With a Catholic Ireland lying to the west of her domain, with a strong Catholic alliance between Scotland and France, with the Scottish Queen married to the French King, with Rome supporting Mary Queen of Scots's claim to the throne of England, and with only one very shaky ally, Spain (and a Catholic one at that), Elizabeth had to play her cards very carefully. This she succeeded brilliantly in doing.

First she tackled the religious question. In her first Parliament a new Act of Supremacy was passed: England became Protestant again, all Mary's Catholic legislation was repealed and the English sovereign once more replaced the pope as Head of the Church in England. The laws of Edward VI were re-enacted and a 'Court of High Commission' was set up to punish religious offenders and insure uniformity of religious conduct. At the same time, the second Prayer Book of Edward VI was altered to make it a shade less Calvinistic.

A few years later the Thirty-nine Articles were issued, setting out the doctrine of the Church of England: they represent a compromise between the doctrines of Rome and those of the German Protestants, and are still in force today. This arrangement satisfied the majority of the English people, but not all of them. The Calvinists were disappointed and felt that the English Church was still far too close to Rome; and as they wished for further purification, they became known as Puritans. Their ranks included a number of fanatical Calvinists who had fled to Switzerland and north Germany during Mary's reign and now came streaming back, full of ideas they had picked up from the continental Calvinists. These Puritans were to cause endless trouble in the years ahead: democratic in their ideas and their organization, wildly intolerant of all who differed from their views in the smallest degree, they were convinced that it was both their duty and their right to search the scriptures, look in their own hearts and challenge the Queen on any matter – affecting either Church or State – which attracted their attention. These Puritans soon formed a growing and vociferous opposition in Parliament, so that for a time Elizabeth had to deal not only with the forces of the Counter-Reformation abroad, but also with attacks from the Puritans at home.

The next matter to be tackled was Scotland. As we have seen, the Reformation had already made considerable strides north of the border, despite the French connection. Encouraged by the intransigent outpourings of John Knox, the prominent Scottish Calvinist, deploring 'foreign rule' from exile in Geneva, a powerful Puritan party took arms against the French troops supporting the Scottish Queen Mother, Mary of Guise. Elizabeth sent what was left of the fleet to blockade the Scottish ports to prevent French reinforcements from reaching Mary of Guise's troops and at the same time smuggled what arms and supplies she could spare across the border to support the Protestant cause. And at this juncture, most conveniently for Elizabeth, Mary of Guise died. The French resistance collapsed and Scotland's future as a Protestant state seemed secured.

In the same year, however, Mary Queen of Scots – whose husband had died very shortly after he succeeded to the French throne – returned to Scotland. There she discovered that the Scottish Parliament, with Elizabeth's help, had driven out the French and set up an official Scottish Church known as the Presbyterian Church, so called because it was governed not by bishops but by a council of elders or presbyters, all of equal rank.

For a time all went well, despite denunciations by John Knox, the fiery Calvinist preacher. Although she was a Catholic, Mary was young and pretty and popular with the people.

But in 1565, she married Lord Darnley, a Catholic with both Tudor and Stuart connections, and the results were disastrous. Feudal factions, embittered by religious differences, eroded away all Mary's power. Darnley was murdered by a party of nobles under the Earl of Bothwell whom she married shortly afterwards. A rebellion followed: Mary was forced to abdicate in favour of her infant son James, and was imprisoned. After eleven months, in 1568, she escaped to England, posing Elizabeth with yet another almost insurmountable problem.

In England Mary immediately became the focal point of a series of Counter-Reformation plots against Elizabeth. England at this stage was the strongest united Protestant state in Europe; and it seemed to the forces of the Counter-Reformation that if England could be restored to the Catholic faith, Protestantism might yet be wiped out all over Europe. Emissaries from Spain came to England to try to stir up a rebellion, and in 1569 the Earls of Northumberland and Westmorland led a rising in the north against Elizabeth, but without any marked success – Northumberland was executed and Westmorland escaped abroad.

Next the pope intervened. In February 1570, Pope Pius V excommunicated Elizabeth and declared her deposed.

Elizabeth, now forced to look for allies in Europe, made overtures to Catherine de Medicis, Regent to the young French King Charles IX and concluded a political alliance with her in April 1572.

Then an event occurred which made any further alliance between England and France impossible. The French Protestants – or Huguenots as they were called – were a strong minority in France in the 1550s. Catherine de Medicis – who dominated the royal house of Valois which had recently recovered power from the noble Guise family – was a Catholic, but too politically-minded to put her religion above the interests of her family and her country. In 1562 she granted the Huguenots the right to worship in certain areas; then ten years later, on St Bartholomew's Day 1572, the French Court suddenly turned on the Huguenots and massacred 10,000 of them in Paris and 30,000 in other towns throughout France. By this move, the Duke of Guise, who led the massacre, regained for his family the power they had lost ten years earlier. To quote Foxe again:

> At two o'clock in the morning the bell of St Germains l'Auxerrois tolled, at which signal the Duke of Guise led his followers to the slaughter of the Protestants. Soldiers had been appointed in different places of the city to be ready at the command of the King; and upon the watchword being given, they burst out to the slaughter, beginning with the admiral himself [Admiral Coligny, leader of the Huguenots], who being wounded, was cast out of the window into the street, where his head being struck off, was embalmed and sent to the Pope. The savage people then cut off his arms, and drew his mangled body three days through the streets of Paris, after which they took him to the place of execution, and there hanged him by the heels, to the scorn of the populace.
>
> The martyrdom of this virtuous man had no sooner taken place, than the troops, with rage and violence, ran about slaying all the Protestants they knew or could find within the city gates. This continued many days, but the greatest slaughter was in the first three days, in which were said to be murdered above 10,000 men and women, old and young, of all sorts and conditions. The bodies of the dead were carried in carts and thrown into the river, which with other streams in certain places of the city, was reddened with the blood of the slain.

This massacre embittered Protestants everywhere, and, combined with the Inquisition, made all the Protestant states determined to resist the Counter-Reformation at all costs. Specifically, it made any alliance between France and England impossible.

With no other allies in the offing, Elizabeth was forced into clandestine support to the French Huguenots and of the Dutch who at this period were in revolt against Spain because of attempts to re-introduce the Spanish Inquisition. The Netherlands had been part of the Spanish empire from the beginning of the sixteenth century, and it is claimed that some thirty thousand men and women died there for their religious beliefs during the reign of Charles V. In 1555, when Charles V abdicated to spend the remainder of his life in a monastery, his son Philip decided to subject the Low Countries to a new Inquisition.

By this time the Inquisition had come a long way from Innocent III's first, tentative efforts to stamp out heresy. Initially the job of hunting down heretics had been left to the bishops. But they had so many other duties to perform that in 1233 Pope Gregory had appointed a regular, permanent organization to deal with heretics, who were regarded in those days in much the same light as we would regard a carrier of typhus – a danger to the entire community.

The inquisitors – mainly friars, both Franciscans and Dominicans – were for all practical purposes exempt from local authority and took their orders directly from the Papacy. The special courts which were set up had two purposes: to save the soul of the heretic and to prevent him from corrupting others. When a man was accused he was arrested and questioned, sometimes for hours on end, by devious and skilled interrogators, though he was not allowed to face his accuser or even know who his accuser was. Technically, if a voluntary confession of guilt was obtained, the accused was given some form of penance – a pilgrimage, a public flogging, possibly in church, a term of imprisonment, or he might be merely condemned to wear some sort of badge or label as a warning to others to enable them to avoid contamination. A confessed heretic was normally deprived of his possessions, which were divided between Church and State, an arrangement which greatly enhanced the appeal of the Inquisition to Europe's rulers.

If the accused could not explain away the charge and still refused to confess, the inquisitors resorted to torture. If the accused still refused to confess, he was surrendered to the secular authorities with a formal request that he should suffer neither death nor mutilation. The Church knew that this plea would be ignored and the offender in all cases would be burnt at the stake, but the formal request absolved the Church from any overt complicity in his execution. Since those who abjured their errors 'not from conviction but from fear of punishment' were in fact also handed over to the secular authorities not many of the Inquisition's victims escaped burning.

In Spain, where the Inquisition reached its height towards the end of the sixteenth century, these public burnings were known as *autos-da-fé* (acts of the faith) and for years no public ceremony was complete without the public burning of a handful of heretics: A. H. Johnson, in his *Europe in the Sixteenth Century*, remarks that 'the Spaniards preferred one to a bullfight'.

The activities of the Inquisition were based on the Augustinian theory that constraint may be exercised on heretics for their own salvation, out of love for their souls. Death by burning was acceptable to the Church because 'the Church abhors the shedding of blood', though, as we have seen, matters were so arranged that it seemed as if the burnings were taking place *against* the express wishes of the Church. To burn a heretic was, nevertheless, regarded as an act of love both towards the community, as it was likely to deter others who might be tempted into committing the same sin, and towards the sinner himself since 'the fear of fire might result in the salvation of his soul'.

The inquisitors tried to secure a confession of guilt from the heretic by alternating blandishments and intimidation, solitary confinement and torture. If he recanted, he might be committed to lifelong imprisonment chained in a dungeon, or be allowed the luxury of being strangled before being burnt at the stake. If after recanting he again lapsed back into heresy, he was simply burnt alive. Instruments of torture included the rack; water torture, in which a funnel was placed in the mouth of the accused and gallons of water poured down his gullet until the bladder could withstand the strain no longer; an iron cage with spikes inside it in which the victim was rolled around; a system by which the accused was hoisted on a pulley by a rope tied to his wrists, bound behind his back, so that both shoulders were dislocated; a very simple arrangement whereby a plank was placed on the accused's chest and loaded with ever-increasing weights until he either recanted or was squashed flat; and an even more ingenious arrangement in which the accused was placed in a wooden box like a coffin and a series of wedges slowly hammered into place which splintered and crushed all the bones in the feet and eventually the legs.

Not because it is necessarily accurate, but because much of the fear and dread of popery and the Spanish Inquisition which haunted every English Protestant at this period – and to a much greater extent later, when the Stuart kings' tolerance of popery (and, in the case of King James II, open conversion to Catholicism) led people to believe that England might again become a Catholic country – was based on accounts of the tortures in Foxe's *Book of Martyrs*, let me include here a brief description of one of the tortures as he describes it:

> A prisoner, on refusing to comply with the iniquitous demand of the Inquisition, by confessing the crimes they charged him with, was immediately conveyed to the torture room, where no light appeared but that of two candles. That the cries of the suffering might not be heard, the room was lined with a kind of quilting, covering all the crevices and deadening the sound.
>
> The prisoner's horror was extreme on entering this infernal place, when suddenly he was surrounded by six wretches, who, after preparing the torture, stripped him naked to his drawers. He was then laid on his back on a kind of stand, elevated a few feet from the floor. They began by putting an iron collar round his

neck, and a ring to each foot, which fastened him to the stand. His limbs being thus stretched out, they wound two ropes round each arm and each thigh; these being passed under the scaffold, were drawn tight at the same instant by four of the men. The pains which immediately succeeded were intolerable; the ropes, which were of a small size cut through the prisoner's flesh to the bone, making the blood gush out. As he persisted in not confessing what the Inquisitors required, the ropes were drawn in this manner four times successively. A physician and surgeon attended and often felt his temples, to judge of his danger; but only that he might recover to sustain further torture. During this extremity of anguish, while the tender frame is tearing, as it were in pieces, while at every pore it feels the sharpest pangs, and the agonized soul is ready to burst from its wretched mansion, the ministers of the Inquisition look on without emotion, and calmly advise the poor distracted creature to confess his guilt that he may obtain pardon and receive absolution. All this, however, was ineffectual with the prisoner, whose mind was strengthened by a sweet consciousness of innocence, and the divine consolation of religion. Amidst his body suffering, the physician and surgeon were so barbarous as to declare that, if he died under the torture he would be guilty, by his own obstinacy, of self-murder. The last time the ropes were drawn tight he grew so exceedingly weak, by the stoppage of the circulation of his blood, and the pains he endured, that he fainted away, on which he was unloosed and carried back to his dungeon.

When the Spaniards extended their empire into the Netherlands and overseas, they took the Inquisition with them. Every town in New Spain, South America was required to have a Catholic Church and School and any Protestant found on Spanish territory was burned. The Inquisition persisted in Spain and South America until the early nineteenth century.

## 4

The English people were convinced that if Catholicism was restored to England, with the aid, perhaps, of one of the Catholic European powers such as Spain or France, they would all have to become Roman Catholics again or be burnt at the stake. And even if they did become Catholics, there remained the terrible example of what had happened in Seville to the 'New Christians' – the Jews there who had embraced Christianity to avoid persecution. The worst fury of the

Inquisition was always reserved for 'lapsed' Christians, and Torquemada, the Grand Inquisitor, had devised a series of 'Articles' which would enable his officers and spies to recognize the first signs of any tendency to lapse among these Jewish 'New Christians'. If, for example, a man put on a clean shirt on a Saturday, or his wife used a clean tablecloth, they were liable to find themselves up before the Inquisition on a charge of observing the Sabbath in honour of the law of Moses and thus guilty of heresy. Another article empowered vigilant friars to watch from the rooftops to spot houses from whose chimneys no smoke emerged: the tenants could then be arrested on the charge that they were still observing the Jewish law of not desecrating the Sabbath by lighting fires.

The central figure in the resistance to the Spanish subjugation of the Netherlands and the re-introduction of the Inquisition there was William of Orange, who eventually – with assistance from England in the form of supplies and even fighting men – managed to free the northern province (roughly corresponding to the modern Netherlands) which declared its independence in 1581, promising religious liberty for Catholics, Lutherans and Calvinists alike.

It was now clear that a showdown with the forces of Catholicism could not long be avoided, but in the interim Elizabeth was beginning to run into trouble at home with the Puritans. Initially, they had been willing enough to to go along with her religious settlement in the hope of later modifying it from within, but they disliked the whole idea of religious uniformity and proceeded to form their own communities with their own ministers and their own forms of worship. To the Puritans, the Anglican Church with its liturgy and doctrines, its bishops and ceremonials, seemed still far too close to Rome. Also, many of the Anglican clergy had been Protestant under Edward VI, had turned Catholic again under Mary, and were now continuing to earn a living from the Church by administering the word of God according to Elizabeth's Thirty-nine Articles, and hardly represented reassuring mentors for people in need of firm spiritual guidance in a difficult period. The Puritans were also great pamphleteers, and now started flooding the country with leaflets and other literature ventilating novel ideas of freedom which struck not merely at the Church, but also at the stability of the State itself. Elizabeth replied by using the Court of High Commission, which had been set up in 1559 to deal with offences against the Church Settlement, as a censorship body.

This infuriated the Puritans who redoubled their efforts and still more inflammatory pamphlets poured from clandestine printing presses.

Meanwhile the Catholics – and in particular the Jesuits, who have been described as the militia of the Papacy – were stepping up their attempts to re-establish the Catholic faith in England, and some at least of these attempts included the assassination of Queen Elizabeth as a prior step to putting Mary Queen of Scots on the English throne. Elizabeth was reluctant to make the necessary decision to do away with another queen, but all logic now pointed that way: the execution of Mary would make her son James heir to the English throne, and James was being brought up as a Protestant. So, to avoid the restoration of Catholicism in England, all Elizabeth had to do was to get rid of Mary Queen of Scots before the Jesuits or their emissaries eliminated Elizabeth herself.

Spanish feeling against England, already enraged by the assistance England had been giving to the Netherlands, was daily becoming more hostile, and Elizabeth was obliged to send an English army under Leicester to Holland to prevent it from being used as a base for an attack on England.

In 1586 a conspiracy was uncovered involving Mary Queen of Scots and at long last Elizabeth was prevailed upon to agree that her death had become a political necessity. The Scottish Queen was found guilty of treason and was executed in 1587. She was only forty-four and had spent nineteen of these years in captivity.

## 5

In Ireland, the effect of Mary's 'plantations' in Leix and Offaly caused considerable alarm throughout the whole country, so that it was all more or less poised on the edge of revolt, and prepared to resist further 'plantations'. Furthermore, England's return to Protestantism immediately provided the Irish – or so they believed – with a number of powerful allies on the continent of Europe to whom they could apply for arms and even reinforcements when the time was ripe. Throughout Elizabeth's reign, rebellions large and small broke out, but there was little cohesion between the Irish leaders, and the rebellions were easily quenched by the army of occupation.

The most serious of these came in 1579 when James Fitzmaurice

Fitzgerald, member of a powerful Munster family, tried to achieve a Catholic alliance of Irish and Anglo-Irish nobles. He went to the Continent and drummed up a mixed force of Italians and Spaniards, financed jointly by the Pope and the King of Spain, both anxious at this juncture to attack Protestant England via the back door, as it were.

Returning to Ireland with a small force accompanied by a party of priests who preached rebellion as a sacred duty, he landed at Kerry. His army dug themselves in on the Dingle Peninsula, but the force was not big enough to hold out for long, and as no further reinforcements came from over the sea, the rebellion was routed. Soon afterwards his kinsman the Earl of Desmond was pronounced a traitor, defeated and killed. The Lord Deputy systematically destroyed all the food in Munster and succeeded in achieving a famine of considerable proportions. As a further reprisal for the rebellion, Elizabeth followed Mary's lead by confiscating vast tracts of Catholic-owned land in south-west Ireland and turned it over to Protestant English planters.

These events in Munster were being keenly watched by two of the most powerful and most independent families of the old Gaelic aristocracy, the O'Neills of Tyrone and the O'Donnells of Tyrconnel, whose final, fatal stand against the forces of the Queen was to pave the way for today's disturbances in Ulster. But, in the meantime, Queen Elizabeth had the Spanish to contend with.

Queen Mary had burnt about three hundred Protestant martyrs in the last years of her reign. In the last years of Elizabeth's reign plots against her person forced her to execute about the same total of Catholics for treason. This further increased the hostility of France and Spain. War with France was averted, but war with Spain now became inevitable and the drama of the Spanish Armada – sent by Philip II to re-convert England to the Catholic faith – is well known. Even today, parties of skin-divers are recovering relics of the stately Spanish galleons which were wrecked off the western coasts of Scotland and Ireland as they tried to make their way back – the long way round – to Spanish waters after a resounding defeat both by Drake's own tiny fleet and by the elements.

Of the crews of the Spanish galleons which were driven ashore on the Irish coast, a few found shelter but most were slaughtered – more, admittedly, for the sake of plunder than out of loyalty to the English throne. Only in the north – in the area controlled by the O'Neills and the O'Donnells – were the Spaniards well treated; for there, by now, the Queen's power was negligible, and the two families were already in touch with Spain.

The Irish in Ulster had an outstanding leader in Hugh O'Neill. He had been brought up in the English Court and knew how to deal with the English. He had taken his time building up his arms, strengthening his relations with his Irish neighbours, and preparing for rebellion. He took the ancient title 'The O'Neill' in place of the title Earl of Tyrone which had been conferred on his grandfather by Henry VIII, and in effect he defied the Crown. Elizabeth's chronic shortage of cash was one reason why she tolerated this defiance. But eventually, in 1597, a full-scale attack was launched on Ulster. It failed, and the following year the English took the worst beating they ever received at the hands of the Irish, at the Battle of the Yellow Ford.

All over the country other Gaelic chieftains rose in revolt. Within a few weeks the Munster plantations were seized back by the native Irish; and there was a promise of help from Spain. The Earl of Essex failed ignominiously to achieve any success at the head of the largest army England had ever sent to Ireland. He deserted his command and was replaced by Lord Mountjoy, a much tougher commander who soon had the rebellion under control. When the promised Spanish force 4,000 strong, landed at Kinsale in 1601, they were already too late; there was no longer any rebellion to support. The Spaniards were glad to be allowed to return home as the price of surrender. O'Neill agreed to come to terms, and O'Donnell, his greatest ally, fled to Spain to urge Philip to send further forces to Ireland.

For a while the surrender negotiations dragged on. Tyrone had to abandon all rights to rule as an Irish king and he could get no pledge of equality for the Catholic religion, but he was allowed to remain on in Ireland as Earl of Tyrone and retain his former possessions. During these negotiations Queen Elizabeth died and the Tudor dynasty came to an end.

CHAPTER EIGHT

# Divine Right—— and the Puritans

## 1

By the beginning of the seventeenth century, the religious turmoil in Europe was beginning to sort itself out along some sort of territorial lines. Several versions of the Christian message were tolerated side by side in Switzerland, Germany and Holland, while in France, after the disaster of the St Bartholomew's Day Massacre, Catholicism and Calvinism co-existed in separate areas. In France, in fact, when the last male member of the Valois family died, the Protestant Henry of Navarre, head of the Bourbon family, became heir to the throne. To avoid conflict, he became a Catholic and in 1598 issued the Edict of Nantes which allowed the Huguenots freedom of worship in certain cities. In Spain and Italy, Protestantism continued to be banned while in Scotland and England Catholicism was proscribed. After the Spanish Armada, no serious attempt to alter Britain's religion was made from outside the country; the trouble now came internally, from the Puritans.

Towards the end of her reign, Elizabeth had been having great difficulties with the Puritans in the Commons. They objected to the power of the bishops; and, encouraged by the outspoken Puritans, the Commons as a whole were beginning to show signs of increasing independence of the Crown. Elizabeth had severe laws passed in an effort to control the Puritans, and some of the more independent of them, men who strenuously objected to any form of Church government, left England and settled in Holland. But Elizabeth had been a natural instinctive ruler: she knew how to handle the Commons. The real trouble was to come when she was succeeded by lesser monarchs.

King James VI of Scotland, who according to Godfrey Davis's book, *The Early Stuarts (1603–1660)*, only came to the throne 'through heredity and the absence of any suitable alternative', soon convinced himself that his accession was due entirely to his own inherent kingly qualities. He was infatuated with his own theory of the Divine Right of Kings and was quite the wrong type of monarch to deal with the ever more vociferous Puritan element in the Commons. In fact, it was he who was responsible in large measure for the trouble which exploded over the head of his successor, Charles I.

When he became King of England he immediately took up residence in London and thereafter Scotland saw little of her sovereigns. He called himself King of Great Britain and would have liked to have seen England and Scotland united under one Parliament, but neither Parliament would agree to this proposition, and it was another century before complete union took place. He had suffered so much from the opinionated Presbyterian clergy in Scotland, that he inclined to favour the rule of the bishops, a notion which didn't go down at all well with the Puritan element in Parliament.

In 1604, James presided over a conference at Hampton Court to discuss the differences between the Puritans and the Established Church of England. The demands of the Puritans were so extreme that no agreement could be reached, and the only concrete result of the conference was a new translation of the Bible, the present Authorized Version, which was published in 1611. If the Puritans who attended the conference thought that they could expect sympathetic treatment from a king brought up in a strict Calvinist household, they were wrong: James was very quick to see that if he allowed men to decide for themselves on major religious questions, it was but a short step until they decided major political questions for themselves as well. 'No Bishop, no King' was his slogan and from this time onwards the Church remained on the side of royalty and upheld the principle of the Divine Right of Kings.

The Catholics in England had also hoped for some relief under James – after all, his mother, Mary Queen of Scots, had been the focus of all their principal ambitions at one period – and indeed, if the Pope had been prepared to allow English Catholics to pay a lip-service secular allegiance to the king, James would probably have permitted them to worship in peace. But the Pope would not yield an inch and as a result Catholics were fined for refusing to attend Anglican services and their priests were banished.

This set-back led a small group of Catholic gentlemen to make a plan to blow up Parliament, King, Lords, Commons and all, as a protest. They had a vague idea that this action might be followed by a Catholic uprising, and the re-establishment of a Catholic state in

England with assistance from Spain. But as every schoolboy knows, details of the infernal plot leaked out, and Guy Fawkes, a veteran of the Spanish Wars in the Netherlands, was caught red-handed among his gunpowder barrels, and he and his fellow conspirators were all captured, tortured and executed. The only result of the affair was to add to the general distrust of popes and popery.

From the beginning of his reign, James was in constant trouble with the Commons. He did no more than the Tudors had done, but he did it with far less tact. The quarrels were mainly about money. Elizabeth had died in debt and James's attempts to raise money, by reviving the prerogative rights of taxation of the medieval kings, irritated the House. James dissolved Parliament – which he regarded as little more than an instrument for providing him with money – in 1611.

It was in that same year the Plantation of Ulster was undertaken – the most successful plantation of all, in the sense that the descendants of the original planters are still there after more than three hundred years, and yet at the same time the seed and root cause of all Ulster's current troubles. It came about in this way.

When the rebellion of the O'Neills and the O'Donnells was crushed, their successors settled down to resume their lives in a country which had utterly changed. English law, administration and justice were now imposed; the ancient Irish 'Brehon' laws were abolished. The old Gaelic kingdoms and Norman earldoms with their own local armies had also disappeared; the only army now allowed was the army of the Crown. Until this period many of the petty Irish rulers held a traditional right to maintain their own armies, and there were men in the country who regarded any work other than fighting as degrading. Since these men would not in any circumstances join the forces of the Crown, most of them now began to emigrate to the Continent, to look for employment in the armies of France, the Catholic Netherlands or Spain.

But even if these fighting men had been willing to remain in Ireland and enter the professions, this was impossible because no education was provided in Ireland for Catholics. For education, they had to go abroad and, once abroad, the tendency was to make their lives there.

In the last years of Elizabeth's reign, the English Government had established Trinity College, Dublin's university, on the pattern of one of the Cambridge colleges, but according to the rules of that university, only Protestants could be teachers. This regulation was part of the rather half-hearted efforts that were made to spread the Reformation in Ireland and was designed to turn Irish Catholics into Protestants. The only result, of course, was that Catholics could not attend Trinity. A commission set up by James to look into the whole question of education in Ireland closed many schools because they persisted in teaching according to the doctrines of the Catholic Church.

Yet another profound change occurred in Ireland during the reign of James. Until then, ever since the Norman conquest, the rulers of Ireland had drawn a definite distinction between their Anglo-Norman subjects and the 'mere' Irish. From the time of James I, the mere Irish could have all the privileges of their 'betters' if they agreed to become Protestants. This arrangement had the effect of causing great bitterness between the bulk of the Irish Catholics, who stuck to the old religion and the few who 'defected'.

Unhappy about the shape of things in Ireland under James I, and half afraid that they might be seized and imprisoned on some trumped-up charge, O'Neill, Earl of Tyrone, and O'Donnell, Earl of Tyrconnel chartered a ship in 1607 and fled to the Continent, taking with them into exile ninety-eight other leading Irish Catholic chieftains from Ulster.

This 'Flight of the Earls', as it was called, was held to be treason and left the way wide open for another plantation, the Plantation of Ulster: almost all the Irish landowners in the area were dispossessed of their farms and the entire area repopulated with 150,000 Scottish Presbyterians and 20,000 English Protestants. The introduction of these non-Catholic settlers laid the foundation for the partition of Ireland over three hundred years later, and sowed the seeds of the bitter dissension whose effects we have witnessed over the last four years. After the Plantation, Ulster was largely in the hands of a people utterly different in religion and outlook from the remainder of the Irish nation.

## 2

Right at the beginning of his reign, James had made peace with Spain. Now in Germany, the Protestants of Bohemia were in rebellion against the Holy Roman Emperor, a Habsburg, and on the death of the Emperor in 1619, made the Elector Palatine king of Bohemia, instead of the new Emperor. In January 1620, the Elector Palatine, who was married to James's daughter Elizabeth, was defeated by the imperial army, driven from Bohemia and lost his own territory on the Rhine as well. England was eager to help the Protestant cause – and her own Princess – and many Englishmen and Scots went over and fought as volunteers. But James was not prepared to declare war officially, because Spain would naturally side with the Emperor, and he still clung to the hope that if he could get his son Charles married to a Spanish Infanta, Spain might be persuaded to intervene with the Emperor on the Elector Palatine's behalf. Parliament, always anti-Spanish, was furious but James went ahead with his plans.

He sent Prince Charles and the Duke of Buckingham to Madrid to view the prospective bride and arrange the wedding. The visit was a total disaster. The Spaniards demanded concessions for English Catholics which the Commons, as James well knew, would never allow, and refused to intercede with the Emperor on behalf of the Palatinate.

A marriage with a Protestant Princess would have united King and Parliament, but to James's way of thinking, if he could not have an alliance with Spain, he must have one with France. The Duke of Buckingham came up with the answer. When he and the Prince of Wales had been passing through Paris en route for Madrid they had both met and admired Marie de Medicis's fourteen-year-old daughter, Henrietta Maria, sister of Louis XIII. Arrangements were accordingly made and James ratified the marriage treaty three months before he died in 1625.

## 3

Charles was twenty-four when he began his hapless reign. He had inherited his father's belief in Divine Right and his hatred of the Puritans.

He had no sooner succeeded to the throne than he carried through his marriage with the French Princess Henrietta Maria, and her arrival at the port of Dover, accompanied by a retinue of French Catholic courtiers and priests, was the first of many shocks to his popularity. Later he enraged the Puritans further by allowing English Catholics to attend her 'Romish' services. Laud, whom he made a bishop and subsequently Archbishop of Canterbury, was introducing 'High Church' doctrines and practices which seemed to the Puritans to be not very dissimilar from those of Rome. By now the English people as a whole were convinced that their survival and their freedom were bound up with the survival of the Reformed faith, and they watched nervously for any sign that it was being put in jeopardy. The fact that the Reformed Church had defied the pope and had survived made men that much less inclined to accept the Divine Right of the king; and the Puritans in particular, who were managing to run their own cheerless offshoot of the Christian Church without the aid of any elaborate hierarchy of bishops and deans and deacons and rectors and canons and prebendaries and parsons, were not slow to realize that the country as a whole could be run on equally democratic lines. So to a very great extent the religious reform movement paved the way for the movement towards parliamentary government. And it was in the reign of Charles I that this movement reached its irresistible climax.

The Parliament's first stroke was to resolve that the customs duties, without which the King could not live in peace-time, much less conduct a war with Spain, should be voted, not for the King's lifetime, which was normal, but for one year only.

Buckingham led an expedition to Cadiz which was a total failure, and Charles had to dissolve Parliament in order to save his friend's life.

Buckingham then led an equally disastrous expedition to relieve the Huguenots then being besieged by Cardinal Richelieu at La Rochelle; despite Charles's marriage to Henrietta Maria, France and England had by now drifted into war. Charles was in a very awkward position; he needed money to conduct the war, but he knew that if he summoned a Parliament it would impeach his friend. In his desperation, he demanded forced loans from various wealthy citizens, and, when they refused to give him the money, threw them into prison. Five of these prisoners appealed against their sentences, but the King's Bench ruled in favour of the King.

Since forced loans were insufficient to keep the King going indefinitely, he was obliged to summon another Parliament in 1628, having first secured a promise that Buckingham would not be impeached. This Parliament – which, among its members included an obscure backbencher called Oliver Cromwell – immediately set about limiting the King's power, framing a Petition of Right which aimed to put an end to forced loans, imprisonment without trial, the billeting of troops on ordinary homes, and martial law. The Parliament also passed a number of resolutions including one that the writ of habeas corpus* should be granted to every man imprisoned, even by the express orders of the King or the Privy Council, and another that no one should have to pay any loans or taxes without the consent of Parliament. Charles accepted this Petition, without ever really intending to keep his word, and the money was granted. Buckingham set out to make another attempt to relieve the Huguenots at La Rochelle but was murdered at Portsmouth before he set sail.

When Parliament met again in 1629, it concerned itself chiefly with religious grievances: the Commons were distressed at the slack way in which the laws against the Catholics were being enforced. In a comprehensive resolution, or Remonstrance, Parliament condemned the encouragement of popery and the collection of tonnage and poundage before it was granted by Parliament. This was a slap at Charles, who, when his first year's tonnage and poundage was exhausted, simply sent his officials out to collect the next year's without recourse to Parliament. Parliament also censured the Lord Treasurer for exacting taxes illegally. When the Speaker tried, on the King's instructions, to adjourn the House to prevent the Remonstrance from being passed, he was forcibly held down in his chair by two members, the doors barred against the Black Rod, and the Remonstrance carried with acclamation. It was clear that Charles could no longer work with Parliament; he now resolved to go it alone.

During the period of Personal Rule, Charles used every device, even obsolete feudal customs, to raise money. His chief minister was Sir Thomas Wentworth, later Earl of Strafford. Strafford's policy, known as 'Thorough', consisted of ruthlessly crushing all resistance.

Because there was no money to fight wars, peace was made with France and Spain. The Huguenots, thus abandoned, surrendered; and the Elector Palatine died soon after without ever recovering his lands.

Puritans, suffering at the hands of Strafford and Laud, now began to emigrate in large numbers to New England; and also a Catholic colony was founded in the north of Virginia, known as Maryland.

In Ireland the King called an informal assembly, to which he pledged certain 'graces'. One of these promised a greater measure of

* Although the first Habeas Corpus Act was not put on the Statute book until 1679 (see page 142) nominally such a right had existed from Magna Carta.

toleration to Catholics; another pledged that the Crown would not claim lands which had been held without challenge for sixty years. In return for these promises, substantial subsidies were paid, but the 'graces' were not granted and Strafford was made Lord-Deputy of Ireland.

He was a vigorous ruler, and he succeeded in putting down piracy – from which the Irish coastal towns had greatly suffered – and in reducing the country to a greater submission to the Crown than ever before or since. He produced an Irish army and a substantial Irish contribution towards the Crown.

## 4

Still Charles managed to do without a Parliament, but he was forever short of money. Now his lawyers came up with a new notion. According to the ancient laws and customs of England, the whole land had been in the habit of paying for the upkeep of the fleet. This was logical enough, for in a small island like Britain, everyone was exposed to attacks from the sea. In recent years, however, only the counties actually on the coast had been paying this ship-money; even at the time of the Armada, Queen Elizabeth had not taxed the inland counties for the upkeep of the fleet. Now Charles decided to change all that: in 1635 he levied ship-money on the whole country.

Immediately a Buckinghamshire county gentleman and former member of Parliament, called John Hampden, refused to pay, though the amount was no more than one pound. The King won his case but a sense of grievance remained and people began to think more deeply about the need to constrict the Divine Right of Kings.

But it was once again on the question of religion that the final break with the King came. Laud, who had been busying himself increasing the gulf between the clergy and the congregation, and using various means, such as the railing off of the altar, to place a new emphasis on the dignity of the clergy, now found a new source of revenue for Charles. Under Elizabeth's Religious Settlement, everybody was obliged to go to Church; they might think as they wished, but they were required to attend public worship once a week. In practice these laws had never been enforced: many people simply did not bother to go to church, and others refused to go. They now found themselves hauled before the courts and fined a shilling for each time they missed divine service. The Puritans, needless to say, regarded this as persecution and felt that it could only lead to a revival of the burnings at Smithfield.

The prosecution, pillorying, branding and lopping-off of ears of Puritan writers was another disquieting feature of a mainly benevolent reign.

But it is doubtful if any of these things would have been sufficient to break Charles if he had not allowed Laud to persuade him to force uniformity on the Scottish Church. An attempt to foist a new prayer-book on the Scots was ignominiously defeated, and the Scots signed a Covenant – many of them opening their veins to sign it with their own blood – pledging themselves to 'adhere to and defend the aforesaid true religion and forswear the practice of all novations in the matter of worship of God till they be tried and allowed in free Assemblies and in Parliaments'. The King found himself confronted with a hostile Assembly, led by armed elders, whose demands amounted to the abolition of the whole episcopalian structure of the Church. He ordered the dissolution of the Assembly, but it declared itself resolved to continue in permanent session in defiance of the King.

The King had ruled for ten years without a Parliament: now he was being openly defied. He looked for military assistance to Strafford's Irish army and even contemplated raising an army of mercenaries in Spain. The Scottish Covenanters – who had sent Scots brigades to fight on the Protestant side in the Thirty Years War in Germany – now began to recall these troops, trained officers and men all hardened and experienced in battle. By May 1639, this army, 30,000 strong, stood on the Scottish border waiting to repel the onslaught of whatever Charles could produce in the way of an army. No fighting took place; the Scots agreed to disband their army and return the royal castles which they had seized, and the King, for his part, agreed to summon both a General Assembly and a Parliament, and furthermore agreed that in future these would be regularly summoned, the one to take decisions on ecclesiastical and the other on temporal matters.

But the peace was short-lived, because Charles could not reconcile himself to what amounted to open defiance of the Crown on the part of the Scots. He recalled Strafford from Ireland. As Lord-Deputy of Ireland, Strafford had raised and trained an army of 8,000 men, in the nature of things mainly Catholic, and the fear began to grow in Scotland – and even in England – that Charles would not hesitate to use this army, if necessary, against the Covenanters in Scotland or even the Puritan Parliamentarians in England.

Unaware of this fear, and convinced that the old antagonism between the English and the Scots could be aroused, Strafford advised Charles to summon another Parliament. This Parliament, the first summoned for eleven years, met the King's demand for money to fight the war against Scotland with a counter-demand for a Statute making Ship-money illegal and was dissolved by Charles within three weeks. The Scots army invaded England, got as far as Newcastle, and appealed for assistance from all who favoured the Puritan and Parliamentary cause; by now, Puritanism was becoming associated with rule by Parliament rather than by the King. Again, Charles was forced into a position in which he had to summon another Parliament: without Parliament he could not defend the country against the Scottish invasion.

Two-thirds of the members of the Parliament, which met on 3 November 1640, were now opposed to the King and his Ministers. Strafford had hoped that Pym, leader of the opposition in the Commons, could be impeached for treasonable correspondence with the Scots, but Pym struck first and impeached both Strafford and Laud.

The main charge against Strafford was that he had advised the King to bring over the Irish troops. His defence was that they were to be used against the Scots, but the Commons felt that, once over in Britain, they might very well be turned against the forces of Parliament. Charles hesitated as long as possible before giving his assent to the Bill of Attainder, but when rioting mobs began to appear in front of the palace demanding Strafford's execution, he gave in, and three days later Strafford was executed. Laud was kept in the Tower and executed four years later, in 1645.

The Commons now proceeded to ventilate their grievances. They forced the King to agree that the Parliament could not in future be dissolved except by its own consent. They also forced the King to abolish the Star Chamber – a device of Henry VIII's by which Common Law on evidence could be short-circuited and persons brought in to give evidence were simply interrogated, often without even taking an oath – and the Court of High Commission, which had been used to establish religious uniformity. The principles set out in the Petition of Right, guaranteeing personal liberty and freedom from arbitrary arrest, were confirmed. They also demanded the abolition of the bishops. But by this stage many of the Commons, some of them churchmen, began to get nervous and a second petition signed by seven hundred clergymen proposed instead the restriction of the bishop's powers to spiritual matters. The King and many of the clergy regarded the hierarchical system of Episcopacy, based on the Apostolic Succession, as an essential feature of the Christian religion. It had, it will be remembered, been introduced by St Augustine who was sent over from Rome to bring the English Church into line with the Church in Europe; and Henry VIII's break with Rome had not interrupted its continuity. The King was determined to maintain his ancient hereditary right of nominating bishops; the Puritans saw in this system a dangerous extension of the King's power.

But before this matter could be resolved, something happened in Ireland which altered the whole course of that island's history and which poisoned for three hundred years the relations between Catholics and Protestants there.

CHAPTER NINE

# The Massacre of the Protestants

## 1

With Strafford gone, the government of Ireland fell to the Lords Justices, Parsons and Borlase: well-meaning men, but far too weak to control a country seething with fear and resentment which had been kept in control only by Strafford's system of 'Thorough'. The landowners of Ulster who had been dispossessed in the Plantation of Ulster less than forty years earlier, and their descendants, were spoiling for a chance to get their lands back and Irish Catholic landowners elsewhere feared – and with very good reason – that if the Puritan element in the British Parliament came out on top, they would bring in further repressive measures against the Catholic religion and seize yet more Irish land for Scottish and English planters.

The King still had Strafford's Irish Army, but Pym argued that it was undesirable to keep such a vast and expensive force in a country which – until that moment – was more peaceful than it had been for centuries, and further that, since it was largely composed of Catholics, it could not be trusted to fight to maintain the Protestant connection. The King agreed to a partial demobilization, reducing the force from Strafford's 8,000 to a mere 3,000. The remainder, 5,000 well-trained, disciplined, native soldiers, were disbanded. Their arms and ammunition were stored in the vaults of Dublin Castle, and although some of the men went abroad to serve as mercenaries, the bulk of them stayed on in Ireland to form the nucleus of a rebel army, encouraged to plot by the success of the Scots' rebellion.

One of the descendants of The O'Neill, Earl of Tyrone, Owen Roe O'Neill – serving with the Spanish Army in Flanders – heard rumours of a forthcoming revolt in Ireland and promised to return as soon as firm plans had been prepared; and one of the disbanded commanders was Roger O'More, a member of the clan that had been dispossessed by Queen Mary's plantation of Leix (see p. 90).

At this juncture, recusancy fines – that is, fines for failing to attend

Protestant divine service – were reintroduced in Ireland. When they were enforced in England (see p. 109) Strafford very wisely had allowed their enforcement in Ireland to be shelved indefinitely because he knew it would inflame the Catholic Irish. It is difficult to understand how the British Parliament could have been so blind to all the potential dangers in Ireland; but they have proved even blinder in more recent, more enlightened times.

Various factions in Ireland now began to make plans for rebellion. The rebellion – which is often dismissed in history books as a simple massacre of Protestants by hordes of bloodthirsty Irish Catholics – was complicated by a great many issues. By now the population had four main strains: the native Irish; the Old English (that is, the descendants of the original Anglo-Norman invaders); the New English (who had come over as Planters during the reigns of Mary and Elizabeth, plus of course the English merchants and traders in the seaport cities and the English administrators, both civilian and military); and the Scots-Irish in Ulster. Most of the Old English were inclined to favour the King, but some, realizing how weak his position was becoming, were prepared to throw in their lot with the Parliamentarians in the hope of getting a better deal. The New English and the Ulster Scots-Irish were divided in their loyalties, some favouring the King and some the Commons. The native Irish, of course, wanted to break the connection with England altogether: they planned to evict the English from all their Irish holdings and take over the government.

The original plan was to seize Dublin Castle, capture the arms stored there after the disbandment of Strafford's army, and at the same time stage an uprising of the Catholic gentry and peasants in Ulster who would be overjoyed at the opportunity to take back their old holdings. The remaining provinces would then, it was expected, follow suit within a few days, and if serious fighting broke out, an Irish army could be rapidly reformed from the disbanded remnants of Strafford's army, and re-armed with the arms from the Castle.

In Dublin the plot leaked out, due to drunken incompetence. The English merchants and settlers of the Pale* were armed to defend the Castle, three of the rebel ringleaders were arrested and the attack on the Castle was called off at the last minute.

But nobody told the conspirators in Ulster what had happened,

* The Pale was the name given to that area round Dublin which had remained continually under direct English rule.

*'romwell's extremely free readings from the Old Testament led him to slaughter Irish peasant 'en and women in the belief that he was actually exterminating, by the express order of 'hovah, what Hilaire Belloc called 'those unfortunate small tribes with the odd, Asiatic ımes':* Cromwell as Lord Governor of Ireland. [Mansell Collection]

*In Bohemia in the fifteenth century, John Huss preached a return to the simple faith of the Bible; he was invited to discuss his ideas on Reform with the Church leaders, guaranteed a safe conduct and then seized, tried for heresy and burnt at the stake:* an old engraving of the event. [Radio Times Hulton]

*Throughout the Famine, evictions continued, though the houses from which the starving peasants were ejected were little better than the caves they made for themselves out of the turf bogs:* the village of Mienies in Ireland during the Famine. [Mansell Collection]

One of the caves in the bogs – they were known as 'scalps' – in which the evicted Catholic peasants lived during the Famine years. [Mansell Collection]

*The English newspapers in August 1969 carried front pages of pictures which might have been taken during the 1916 Rebellion in Dublin:* Sackville street after the Easter Week Rising, 1916. [Mansell Collection]

A scene during the Battle of the Bogside, Derry, August, 1969. [Colman Doyle—Camera Press]

*The British people found it hard to credit that such scenes as these were taking place, not in Prague or Budapest, but in a part of the U.K. less than one hour's flying time from London. In 1916, the British public felt exactly the same kind of shock at the sight of British Tommies on 'active service' in the streets of Dublin:* The front line in one of the many battles for Derry, as British troops fire on I.R.A. snipers. [Colman Doyle – Camera Press]

British Tommies firing on I.R.A. snipers in Dublin in 1916. [Mansell Collection]

*'It was old, but it was beautiful . . .' (from the traditional Orange ballad, 'The Sash My Father Wore'):* one of the Derry Apprentice Boys wearing his 'uniform' for the annual march in celebration of the closing of the gates of Derry in the face of King James's Catholic Army in 1689. [Gilles Caron – Gamma]

*In urban guerilla warfare, the women cannot avoid becoming involved:* women in Derry and Belfast have always rattled their dustbin lids on the pavements to warn their menfolk that the police and military are in the vicinity. [Camera Press]

A puzzled paratrooper comforts an equally puzzled girl injured in the random bomb blast in Donegall street, Belfast, on 20 March 1972 which killed four people and injured ninety-seven. [Press Association]

*It was the utter familiarity of the setting – these could be the back streets of Liverpool or Sheffield – which so shocked the British public when pictures like this began to appear in their newspapers:* here, troops rush a house in the Belfast suburbs looking for an I.R.A. sniper. [Camera Press]

and at dawn gangs of armed Irishmen descended on the homes of the English settlers. The evictions were carried out with terrible cruelty. It was late October and the weather was bitterly cold. Without warning, stripped of everything they possessed, often including their clothes, the English settlers were bundled out into the savage winter to take their chance.

Much of the present Ulster Protestant mistrust and fear of Catholics stems partly from the events of that terrible winter, petrified in racial memories; for the Scots Irish and English Protestant settlers share the Celtic Irish propensity for remaining for centuries prisoners of their own past – this is the crux of the whole matter. It is true that the Irish who descended on the English and Scots settlers in Ulster in 1641, and at first evicted and later massacred them in thousands, were all Catholics, but the reason they did so was not because they were Catholics and the settlers Protestants, but because they wanted their land back. Nevertheless, the difference in religion provided convenient and misleading labels which could always thereafter be used to whip up violence in the province.

As the first week wore on, the peasants began to realize the enormity of their offence in the eyes of authority and the sort of reprisals they might expect. D. M. R. Esson writes in his book *The Curse of Cromwell*:

> Within a week the practice of ejection was seen to be stupid: a despoiled and embittered man could return in a very dangerous mood; supported by the law and armed with modern weapons, his enmity could be terrible. . . . In the killing, neither man, woman nor child was spared. Indeed the Irish blood-lust went on to destroy everything English; the farms were burnt, the horses ham-strung, the cattle slaughtered. The Irish were bent on obliterating everything English, or that had even a semblance of being English. Nothing was sacred, nothing was to be spared. Wooden structures were burnt, stone buildings were torn down and it was enough that a dog had prowled around an English midden for it to be killed; sufficient that a hen had laid eggs for an English table for its neck to be wrung.

Naturally, the reprisals were equally savage. The Protestants of Enniskillen, sturdy yeoman stock, began to attack the Irish, burning their cottages, driving off their sheep and cattle and killing any they fell upon.

Within a month, the rising had spread through the remainder of the country; outside the Pale, Wicklow and Wexford were ravaged and most of Munster was in revolt. Refugees pouring into Dublin found there some security from the marauding bands of Irish cut-throats, but few other comforts. And soon, all over the country, famine and disease were exacting as formidable a toll as the Irish rebels.

## 2

When the Irish Rebellion broke out, the King was in Scotland and he communicated with Parliament initially by letter. A Scottish Army of 1,500, under General Munro, was sent to Ulster to reconquer the rebellious province for the Crown. For once King and Commons were agreed: the Irish revolt must be crushed. But many in the Parliament doubted that the King should be given control of an army. To Pym the Irish rebellion offered an opportunity to attack what little remained of the Divine Right, and the replies which Parliament sent to the King included a request that in the future all his counsellors should be appointed by Parliament. At the same time Oliver Cromwell tried to limit the King's control by suggesting that the Puritan Earl of Essex should take over the Trained Bands* in the south.

The King left Edinburgh for London on 18 November 1641. He arrived to find that, during the week it had taken him to travel south, Pym and his followers in Parliament had succeeded in passing a Grand Remonstrance (a repetition on a larger scale of the earlier Remonstrance passed by the 1629 Parliament) which condemned at great length and in great detail all the King's misdemeanours in relation to Church and State, at home and abroad, throughout his reign.

But it was carried by only 11 votes out of a total of 307 at one o'clock in the morning of 23 November 1641, which shows how strong the growing body of Conservatives (or Episcopalians, as they were sometimes called, since they objected to the Puritan plans for lopping the power of the bishops) had become. They were agreed that Parliament needed a greater measure of control over the King, but felt that it could be done more tactfully and delicately. Since many of the two hundred or so absent members could also be relied upon to

* The trained or train bands were small bands of locally trained militia, which were originally formed by order of Elizabeth I in 1573.

support the King, the sensible action, on his part, would have been to ignore the Grand Remonstrance and try to settle the Irish Rebellion.

Instead the King allowed his Queen, Henrietta Maria, to talk him into attempting to prosecute five of his principal opponents in the Commons for High Treason. Accompanied by three or four hundred Cavaliers, he went to the House of Commons on 4 January 1642 – it was the first time a king had ever set foot in the Chamber – and found that the five members, warned of his intention in advance, had embarked at Westminster steps and were safe within the City of London.

The mobs which had thronged the streets outside Westminster howling for the execution of Strafford now started rioting in protest at the King's action, and Charles and his Court had to flee the capital for Hampton Court. This was the last he saw of London until he returned for trial and execution.

Within a week, the five members – Pym, Hampden, Holles, Hazelrigge, and Strode – were escorted back to Parliament in a triumphant procession, accompanied by two thousand armed men. The capital was lost to the King, who withdrew by easy stages to Newmarket, Nottingham and then York. Here, he gathered around him the loyalist leaders of Old England, while in London, Pym ruled what was left of Parliament as a virtual dictator. Charles's Cavaliers and the Roundheads (or skinheads, as we would say, so called after the short hair worn by the London apprentices who so vociferously had supported the Parliamentary cause in the early struggles) were now on a course set for civil war.

## 3

In the meantime, the massacres in Ireland were continuing apace. Parliament raised a few companies and sent them to reinforce the Dublin garrison and passed an act depriving Irish rebels of their lands and selling them to holders of a new debenture issue who would advance money to conduct the war and would be rewarded after the suppression of the rebellion either with the rebel lands or with the proceeds of their sale. Among the holders of this debenture issue were John Hampden and Oliver Cromwell.

From the Pale an army of colonists raided the Wicklow mountains shooting and hanging as many Irish as they could find in the process, and seriously depopulating the area; and in Ulster the Scots force, under Munro, began to drive the Irish out of Antrim and Down, exterminating them whenever possible, as a matter of policy.

By the spring of 1642 the English still held Dublin and Drogheda, Kinsale, Cork and Youghal and a number of strongholds like Enniskillen in the north of Ireland. The rebels were in control of the rest of the country, though much of it had been reduced to a wilderness.

To quote D. M. R. Esson's *The Curse of Cromwell* again:

> Here troops of starving kerns [lightly armed Irish foot-soldiers] fought with each other for such scraps of food as their own improvidence had not destroyed. The depopulation of those parts where heavy fighting had taken place naturally reduced the capacity of the warring factions, but not their ferocity. Whenever armed columns entered hostile territory they indulged their destructive capacity to the full. On balance this operated to the advantage of the English since they could always obtain supplies from across the sea, but the Irish were solely dependent on the produce of their own land. Varying estimates have been made of the slaughter which range from 30,000 to 500,000. These figures are based on a total population of a little over a million. [The population of England at this period was about three million.] The smaller number represents a very conservative figure of those actually killed by the sword in the initial uprising; the larger may be a slightly exaggerated total death roll from famine, pestilence and war until restoration of order. Anyway at least a sixth of the total population of Ireland disappeared from the face of the earth that winter, and the survivors swore to continue the killing. The process of depopulation had begun, and it was to continue by these and other methods for another ten dreadful years. Meanwhile, the fortresses could not be reduced; nor could they in their turn eliminate the menace of the Irish.

Another estimate, dealing purely with the initial massacre of Protestants, reckons that about one in ten of the Protestants in Ulster perished in the initial onslaught.

But it would be altogether unfair and inaccurate to suggest that only Protestants suffered in this grisly affair, or that all the atrocities were committed by the Catholics. In December 1641 the Lords Justices issued the following order to the commander of the King's forces in Ireland: 'It is resolved that it is fit his Lordship do endeavour, with His Majesty's forces, to slay and destroy all the said rebels, and their adherents and relievers, by all the ways and means he may; and burn, destroy, spoil, waste, consume and demolish all the places, towns and houses where the said rebels are or have been relieved and harboured and all the hay and corn there, and kill and destroy all the men there inhabiting able to bear arms.' And apart from attacks by the army, small bands of English and Scots colonists armed themselves and carried out ferocious raids on the rebels. For example, Sir Warham St Leger, who had been surrounded by rebels in Cork city, broke out and committed some savage reprisals; he executed fifty men in Waterford without trial, simply because they happened to be Irish.

The Catholic gentry in the Pale were initially disposed to side with the English; during Strafford's time the laws against the Catholic religion had not been very rigidly enforced and in fact Catholicism had been tolerated because Strafford knew it would make his task so much more difficult if he tried to suppress it rigidly. These Catholic gentry asked the Lords Justices if they could be allowed arms, like the Protestant settlers of the Pale, with which to defend themselves. Arms were initially issued to them and were then taken back, because the English Parliament regarded all Irish Catholics, the gentry as well as the peasants, as potential rebels. The result of this was that the Catholic gentry were forced to throw in their lot with the rebels, many of them becoming commanders of the Irish rebel forces.

The already complicated pattern of the Irish rebellion became even more complicated when it became clear that civil war was imminent in England. The commander of the Royal forces, James Butler, Earl of Ormonde, remained loyal to the King; the Lords Justices in Dublin and the civil administration favoured the Parliamentary cause.

All through the early part of 1642, negotiations dragged on between the King and Parliament which were conducted by letter and which could only bring civil war closer. In June, Parliament presented nineteen propositions to the King which amounted to a demand that Parliament should control the country's finances, the Army, the choice of the King's Council, and the Church: in other words the King was being invited to surrender to Parliament all effective sovereignty over Church and State.

Meanwhile in Ireland, guided now by the Catholic gentry, the rebels set up the Confederation of Kilkenny to provide a central government modelled on the Dublin Parliament: it had an upper house consisting of bishops, abbots and the few Catholic peers, and a lower house of county and borough members. In July, Owen Roe O'Neill arrived suddenly from the Netherlands with two hundred trained officers and three boatloads of arms and ammunition, and set about the difficult task of trying to weld the marauding gangs of dispossessed Catholic landowners and peasants into an orderly army capable of facing General Munro's Scottish force. In September of the same year Colonel Thomas Preston, a member of the Anglo-Irish Catholic gentry who had served during the religious wars in Germany, landed at Wexford with further arms and ammunitions and another five hundred trained men. So the Irish rebels now had not only the nucleus of an effective fighting force, but also the leaders.

## 4

By this time, the English people – who had grown accustomed to a peaceful tranquil life – were very slowly and reluctantly sorting themselves out into the opposing factions of Cavalier and Roundhead. Here, as in Ireland, the issues were far from clear. It was partly a religious and partly a class conflict. The Puritans were predominant in Parliament, the Episcopalians at Court. The new merchants and manufacturers and rich tenant farmers were in effect claiming, through their support of Parliament, a share of the political power which had previously been the hereditary right of the aristocracy and the Church dignitaries. But many who felt sympathy with the Parliamentary cause also were conscious of a deep-seated and instinctive loyalty to the monarch; and others who were strongly in favour of curtailing the King's Divine Right preferred their ancient, traditional, hierarchical Church to the cheerless creed of the Nonconformists.

After an unbroken spell of seventy years peace, there was a distinct shortage of trained fighting men in England, and the Civil War dragged on for five years, one indecisive battle following another. The Parliament made the Earl of Essex – son of Elizabeth's favourite – their General, but very soon Oliver Cromwell was training his new model army. At the outset, the King had better troops; but the war was won by the Parliamentarians who had behind them the fleet, the capital, all the wealth of the cloth-manufacturing towns and their new merchants and traders, plus the invincible ardour of the Nonconformist Ironsides under Cromwell.

In the early stages of the Civil War, when his march on the capital was halted at Turnham Green, Charles started to open negotiations with the Confederation of Kilkenny, through Ormonde, the commander of the Royal forces in Ireland. This, of course, held an immediate appeal for the old Anglo-Irish Catholic gentry, who controlled the Confederation, but in the event, they found Charles vacillating, devious and unreliable. He was prepared to make secret pacts with the rebels which he would later deny publicly, and he could not be pinned down to any specific terms.

The class distinctions in the fabric of Irish society were largely responsible for undoing the Kilkenny Confederation and for throwing away the opportunities which trained armies under Owen Roe O'Neill and Preston had given the Irish at a time when the English had their hands full on the mainland. The native Irish accused the Anglo-Irish Catholic gentry in the Confederation of plotting with the King and betraying the rebel cause in order to preserve their own political and social ascendancy; the Anglo-Irish Catholic gentry replied that so far from acting out of self-interest, they were risking the loss of valuable possessions by joining the Confederates, while few of the native Irish had anything to lose other than their lives. It was from the bitter divisions of these days that the phrase 'quarrelling like Kilkenny cats' passed into the English language.

## 5

In England, the Civil War was over, but peace could not be arranged; for Charles would not abandon the Church of England with its hierarchy of bishops and its continuity with the old Catholic Church, and Parliament was bent on turning the English Church Presbyterian.

Charles, vacillating as ever, then tried to win the Scots, who were virtually holding him captive at Newcastle, to his side. But, as he refused to accept the Covenant, they lost patience with him, handed him over to Parliament in return for payment of half their expenses in the Civil War, and went home.

Next a quarrel arose between the Army (which was mainly Independent and Calvinistic in its religious views and almost as strongly opposed to a Presbyterian as to an Episcopalian Church) and Parliament (which was still bent on setting up a Presbyterian Church). The Army was also owed some arrears of pay, the foot for eighteen weeks, the horse for forty-three, and the rank and file were growing restive. A council of officers of the Army sent a regiment of cavalry to capture Charles from Holmby House, in Leicestershire, where Parliament had placed him, and install him in Hampton Court. The Ironside Army, 22,000 strong and flushed with their success in the Civil War, was, as Churchill put it, 'not yet the master but no longer the servant of those who had created it'. But for a time, with the King in Hampton Court, strolling around and chatting with the rebel Army officers, it looked as if a solution to the whole question of a limited monarchy might be reached between Charles and the Army. But Charles was never wholly sincere in his dealings with the Army; he still had faint hopes of help from the Scots. And Parliament would not accept the proposals of the Army and the King. In the delays that followed, the rank and file of the military grew more and more discontented and the City of London, fearful of rule by the Generals, began to press Parliament to put the Army back in its place. Eventually, Parliament withdrew the conciliatory resolution which they had offered the Army, in order to keep the lines of communication open, whereupon Cromwell's troops marched on London, occupied Westminster and entered the City.

But the problems that faced the country all still remained to be solved. So the Army set up a great Military Parliament at Putney to debate these problems. The debates are interesting and some of the ideas expressed – manhood suffrage at the age of twenty-one was one of them – were away ahead of the times. Cromwell thought that such ideas could only lead to anarchy, and promptly sent the agitators back to their regiments, replacing the General Council of the Army with a Council of his own officers. It was soon clear that even with their pay settled, it would not be possible to unite King and Army; already many of the rank and file were talking of him as a 'man of blood' and his assassination in the public interest was being openly debated. Fearing that his life was in danger, Charles rode off in the night and made his way to Carisbrooke Castle on the Isle of Wight. Here he reopened negotiations with the Scots and managed to win the moderate Presbyterians to his side by signing a secret agreement which would ally Presbyterianism and the royalty. And in the summer of 1648 the Scots marched into England.

By this time, fear of the Army was the predominant feeling throughout the greater part of England, and many of the people who had previously been bitterly opposed to the King now saw in him a safeguard against the dictatorship of the Generals. The London apprentices had turned royalist; they supported Parliament, but preferred the King to the Army. Half the Navy mutinied in his favour. But even, with Parliament, King, the City of London, the landed gentry, the Scottish Army and the Welsh nation as well as half the Fleet lined up solidly against them, the New Model Army, their differences all forgotten at the prospect of a fight, were now victorious. They marched and fought and reduced the royal strongholds one by one, finally falling on the Scots Army as it marched through Lancashire, and cutting it to pieces.

The Ironsides – resolute, ruthless, fanatical – returned to the capital determined to execute Charles, that 'man of blood' who, whatever about the first Civil War, was certainly responsible for the second. And Cromwell, who had previously sought some arrangement by which this could be avoided, was now firmly of the same opinion.

When Charles, from the Isle of Wight, began again to negotiate with Parliament, the Army seized him and kept him a close prisoner at Hurst Castle on Southampton Water, then brought him to Windsor, where he was allowed a brief respite and treated with some of the old respect and ceremony before being summoned to Westminster Hall to hear his fate.

In the meantime, all Members of Parliament likely to be unsympathetic to the Army point of view were kept out of the House by an armed force, under Colonel Pride, until the remainder, all Independent Puritans, about sixty in number out of a grand total of about five hundred – and contemptuously called the 'Rump' – had appointed a court of 135 Commissioners to try the King for treason, his offence being that he had made war upon Parliament.

The King conducted himself now with a dignity he had rarely attained during his reign, and refused to recognize the competence of the court to try him. Nevertheless, at one o'clock in the afternoon of 30 January 1649, in front of the Banqueting Hall of Whitehall, an axe blade flashed in the pale sunlight and a groan arose from the thousands present – but kept at a safe distance by the ranks of the Ironsides.

Cromwell and the Army were now in full control of affairs in England; and it was natural that Cromwell's first task should be to restore order in Ireland, and ruthlessly punish both the Irish rebels and the Royalists there who, right up to the end, had been carrying on negotiations with the late King.

CHAPTER TEN

# Cromwell's Solution: 'To Hell or Connaught'

## 1

To the Royalists, the execution of the King meant that his son, Prince Charles, then in Holland, automatically became King Charles II of England; and Parliament's first act after the execution was to declare that any proclamation of Prince Charles as King would count as an act of treason.

A Council of State was next set up to run the country: it consisted of John Bradshaw, President of the Court which had tried the King, Cromwell and another general, Fairfax; and some thirty-eight others.

I have already dealt in some detail (in Chapter One) with the preparations for the Irish campaign, and Cromwell's arrival in Ireland up to and including the infamous siege of Drogheda in September 1649.

The ferocity of Cromwell's troops is to some extent explained, if not justified, by the fact that they believed that they were dealing with the Catholic wretches responsible for the terrible massacre of the Protestants in the winter of 1641, eight years earlier. In England, almost from the outbreak of the rebellion, Parliament had authorized the publication of atrocity stories, and a few weeks later the Dublin Parliament followed suit. As C. V. Wedgwood put it in *The King's War*:

> The Protestant public read with fascinated horror of settlers hanged before their plundered farmsteads, of families burnt alive in their homes, of women raped and murdered, of children drowned in bogs or spitted on long knives before the eyes of their parents. The refugees added to the tales; a woman in Scotland claimed to have seen her husband crucified. The appetite grew with what it fed on. No crime was too atrocious for the 'bloody Irish butchers', and the reputed numbers of their victims had, within weeks, passed a hundred thousand, until Ireland, drowned

in blood, seemed 'scarce tomb and continent enough to hide the slain'.

But, as C. V. Wedgwood goes on to point out: 'There had been deliberate drownings of women and children at Portadown in Ulster and Shrule Bridge in Galway. Even when the leaders wanted to save the lives of their civilian prisoners, they could not always protect them from the marauding bands of raiders who roamed the countryside.'

And, long before Cromwell's Army arrived in Ireland, 'No Quarter' had become the common rule on the other side: Irish rebel prisoners were all hanged, their women drowned. In Leinster the Government troops fired the furze and heather in which the Irish had taken shelter and burnt not only the active raiders, but also their women and children. It is in this context that the events in Drogheda and immediately following it must be judged.

The horror of what happened in Drogheda had the effect of forcing the Irish, the old Anglo-Irish and the New English Royalists to settle their differences, but it was too late. Owen Roe was now a dying man, and there was no other Irish general of sufficient calibre to confront Cromwell. In October, Wexford suffered more or less the same fate as Drogheda. Cromwell next turned his attentions on New Ross and within a few months had sufficiently subdued the rebels to be able to return to England to attend to urgent matters there, leaving Ireton in charge of the task of completing the subjugation of the Irish.

One of Cromwell's first problems was the fact that the Presbyterians of Scotland had proclaimed Charles, still in Holland, as King. But Charles initially – like his father – refused to accept the Covenant and sent Montrose to raise the predominantly Catholic Highlands again; Montrose was defeated by the Presbyterian forces and killed. In 1650, Cromwell marched on Scotland and defeated the Scots at Dunbar. The next year, Charles, who had travelled from Holland to Scotland, marched suddenly into England. Cromwell attacked him at Worcester and, on the anniversary of Dunbar, routed his army. Charles escaped to France.

The war in Ireland was beginning to flicker to a standstill. Only the west still held out but the Irish forces were so disorganized that no commander could speak for all of them. As a result, there was a whole series of separate surrenders, each commander claiming the right to take his men abroad with him.

Puritan England now set about the task of settling the account with the Irish Catholic rebels. The Catholics had already been warned what they might expect, by Cromwell, before he returned to England. 'I shall not, where I have power, and the Lord is pleased to bless me,' he had written, 'suffer the exercise of the Mass . . . nor suffer you that are Papists, where I can find you seducing the People or by any overt act violating the Laws established; but if you come into my hands, I shall cause to be afflicted the punishments appointed.'

But many different people, with many different problems, were calling for satisfaction. The soldiers wanted the arrears of pay they were owed, whether in cash or in land. The English and Scottish settlers who had been bundled out of the lands they had acquired in the Plantation of Ulster wanted these lands back. The English were united in their demands that the dastardly Irish rebels should be suitably punished for their deeds; and both the old and the new settlers were looking for a greater measure of security in their holdings.

The rebellion of 1641 had taken place nine months before the outbreak of civil war in England and, as we have seen (p. 117), a considerable loan – needed to conduct the war in Ireland – had been raised by an issue of debentures which guaranteed, in repayment, two and a half million acres of arable Irish land (out of a total of twenty million, about fifteen million of which could loosely be regarded as arable). Now it was also proposed that soldiers who had served Parliament, either in England or Ireland, and who still had arrears of pay owing, should be recompensed by further confiscations of land in Ireland. In a sense, this meant that the English Parliament was proposing to pay part of the cost of the war in both countries at the expense of the conquered Irish rebels.

An Act of Settlement was passed which decreed that every person in Ireland would lose his property wholly or in part, unless he could prove that he had been constantly faithful to the cause of the English Parliament.

There were about two hundred executions but most of the thirty thousand odd soldiers who surrendered were allowed to go into exile on the Continent. The principal revenge took the form of confiscations of land. 'To Hell or Connaught' was the choice offered to the Catholic land-owners, with the result that when Cromwell's Parliament had done with the country, less than a quarter of all the land in Ireland remained in Irish Catholic hands. Later this was to be further reduced.

It is debatable whether the English really intended to drive all the Irish Catholics into Connaught; in any event, it would have proved impossible. Some areas were wholly cleared of native Irish; in others, workers who owned no land were allowed to stay on to labour for the new landowners. All this transference of population from one area to another caused a great deal of confusion, and took a long time. Cromwell's Government tried to hasten a solution to the problem by transporting several thousands of Irish to work as forced labour on tobacco and sugar plantations in the West Indies, but not in numbers large enough to make any real impression on the situation.

And in the meantime, back in the English Parliament, Cromwell had been having problems of his own.

## 2

On his return to London in 1652, after Prince Charles had fled to France, Cromwell wanted to call a new Parliament to arrange a constitution. But the members of the 'Rump' insisted on retaining their seats, and eventually Cromwell lost his patience with them, came down to the House with his soldiers and threw them out. So, in the end, the Long Parliament – or rather, the last, sad remnants of it – was overthrown by its own creation, Cromwell's Army.

This army was now the only real power in the land. Cromwell next tried to make a Parliament from a list of names sent to him by the Independent clergy, but it contained – as anyone might have guessed – such a collection of impractical fanatics that he soon got rid of it too.

A council of Cromwell's officers next drew up a new 'Instrument of Government' by which Cromwell was to be Lord Protector, with a Parliament (to last only three years) to be elected for England, Scotland and Ireland. Cromwell, after some hesitation, accepted this proposition and moved into the royal palace at Whitehall.

The Parliament which was called in 1654 persisted in discussing his right to call himself Lord Protector; he soon dismissed it. He called his last Parliament in 1656; it proposed that he should be king, with power to name his successor, but although pleased with the suggestion he did not risk incurring the Army's disfavour by accepting it, and had to satisfy himself with the main provisions of the 'Humble Petition and Advice' without taking the title of king. Under the terms of the Petition, he had agreed to allow certain members whom he had excluded to return to Westminster, and as soon as they were back they began again to discuss the demerits of the new regime. Convinced that hostile designs against him were afoot, Cromwell dissolved Parliament in 1658 and decided to go it alone.

A grim, joyless Puritanism now became the English way of life. The execution of the King had meant also the overthrow of episcopacy. During the Civil Wars, wherever Parliament was in control, those clergy who would not take the Covenant or forswear the Prayer Book lost their livings. An attempt was even made to set up a Presbyterian system of church government, as in Scotland. But the Independents objected to any form of church government, however lax. In this period about ten thousand Church of England clergymen lost their livings; many were imprisoned as being papists in disguise, others fled abroad. Some were supported by Royalist gentry and continued to perform church services in secret; others made a living by reciting such offices as they could, from memory.

But besides church services, the Puritans also turned their attention to such potentially papish festivals as Christmas Day, which was abolished. Convinced that virtue could be achieved by drawing up laws against 'vice', they tried to stop such cruel sports as cock-fighting, bear-baiting and bull-baiting, and also curtailed many far more innocent amusements such as dancing, May games and the theatre, for fear that they might lead men into temptation.

Oliver Cromwell died in 1658, at the age of fifty-nine. His son Richard succeeded him as Protector, but at his first attempt to make a decision he was checked by the Army, and his brother Henry stepped in to advise that a Parliament should again be summoned. Cromwell's system had the same defect as Strafford's: it would work only as long as he was there himself to enforce it.

Although the new Parliament was one from which all Royalists were formally excluded, it began at once to raise the principal issues of government in England. It questioned the validity of all Acts passed since the 'Pride's Purge' of 1657 had robbed Parliament of its representative integrity, and it set about trying to regain control of the Army. The Army, however, were determined to retain their independent power for which, they argued, they had shed so much blood – most of it, it might be added, the blood of others. Parliament was equally resolute that the Army should not establish itself as a permanent 'estate' in the realm, and passed a resolution that every officer should sign a pledge never again to interrupt sittings or debates of Parliament.

Once more, trouble broke out between Parliament and the Army, and Commons members who tried to assemble were turned back by the troops, with Lambert and Fleetwood at their head. But the Army still felt in need of some constitutional backing for what they were doing; so they sought out the former speaker, Lenthall, and invited him and those of his colleagues who still survived from the Rump of 1653 to resume their seats. While this attenuated Rump and the Army debated the best way to run the country, a widespread Royalist movement broke out, and was quickly put down by Lambert, who returned to London with his victorious regiments, barred Parliament from Westminster, and began to plan the Restoration of the monarchy on his own terms, which involved the marriage of his daughter to Charles II's brother, the Duke of York. This plan had the immediate effect of dividing the Army: Fleetwood, Lambert's rival general, would not countenance a restored monarchy with Lambert holding so privileged a position. Divided, the Army turned to Parliament for guidance, expressing penitence for interrupting so many sittings of the House.

The Cromwellian commander in Scotland, George Monk – a former supporter of the King's who had gone over to their side while imprisoned by the Roundheads, and soon gained important Parliamentary commands – was known to be opposed to the Army's interference with Parliament in London. And when the Roundhead veteran commander Fairfax appeared in York to raise a following for a free parliament, Monk marched south with his well-trained army of 7,000 and joined him. In York, he received an invitation from the attenuated Rump to continue on to London. He arrived to find that the City of London had now turned Royalist, and the Rump instructed him to pull down the City gates preparatory to reducing it. Instead of dissolving the Rump, or excluding it from the House by force, as Cromwell and his generals had done with previous parliaments, Monk decided to dilute its Parliamentary fervour by recalling all the members excluded at the time of Pride's Purge, most of them Presbyterians and many of them now confirmed Royalists. Their first move was to declare invalid all Acts passed since the Purge. Monk was made Commander-in-Chief, the Long Parliament finally dissolved itself by its own consent, and a free Parliament was summoned which now would almost certainly vote for the return of the monarchy.

Monk sent word to Charles in Holland suggesting that he should offer free pardons, except for those whom Parliament had decided to punish, that he should guarantee the Army payment of any arrears still owed, and confirm new landowners in lands they had acquired during the Civil Wars. Charles went even further: he promised freedom of conscience for all.

The elections were held, Presbyterians and Royalists found themselves in the majority, and when the new Parliament assembled the Peers met again as if nothing had happened. On 1 May 1660, the new Parliament – which significantly didn't call itself a Parliament but merely a Convention, since Parliament as such can only be summoned by a monarch – voted that Charles II should be restored as King; and on the 29th he landed at Dover amid scenes of universal joy and relief. But although the monarchy was restored, it was a very different monarchy. All the remonstrances and petitions and propositions which had been put to Charles I before the Civil Wars were now more or less taken for granted by everyone: there was never any question of reviving the criminal jurisdiction of the Privy Council, the Star Chamber or the Court of High Commission. The whole question of levying taxes and making legislation was now unquestionably Parliament's concern. The monarchy that was restored in 1660 was, in effect, a constitutional one.

Feelings now began to run high against the men who had executed the King's father. Of some sixty men who had condemned the late King, about a third were dead, and another third had fled abroad. King Charles II, a very humane man, tried to save as many of the survivors as possible. In the end, nine paid the extreme penalty for treason. Most of them went to the scaffold glorying in what they had done, with a superb confidence, says Ivan Roots in his *The Great Rebellion 1642–1660*, which 'would carry them through the appalling destruction that lay concealed in the flat syllables "to be hanged, drawn and quartered"'.

To assuage the public feeling that this total of scapegoats was far too low, on the twelfth anniversary of the execution of Charles I the corpses of Cromwell, Ireton and Bradshaw were taken from the coffins in Westminster Abbey in which they had been buried in state only a short time before, dragged through the streets to Tyburn, hanged on a gibbet there, their heads spiked up on Westminster Hall, and their bodies thrown upon a dung-heap. For good measure, Pym and a score of other prominent Parliamentarians were disinterred and buried in a pit. It was an unedifying and tasteless exhibition, but at least no further lives were lost in pandering to the mob in this way.

## 3

The Acts under which the Irish lands had been confiscated were now invalid, but if the Irish expected any consideration for the support they had half-heartedly and intermittently given to the Royalist cause, they were to be disappointed. So little did the Irish grievances concern the English that the issue was not even debated in Parliament but was resolved by direct action; a proclamation in the spring of 1660 allowed current holders of lands formerly owned by native Irish involved in the Rebellion of 1641 to retain them pending a final decision.

> A declaration of November 1660 [I am quoting Ivan Roots's *The Great Rebellion* again] confirmed later by the Acts of Settlement of 1661 and an Explanation of 1665, confirmed soldiers and adventurers (there were more of the latter) in possession of lands held in November 1659. More than half the best land in Ireland was thereby lodged in the hands of Protestants, often absentee, marking the indestructibility of the Cromwellian settlement. The native Irish were condemned to be hewers of wood and drawers of water on land they regarded as rightfully their own. The ascendancy class which dominated Ireland for more than two centuries was being created.

To this H. A. L. Fisher (*A History of Europe, Vol. 1*) adds:

> The Cromwellian settlement only aggravated the evils of Ireland. The native Irish, driven from their homes to make way for soldiers and land speculators from England, found a refuge among the desolate bogs of Connaught, where their descendants continue to this day, despite all that has been done for the congested districts, to afford a spectacle of material wretchedness nowhere else to be paralleled in the British Isles.

Charles cared nothing for Ireland and very little for the dispossessed Royalists in Ireland; he tried to compromise but in practice he had far more to fear from the Cromwellian settlers in possession of the new lands, than from the few remaining dispossessed Catholic gentry. In religious matters, at the beginning of his reign at any rate, he went back to Strafford's system of *de jure* strictness – to keep the English Protestants quiet – combined with *de facto* laxity to avoid trouble from the Catholics.

Throughout Charles's reign, although there was inevitably much misery and discontent in Ireland, it was never sharp enough to provoke a rebellion; and in all conscience, after the trouncing they had received from Cromwell's troops, the Irish were not yet in any position to plan another rebellion, even if the provocation had been sufficient.

## 4

The surge of relief that shuddered through England at the Restoration was not merely a reaction against the joyless Puritanism of the Commonwealth, though that was an important factor in it. The Puritan Parliament punished adultery with death; the new King's adulteries were common gossip and the English people much preferred to have sinners, rather than saints, in charge of things.

But there was more to it than that, and the recent religious conflict had had a deep effect on the administration of the country. At this period in history, apart from the Royal Mail, there were no national public services outside the Courts of Law, the Exchequer and the Army. All administration which in these days is carried out by corporations and borough councils was then the concern of the parish, whose officers were expected to preserve the peace, maintain the highways, administer the poor law and public relief and so on. Outside the towns, these duties were unpaid: each householder in the parish, unless exempted for one reason or another, was expected to serve his turn for a year in one of these parish offices or provide a substitute. The overseers of the poor were expected to give weekly relief to the aged and infirm, to find work for the able unemployed, to provide houses for the homeless, and in fact to carry out a whole host of duties now administered by a vast army of civil servants and county council officials and administrators. At this period, there wasn't even a police force; one of the parish officers was the constable, appointed by the court and sworn in by the justices. His principal duty was to preserve the peace, and in attempting to do so he could call on any citizen to assist him, and it was an offence to refuse.

The change from the Roman Catholic religion to the Anglican version of it which became the religion of the bulk of the people in Elizabeth's day, did not threaten this parochial system of local government and administration, but the efforts of the Commonwealth parliaments to substitute in some cases Presbyterianism and in some cases what amounted to anarchy – because the Calvinist Independents didn't believe in any system of church government whatsoever – had the effect of upsetting the whole pattern of life in rural England. Thus the restoration of monarchy and the restoration of the episcopacy was welcomed because they meant also the restoration of a stable system of local government which had been developed over the years to meet the needs of the English people.

But the religious troubles in England – and Ireland – were far from over. For although the bulk of the people were overjoyed at the return to the old Anglican system of worship and parish control, there remained a hard core of Nonconformists of all sorts: Presbyterians, Calvinists, Independents, Levellers, Quakers, and so on; as well as a number of Roman Catholics. Both Charles himself and his brother James, Duke of York, were Roman Catholics at heart, from the influence of their mother Henrietta Maria, and the Jesuits saw in the Restoration a faint hope of restoring the Catholic faith in England. Since the foundation at Douai, sanctioned by Pope Pius V, of a seminary dedicated to the reconversion of England to the Roman faith, the Papacy had never abandoned hope.

At the beginning of Charles's reign, with a balanced and representative Convention at Westminster, it might have been possible to weld all these diverse religious elements into some sort of unity. The fear of Puritan domination was removed when the hated army, helpless without leaders, was paid off and disbanded, although Charles kept one regiment of Monk's men as personal guards: the horse known as Life Guards, and the foot-soldiers known as the Coldstream Guards (from a village on the Tweed where they were raised during Monk's march south to London) – this was the beginning of the British Army as it now exists. The Customs were voted to Charles for life, and all seemed set fair to attempt to resolve the religious differences.

The Convention itself, however, felt that it lacked constitutional status since it had not been summoned by the King's writ. Realizing the hazards of another election at this particular period, the King tried to suggest that he might issue his writ retrospectively, but they wouldn't have it, and in 1660 the Convention was dissolved.

The Parliament which replaced it has been called the Cavalier Parliament. It consisted mainly of landed gentry, some of whom had lost their lands in the Civil Wars, and all of whom were determined to use the parliamentary rights which had been gained in the immediate past to the advantage of their own class. They conceded that it was necessary to provide for the defence of the country by armed militia, and agreed that the King had supremacy over these forces, but insisted that the militia be controlled by the Lord-Lieutenant in each county. Having ensured that control of the armed forces would henceforth be in the hands of the county families and local gentry, they went on to consider the question of religion.

As Clarendon was Lord Chancellor and chief minister at this time, his name is associated with a whole series of Acts which the Cavalier Parliament passed, re-establishing the Anglican Church on terms which drove a deep and enduring wedge between the established Church of England and all the other Protestant sects, and united the latter into a solid Nonconformist opposition bloc with two objectives: the securing of toleration, which was achieved with the Revolution of 1688; and the reduction and eventual abolition of the privileged status of the Church of England.

But for the moment the landed gentry of the Cavalier Parliament had won another victory: they now had their own Church and their own bishops, as they already had their own militia.

Charles had promised freedom of conscience for all, and would have been happy to have allowed such a situation; but the Clarendon Code ruled this out. It included the Corporation Act of 1661 which effectively excluded Presbyterians, Republicans, Roman Catholics and some Nonconformists from holding municipal office, which meant in effect that the management of elections for parliament became confined for all practical purposes to Royalist Anglicans. The Act of Uniformity of 1662 imposed upon all the clergy the Prayer Book of Queen Elizabeth, with some deletions and additions, with the result that one-fifth of the clergy, nearly two thousand ministers, were deprived of their livings. Other Acts prevented these clergy from preaching to their own congregations and from going within five miles of any parish or place where they had ever preached or held a living.

Throughout his reign, Charles did his best to achieve the religious tolerance he had promised before the Restoration. In May 1663, he tried to suspend the Act of Uniformity, and in December of the same year he issued a Declaration of Indulgence, relieving dissenters from the laws enforcing religious conformity or requiring religious oaths. He did this, he claimed, by virtue of power inherent in the Crown, but the Commons protested. In 1672 he issued a second Declaration of Indulgence to suspend 'the execution of all manner of penal laws in matters ecclesiastical against whatsoever classes of Nonconformists and Recusants [Roman Catholics]'. The Commons ruled that Penal Statutes in ecclesiastical matters could not be suspended except by Act of Parliament, and King Charles finally got the message and desisted from further interventions on behalf of the oppressed minorities.

## 5

At the Restoration, the union of the parliaments accomplished by Cromwell was undone and Ireland ceased to be represented at Westminster; she became a foreign country for some purposes, as D. M. R. Esson puts it in the Epilogue to *The Curse of Cromwell*, and a conquered dependency for others. He goes on:

> The English Navigation Acts required all cargoes for the colonies to be carried in English bottoms, and this excluded the Irish; other forms of protection struck hard at Irish agriculture; this was justified in England by saying that the Irish were just a lot of rebels, but the English were really striking at their own kith and kin, driving them into the arms of the hated Papists. The settlers had gone to Ireland to seek prosperity, but the home country were denying them an opportunity. As a result of these and other pinpricks the Cromwellians began to throw in their lot with the old Irish. Not for the first time and not for the last, the new leadership which had been grafted on to Ireland displayed sentiments which were distinctly Irish. Many had acquired Irish wives; for the Cromwellian inhibitions had gone with the Restoration; more had imbibed Irish thoughts; most were as firmly attached to the soil as their predecessors. The old leadership of the nation had gone; in its place the Irish could look to the triumphant veteran of the Puritan Revolution, and due to the crass idiocy of the English administration, he did not look in vain.

This is true only to a limited extent. Many of the subsequent struggles for Irish freedom were led by Protestant settlers, a few dating from this period, perhaps, but more dating from earlier settlements. But there is no doubt that some of the Cromwellian settlers resented the way in which they were treated by the English Parliament, and may have mingled their resentment with that of the Irish, smarting under other, more enduring wrongs.

CHAPTER ELEVEN

# Popish Plots—— and the Last Catholic King

## 1

In their intransigence, in their fear of foreign domination, and above all in their deep and abiding distrust and detestation of Roman Catholicism, the people of Charles II's time have parallels among the more militant Ulster Protestants today. And yet much of their fervour was a direct outcome of their medieval Catholic faith.

In his social history of England during this period, *Protestant Island*, Arthur Bryant makes the point that although England had broken her last links with Rome a century before and was, politically speaking, militantly Protestant, her simple country folk were still instinctively rooted in the faith of the medieval church.

> Faith [he writes] was the air its people breathed. To them it explained everything; even affliction was a visitation sent to test the spirit and teach patience and resignation. 'If you be taken away by this dreadful pestilence,' a correspondent wrote during the plague of 1665, 'you have had a fair warning and a very long time to prepare yourselves for Heaven. It seems that every day at London is now a day of judgement, and that all our thoughts are placed on death, on Hell, on Heaven and upon eternity. Thy will be done on earth as it is in Heaven is the balsam that cureth all.'

To write in such terms at a time when London's population was dying at the rate of six or seven thousand people in a single week, calls for faith of a kind that is difficult to comprehend today.

And no sooner was the worst of the Plague over than the Great Fire engulfed the centre of the capital. It broke out near London Bridge – in those days a bridge like Florence's Ponte Vecchio, with houses and shops built on top of it – and, fanned by a summer gale blowing in from the east, blazed away for four days and nights during which a third of the city disappeared. When the fire was eventually halted, just short of the Temple and the present Holborn Viaduct, by blowing up whole streets of houses to prevent it from spreading further, a total of more than 13,000 dwelling houses, the Guildhall and eighty-four churches had been destroyed, including St Paul's Cathedral, which in any event was in a ruinous state. The spire of the cathedral had fallen down many generations before, and Cromwell's troops had used the nave as a stable during the Commonwealth, a gesture of their contempt for Anglicanism.

But the point about both the Great Plague and the Great Fire was that they confirmed an uneasy suspicion that popery was about to be reintroduced into England, which had begun to dawn in the minds of the ordinary English people, and particularly the London people around this time. It was partly the fact that Charles II was known to be very lenient with the Catholics, and indeed there were rumours that he was in fact still a Catholic himself. He was the son, after all, of Henrietta Maria, a French Catholic, and his brother the Duke of York, next in line for the throne, was now openly a Catholic. It was felt in some vague way that the Papishes were responsible for both the Plague and the Fire and, indeed, for all other ills that befell the plain people of England at this time. Of the aftermath of the Great Fire, Arthur Bryant writes:

> This devastated area, into which the Londoner passed as he came out of the populous streets of Tower Hill or left the prosperous western faubourgs at Temple Bar, was the key to the political feelings of a generation which, twenty-two years later, swept away, in a frenzy of Protestant hysteria, the last English sovereign who dared to avow the Catholic faith . . . It spelt a legend of nightmarish fears, of popes and red cardinals, priests and foreign dragoons threatening stake, massacre and wooden shoes [always regarded in seventeenth-century England as a symbol of poverty and popery] to the people of England. And even when a new city of warm-coloured brick and pleasant well-ordered streets had arisen out of the ruins, the legend persisted. On the wall of the house in Pudding Lane on the site where the Fire began, the Lord Mayor of the most bigoted city in the world inscribed the words: 'Here by permission of Heaven Hell broke loose upon this Protestant City from the malicious hearts of barbarous papists.'

Bryant continues:

> Popery was the bugbear with which seventeenth-century children were brought up by their mothers and nurses: a terror they never

> outgrew. They had learnt their religion from the crude woodcuts of Protestants burning at the stake in Foxe's *Book of Martyrs* and their history from tales of the Massacre of St Bartholomew, the Gunpowder Plot and the Irish Rebellion of '41. The Great Fire seemed to them but one more page in that bloodstained mythology, a prelude to some gruesome popish plot of assassination, midnight massacre and foreign invasion.'

Pamphlets which exposed, often erroneously, the fallacies and false claims of Rome were popular reading, and once a year there was a procession through the streets of London in which the mob carted effigies of popes, cardinals and devils, stuffed with live cats so that they would squeal realistically when later burnt at the stakes in Smithfield.

At this period Louis XIV was bent on increasing France's territorial possessions in Europe, and when eventually – to the great joy of the English people – Charles II arranged a triple alliance against France with the two Protestant countries, Holland and Sweden, Louis decided to buy off one of Europe's two principal maritime powers before resuming his war. He chose England, and in 1670 began secret negotiations through Charles's sister Henriette, who was married to Louis's brother, the Duke of Orléans. Charles was after money and had inherited his father's fatal penchant for bargaining. He put it to Louis that Parliament was prepared to vote him all the money he needed if he would make war on France, and suggested that if Louis were to pay him the money instead there would be no need to call Parliament. Although a Parliament of sorts had existed from the time of Edward I, it could not meet unless summoned by the king, and during many reigns was only summoned whenever the king was short of money. Earlier parliaments had insisted that the king could not raise any additional taxation without Parliament's consent; consequently Parliament had to be assembled and consulted whenever a king needed more money. And naturally, once summoned, it could refuse to grant the king permission to raise the extra funds unless and until he had first redressed whatever grievances Parliament chose to bring up. This was the uneasy relationship which existed between all the Stuart kings and the many parliaments, long and short, which they summoned.

The Treaty of Dover, as this secret agreement was called, also included a clause to the effect that King Charles, 'being convinced of the Truth of the Catholic Faith is determined to declare himself a

Catholic . . . as soon as the welfare of his realm will permit'. In return the King was to receive from France a sum of about £166,000 a year, some of which would be devoted to the upkeep of his mistresses, and there was also a military alliance.

War then broke out again between France and Britain on the one hand and Holland on the other; this was the war that ended for Holland with a revolution at The Hague which put William of Orange in charge as Stadtholder. The dykes were opened: the North Sea poured in over the flat lands of the Low Countries and Amsterdam was closed off to the French army. William of Orange had saved Holland's honour – but Charles's troubles were just beginning.

A meeting of Parliament in 1673 had informed Charles of the Commons' disapproval of this war against the Protestant Dutch, with Britain ranged on the same side as papist France, now the strongest force in Europe. Rumours that the King had made a secret treaty with France, the King's continuing and increasing laxity towards Papists and the open conversion of the Duke of York to Roman Catholicism, combined for once to unite all the disparate Protestant elements in the country. Much as they hated one another, Anglicans and Calvinists were prepared to work together to fight the threat of a return to Rome Rule.

Parliament next introduced a bill under which no man could hold an official position, or a king's commission, afloat or ashore, without first taking a test which entailed declaring his disbelief in the doctrine of transubstantiation. These Test Acts put the Duke of York in a very tricky position; a Catholic and about to marry a Catholic princess, Mary of Modena, he was also Lord High Admiral. When he relinquished his post rather than deny the doctrine of transubstantiation, it confirmed the public in their worst fears. Since Charles II's wife, Catherine of Braganza, seemed unlikely ever to bear him a son, it looked as if the next English king would be a declared Catholic and a convert, at that. As we have seen, all the armed forces in the country were under the control of the Royalist gentry, and Cromwell's army, though disbanded, could be very quickly mobilized again; and this time the Roundheads and Cavaliers would be on the same side, against popery and foreign domination.

A marriage was now hastily arranged between Mary, the Duke of York's daughter by his first (and Protestant) wife, to the now famous Protestant hero of Holland, William of Orange. This match offered an immediate – and to the violently anti-Catholic people and Parliament of England, an irresistible – alternative succession to the throne, since not only was Mary daughter of the heir to the English throne, but William of Orange's mother had been Charles's sister, so that he too had British royal blood in his veins.

Louis XIV, angered at the Dutch match and the strengthening by marriage of the Protestant alliance, decided to avenge himself on Charles's chief minister, the Earl of Danby, who had arranged the match. He did this by leaking the fact that France had been paying money to Charles II under a secret treaty. Dark fears of underground foreign alliances and the arrival in England of a new inquisition turned to terror when news of a popish plot to murder Charles, and make the Duke of York king in his place, burst upon the country. The plot also involved a French invasion of England. The story was concocted and spread by a renegade priest called Titus Oates, who represented himself as a champion of the Protestant cause. The evidence he offered consisted of letters written by Catholics and Jesuits in England to their colleagues in St Omer and other French Catholic seminaries.

To save Danby from impeachment, Charles dissolved the Cavalier Parliament which had been sitting off and on for eighteen years. The new Parliament which replaced it contained a much higher proportion of prominent opponents of the King and Danby went to the Tower.

Acutely aware of the delicacy of his own position and remembering only too clearly what had happened to his father, King Charles advised the Duke of York to leave the country: his presence in England was becoming an increasing hazard to the monarchy. James went to Holland obediently enough, there to await the next turn of events, and Charles stood by powerless as an anti-Catholic wave of popular feeling swept the country into another great series of savage persecutions during which a number of blameless Catholic gentry went to the scaffold.

Parliament now set about trying to exclude Charles's brother, the Duke of York, from the succession to the throne. There were two possible alternatives: William of Orange and his wife Mary, both with very close ties to the throne; and the Duke of Monmouth, Charles's illegitimate son by Lucy Walters. Charles had given way on the Popish Plot; he refused to give way on the question of succession, and dissolved Parliament – but not before it had passed an Act which was perhaps the final milestone on the road to democratic liberty:

the Habeas Corpus Act, which guaranteed that no Englishman could ever be imprisoned for more than a few days without being produced in an open court where the grounds for his arrest must be shown. Churchill wrote: '. . . wherever the English language is spoken in any part of the world, wherever the authority of the British Imperial Crown or of the Government of the United States prevails, all law-abiding men breathe freely.'

The new Parliament which was elected did not contain a much higher proportion of Charles's supporters than the former one, and he did not summon it for nearly a year. It was during this interval that the party names 'Whig' and 'Tory' were first introduced, and politicians first began to group themselves, not according to their religious views, but in political 'parties'. Those in favour of excluding James from the succession were called Whigs, after the Scottish Covenanters, and they called their pro-Catholic opponents 'Tories', a word which had previously been used to describe Irish Roman Catholic brigands. To say that the Tories were pro-Catholic is perhaps overstating the case; what had happened was that petitions for the exclusion of the Duke of York from the royal succession were being signed by thousands of people up and down the country, and the Royalist-Anglican elements in the community saw in these demands on the Crown the faint threat of a return to some form of Commonwealth, and consequently opposed them. But the names stuck and eventually were used with pride on both sides of the House.

When the Parliament met in 1680, the debates on the Exclusion Bill continued and a stout effort was made to persuade Charles to declare Monmouth legitimate. Charles would not have tolerated it, but in any event, the Peers – who all held their own valuable estates by virtue of unassailable hereditary rights – defeated it.

Yet another Parliament – not differing greatly in composition from its immediate predecessors – met at Oxford, where Charles felt he would be freer from intimidation by the London mobs. Before summoning Parliament, Charles worked out exactly how much money he would need to maintain the Navy and his own household, and arranged with Lawrence Hyde, the Duke of York's brother-in-law, to reopen negotiations with Louis XIV. Louis eventually agreed to finance Charles to the tune of £200,000 a year in return for a promise that England would never interfere with France's activities on the Continent. The King did not, however, intend to take up the French King's offer, unless Parliament proved recalcitrant. So he began by trying to win Parliament over. He would not agree to interfere with the ancient system of succession, but James, when he came to the throne, would be King in name only, and the country could be governed by a Protector. The conversion of James would not strip his hereditary royalty, but the administration could remain in Protestant hands, and he was even prepared to go so far as to promise that if James had a son, the child would be brought up a Protestant. It is doubtful if he consulted James before making these promises on his behalf, and it is even more doubtful whether James would have entertained them for a moment, but in the event, Parliament was now set on Monmouth as heir to the throne. Charles would have nothing to do with this; what little remained of the Divine Right of the Stuarts was now enshrined in the principle of strict heredity. And when the Commons passed a resolution in favour of excluding the Duke of York from the succession, Charles summoned them to the Peers, where they found him robed and enthroned and where the Lord Chancellor announced that Parliament was dissolved yet again.

The fears of a return to popery – which most people in England by now believed would mean that they would have to turn papist again immediately, or be burned at the stake – were greatly increased when James returned from exile in 1682.

The next year an event happened which turned the tide of public feeling. It was alleged that a party of Whigs planned to murder King Charles II at a farm called Rye House, on his return from Newmarket races. The farm belonged to an ex-officer of Cromwell's Roundheads, who, significantly, had been on duty at the scaffold when King Charles I was executed. A fire at Newmarket caused Charles to return a few days earlier than he had originally planned to do, and the plot was foiled and, in a few days, leaked out. Two leading Whigs were executed, and throughout the country, by pressure of one sort or another, Tory-controlled sheriffs and corporations took over from the Whigs. Monmouth was banished, and went to Holland. Horror at the plot considerably strengthened Charles's position: he ruled as he liked without summoning Parliament – thanks to funds from France – and even restored the Catholic Duke of York to his former command in the Navy, in all but name, ignoring the Test Acts.

Talk of excluding James from the succession died away and all seemed set fair for King Charles again when suddenly, in 1685 at the age of fifty-six, he had a stroke. A priest was smuggled up the back stairs by his brother James, and King Charles II died a Catholic.

## 2

As the Whigs had not recovered from the set-back they suffered after the Rye House Plot there was no effective opposition to King James II's succession to the throne at the age of fifty-two. He summoned a Parliament and promised to preserve both Church and State; and the Parliament inexplicably granted him a larger revenue than Charles had ever enjoyed. It is doubtful whether the religious toleration which James offered was more than a first step towards the revival of Roman Catholicism: he was a bigoted convert and had already shown that he was prepared to make considerable sacrifices for his faith.

Monmouth, still in exile in Holland, had gathered a number of conspirators who had fled England after the Rye House Plot. They now urged him to return home and see whether the English people would not prefer a Protestant duke to a Popish king.

In June 1685, Monmouth landed at Lyme Regis, and issued a proclamation announcing the validity of his mother's marriage to Charles II and denouncing King James II as a usurper. Many of the common people rallied to his side; but he was easily defeated at Sedgemoor, where most of the West Country peasants and Mendip miners who had supported him were slaughtered in the field or executed immediately after the battle. Monmouth, captured a few days later, was also executed, and Chief Justice Jeffreys was sent down to the West Country to deal with such prisoners as had not been disposed of at the time. In what were known as the Bloody Assizes, he hanged two or three hundred and deported eight hundred to Barbados.

King James had already openly attended Mass, and during the threat of Monmouth's rising – ignoring the Test Acts – had commissioned a number of Catholics as Army officers. He now set about trying to have the Habeas Corpus and Test Acts repealed. The King was warned that he was treading on dangerous ground but, flushed with his success over Monmouth, he refused to listen to reason.

When Parliament met for its second session he pressed for a strong standing army to replace the militia, and made it plain that he had no intention of dismissing the Catholic officers who had served him well during the fight against Monmouth. The Commons, with great misgivings, voted him a further £700,000 to strengthen the royal forces, but asked for a solemn assurance that Acts of Parliament would not in future be set aside by Royal Prerogative. The King's answer was to summon the Commons to the Bar of the House of Lords and dissolve Parliament.

He now assiduously set about his main task: to free his fellow Roman Catholics from their oppressions. By manipulating the Bench, he managed to get a verdict in favour of the Royal Prerogative in a case against a violator of the Test Acts. With this as a precedent, he then granted a dispensation to the curate of Putney to continue in office, though he had become a Catholic; went on to admit Catholic peers to the Privy Council; and finally set up an Ecclesiastical Commission similar to the old Court of High Commission – alarming signs of a new autocracy, which had the effect of drawing the Whigs and Tories close together. To give his actions the outward appearance of general tolerance rather than a bald attempt to reinstate the Catholic Church, and perhaps – though unsuccessfully – to get the Nonconformists on his side against the Anglicans, James also attempted to reduce the oppression of the Nonconformists, by issuing a Declaration of Indulgence which included them with the Roman Catholics.

These signs of a return to popery were all the more anxiously watched in Britain because in France, soon after James's accession, Louis XIV had revoked the Edict of Nantes which granted freedom of worship to the Huguenots, many of whom now fled to England, fearful of another St Bartholomew's Day.

In Ireland, hopes ran high that the accession of a Catholic king would undo the Cromwellian plantations; and indeed James did send to Ireland as Governor a Roman Catholic called Talbot, to whom he gave the title, Earl of Tyrconnel. Tyrconnel set about replacing the Protestant officers in the Irish regiments with Catholic ones. Also, many of the existing corporations were dismantled and new ones – with Catholics in the majority – were established in their place.

By now James had both Whigs and Tories against him, had angered Parliament as a whole by overriding its Acts with the Royal Prerogative, and had irritated the Nonconformists by including them alongside Catholics in a single Declaration of Indulgence. He next set about antagonizing the two universities, Oxford and Cambridge, by forcing Roman Catholic Presidents on some of the colleges, and expelling the Fellows when they resisted. He made further enemies by officially entertaining the Papal Nuncio.

Finally in April 1688 he took the step which ultimately ruined him: he alienated the one group in the whole community which still supported the doctrine of Divine Right – the Anglican hierarchy. He ordered that the Declaration of Indulgence, which he now reissued, should be read in all churches in the realm. Seven bishops petitioned him to withdraw the order, most of the churches ignored it, and the seven bishops were imprisoned in the Tower on charges of sedition.

And on 10 June, while the bishops were still awaiting trial, James's Catholic Queen gave birth to a son. Until the birth of this child, the people had been hoping that the King, who was now fifty-five, would be succeeded by the Protestant Princess Mary, but now it seemed as if a Roman Catholic dynasty was about to be established in England. Something would have to be done.

The bishops, never too popular with the mob, now became their heroes. For the first time, the episcopacy found the people of London firmly behind it in its refusal to accede to James's order. The trial at Westminster Hall on 29 June lasted until late at night, and the verdict of 'not guilty' was resoundingly welcomed from one end of the country to the other.

With Monmouth out of the way, the only possible alternative to James was William of Orange and his wife Mary. The Whig leaders had already been in touch with Holland. William, who was primarily interested in the project to secure England's aid in his lifelong struggle against Louis XIV, indicated that he would be prepared to come to England if invited by both political parties.

On the same night that the bishops were declared 'not guilty', the Whig Admiral Herbert, disguised as an ordinary seaman, left for The Hague carrying an invitation to William of Orange signed by seven men, representing Whigs, Tories, Church, Army and Navy.

It was clear that Louis XIV was contemplating another campaign, and William of Orange was bottled up in Holland until he saw where Louis planned to attack. If this was through the Low Countries, William of Orange would not be able to remove his armies from Holland. But Louis marched instead on the Rhine, and William of Orange was free to take up the English invitation. He landed at Torbay on Guy Fawkes Day, 1688, with an army of 15,000 men which included some British and Scots regiments in the Dutch service. In a proclamation he claimed that he had come in the defence of the liberties of England and the Protestant religion.

James, who had been making last-minute efforts to undo the damage but at the same time had been augmenting his army with Irish troops – an action which further increased his unpopularity, for the memory of the massacre of 1641 was still fresh in English Protestant minds – marched west with his army to meet the challenge. Large-scale desertions soon began, and when Lord Churchill (later Duke of Marlborough – and an ancestor of Sir Winston's), the best officer in his army, went over to the Protestant side, what amounted to a revolution took place, and James lost heart and returned to London. He sent his wife and son to the Continent and on the night of 11 December left the Palace of Whitehall for the coast.

After one unsuccessful attempt, when he was stopped as a supposed Jesuit and hauled ashore again by fishermen, James succeeded in escaping to France. He never returned to England.

## 3

As soon as he heard that James's flight had left him in undisputed control of England, William of Orange ordered the French ambassador out and began preparations to make war on France. A Convention Parliament summoned to find some constitutional basis for the new succession ran into difficulties immediately. Many Tories were alarmed at upsetting the succession and were openly in favour of some arrangement under which William of Orange would merely act as regent, with James still as titular king. Eventually a formula was found in dual monarchy – dubbed the reign of WilliamandMary in Sellar and Yeatman's *1066 and All That* – and Princess Anne, Mary's younger sister, surrendered to William her right to succeed should Mary die first, which meant that William III of England, as he now became, would be certain of the throne for his lifetime.

In France, James was received with all honours by Louis XIV who provided him with a French army, some French officers, plus munitions and money. And before long James was on his way to Ireland to renew the fight from that staunchly Catholic quarter.

When James reached Ireland in 1689, he found that Tyrconnel, as Viceroy, had refused to acknowledge the new sovereign, and three provinces of the country were prepared to flock to his support. An

Irish Parliament was summoned, consisting almost entirely of Catholics, which immediately repealed the Act of Settlement that had been passed nearly thirty years earlier. This had the effect of taking from the Protestants all the land given to them during the Cromwellian confiscations, but did not affect property held by Protestants before 1641. In point of fact, the repeal of this Act, which amounted to a re-confiscation of all the land held by the Cromwellian settlers, was never carried out, because James was defeated before the machinery could be put in motion to implement it.

This predominantly Catholic Parliament – possibly echoing James's own old ideas of religious toleration – also decided that there would be freedom for all religious denominations and that no man would ever be barred from any post because of his beliefs. In this respect it was away ahead of any British parliament of the period.

The one province which had not succumbed was, of course, Ulster, which remained as defiantly anti-Catholic as ever. A good deal earlier, towards the end of 1688, rumours of another massacre of the Protestants had begun to fly around the province, and the Protestants had flocked into the fortified cities for safety. There they proclaimed William and Mary King and Queen, and although they had no army to put into the field against James, they controlled a number of places where William's army might land. They held Enniskillen, a strategic stronghold between the lakes which separate Connaught and Ulster, and also Londonderry,* the chief port of the province, since Belfast at this period was no more than an unfortified village on the Lagan.

Tyrconnel had already moved some of his troops towards the north with the intention of stationing them in the strongly Protestant areas to prevent any movement in sympathy with the English Protestant Revolution. He now withdrew a Protestant regiment from Londonderry and ordered Lord Antrim, with a Catholic regiment, to replace it. Antrim's soldiers approached the city along the east side of the estuary of the Foyle and were being ferried across to the hillock on which it stands, when suddenly a mob of apprentice boys seized the keys of the city and locked the Ferry Quay Gate in the face of Antrim's troops. This event occurred on 18 December 1688, and is still commemorated by a march of the 'Apprentice Boys' through Londonderry. (These days they are represented by stern, tight-lipped,

* The old town of Derry was thus renamed when it became a plantation settlement in 1613, undertaken by the City of London guilds.

middle-aged members of the Orange Order, wearing the sashes their fathers wore over their dark Sunday suits, and bowler hats at a curiously defiant angle; they walk in procession with an aggressive strut unique to this corner of the world.) The Enniskillen people also drove off the troops which Tyrconnel sent to occupy the town, and a few other strongholds in Ulster stood by King William.

The troops which had been locked outside Derry's walls now threw a boom across the River Foyle to prevent relief from reaching the city from the sea, and settled down to starve the inhabitants into submission. The townsfolk suffered terribly from hunger and thirst, but they held out for 105 days, until at last a frigate and three provision ships – which had been standing off, in full view of the starving garrison for six weeks – burst through the boom and lifted the siege.

Meanwhile, the Enniskillen men had been driving off all attacks and making raids on the surrounding countryside. They had two able commanders against them: the Duke of Berwick, an illegitimate son of King James; and Patrick Sarsfield, a member of an old, propertied Anglo-Irish family, who had been in the Life Guards under King Charles II and who had fought for King James in England.

Later in the year, 10,000 troops from England, under one of William's Dutch generals, Schomberg, landed in County Down, and the following year, 1690, William himself arrived with English troops and some from the Army of the Netherlands. James, with some 30,000 men, now confronted William – who probably had about 40,000 men and more cannon than James – on the River Boyne, thirty miles from Dublin and about eight from Drogheda, the scene of Cromwell's first, ferocious Irish siege. James took up a defensive position along the river. William simply had to attack the enemy; if he could cross the river he could carry on to the capital.

The battle began on 1 July.* The main attack was frontal but a smaller force forded the river upstream and attacked along James's flank. James was driven from his position with about 1,500 casualties, and his army retreated towards the River Shannon. It is quite possible that Sarsfield might have regrouped to fight another day; James did not wait to see but fled almost immediately for France where his renewed appeals for a fresh army to retake England were ignored by Louis. The Irish Jacobite army – King James's supporters were

* It is now commemorated on 12 July because of a subsequent correction of the calendar. The closing of the gates of Derry is celebrated on 12 August, the anniversary of the lifting of the siege.

known as Jacobites – fell back on Limerick and relieved Athlone, which was being besieged. The French-led section of the Jacobite army withdrew to Galway, and William III pressed on against Limerick City. After a prolonged and bloody siege at Limerick, which was repulsed on the third break-through, and a series of battles at Athlone, Aughrim and Galway – William himself had returned to England after the siege of Limerick – Sarsfield decided to negotiate for peace, when the Protestant troops, under a Dutch general called Ginkel, laid siege to Limerick for a second time.

The Treaty of Limerick was signed on Thomond Bridge in August 1691. It had both military and civil provisions. The military provisions were simple and straightforward enough and were promptly carried out. It was agreed that those Irish soldiers who wished to enter the French service would be transported to France; some 14,000 of them took this course and joined what were known as the 'Wild Geese' – Ireland's flock of exiled soldiers, serving as mercenaries all over the Continent.

The civil provisions, however, were not so readily arranged. Sarsfield had asked for full toleration for Catholics and the restoration of their estates. Ginkel would not agree to this, but did agree that the Roman Catholics in the kingdom were to enjoy 'such privileges as are consistent with the laws of Ireland [a vague phrase which would cover every eventuality], or as they did enjoy in the reign of King Charles II, and their Majesties, as soon as affairs will permit them to summon a Parliament in this Kingdom, will endeavour to procure the said Roman Catholics such further security in that particular as may preserve them from any disturbance on account of the said religion.' The Treaty went on to guarantee that the Lords Justices would undertake that their Majesties would ratify these articles within eight months and 'use their utmost endeavour to see that they were also ratified in parliament' – nothing about the repeal of the Elizabethan Penal Laws, and no formal guarantee that the Laws would be left in abeyance, as they had been in the time both of Charles I and Charles II.

In his volume *The Later Stuarts, 1660–1714* (in *The Oxford History of England*), Sir George Clark adds:

> And there were those among the conquerors who needed no verbal loophole to break away from their duty to the conquered. On the Sunday after the Treaty was signed, the Lords Justices went to

> service in Christ Church Cathedral in Dublin, and heard a sermon from Anthony Dopping, bishop of Meath. This preacher maintained that with such faithless people, no faith need be kept. King William removed him from the privy council, but in the end it was not the king's spirit but Dopping's which prevailed.

Once again the Irish had backed the wrong side; and once again the reprisals would be terrible and far-reaching in their effects.

CHAPTER TWELVE

# The Penal Laws, and the Rebellion of 1798

## 1

After the departure of King James II, the last Catholic king to reign in England, the English people had no further reason to fear popish plots or any outside attempt to reconquer their country for the Papacy. Although some of the Elizabethan Penal Laws remained on the Statute Book in England until the nineteenth century, they were never strictly enforced, and indeed there was no need to enforce them in a predominantly Protestant island where the Catholics now numbered a very small minority hardly worth oppressing. There was no need to oppress the other minorities either. Most of the sects into which the Protestant movement had splintered were so independent and so lacking a strong central organization that they represented no menace to the establishment. From time to time some of the more extreme splinter groups, such as the Quakers and the Anabaptists, drew attention to themselves by their behaviour and suffered accordingly, but from the beginning of the eighteenth century England became more and more tolerant of religious differences* and the minorities were allowed to worship as they pleased without interference, while the established Church lapsed, as the Catholic Church had done before it, into pluralism and complacency.

But the situation in Ireland was very different. After the defeat of the remnants of the Jacobite army and the Treaty of Limerick – which, as we have seen, resulted in the departure for foreign shores of an army of 14,000 trained fighting men – the Irish Catholics were without an army to defend their cause. It is hard to get accurate figures for this period, but there were probably between two and four million people in the country, three-quarters of them Irish and Catholic, and

* There were, of course, odd, isolated outbursts of religious bigotry, such as the anti-Catholic Gordon riots in London in 1780 which led to 285 deaths from violence and twenty-five judicial hangings.

the remainder English, Scottish or Anglo-Irish and Protestant; and the latter were confined very largely to two areas, Ulster and the Pale (around Dublin).

It was now clear that the policy of removing the Irish from their lands and planting these lands with English and Scots settlers had failed to achieve peace in Ireland, and no further attempts at colonization on a large scale were made. The Protestants, who looked to the English government for support, had to be content with their situation as a minority set amid a hostile native population, constantly on guard against attempts to unseat them. Their aim, therefore, and the aim of successive British parliaments, was to bring about a situation in which the Catholics would never be able to gain any political power. This was achieved by a whole series of new Penal Laws, which began under William III and continued under Queen Anne, and which for all practical purposes deprived Irish Catholics of what we should now call their civil rights.

Under these Penal Laws, Catholics could not vote or hold military or civil posts. They could not become lawyers or teachers or sit in Parliament. One of the Penal Laws prevented a Catholic landowner from leaving all his land to one son: it had to be equally divided between all his sons – a ruling which, combined with the existence of so many small tenant farms rented out by the 'absentee' landlords, produced a multiplicity of meagre and utterly uneconomical holdings from which Irish agriculture is still suffering. Catholics were not allowed to buy land, or inherit it from Protestants. They could not sit on juries or become constables. An Irish Catholic could not even own a horse worth more than £5, and if he did, it was perfectly legal for a Protestant to buy it from him for £5.

Bit by bit these laws were chipped away, but many of them remained in force for about a hundred years, though in practice they were not, and could not be, all strictly enforced. Certainly they were never equally enforced in all parts of the country. And there were as many evasions of the law as there were laws. Some Catholic landlords, for example, with the connivance of Protestant friends or relations, continued to enjoy the estates they could no longer formally own. In *The Later Stuarts 1660–1714* Sir George Clark makes the point that 'the Protestants regarded the code not as laying down the exact condition to which they would reduce the Catholics; but as giving them a reserve of power, an armoury of weapons to which they might resort at need. There was, however, sufficient enforcement to effect the main purpose of the laws, and the existence of the reserve of power continually aided in this. The Catholic population acquired the qualities of a subject population.'

One reason for this was the fact that the Irish were now leaderless. The principal effect of the Penal Laws was that the ablest and most energetic of the Catholic gentry emigrated and those who remained were prevented by the laws from playing an active part in the political, economic and social life of the community. Thus, in the absence of an intelligent, professional middle class, such intellectual and political leadership as there was, passed into the hands of the clergy. Also since the Irish react sharply against compulsion in any form, it is likely that the Penal Laws are partly responsible both for the religious ardour of the ordinary Irish Catholic, and for the political power of the Church in Ireland.

For about a century, intermittent efforts were made to crush Catholicism and to destroy the Catholics as a social class. The ordination of priests was forbidden, Catholic bishops were banished and religious orders formally expelled. The punishment for returning was death. On the other hand, Catholic priests who turned Protestant were given a State pension. Education was denied to Catholics, Catholic schools were prohibited, and no person was permitted to act as tutor to a Catholic family. Furthermore, Catholics were forbidden from sending their children abroad to be educated. A reward of £10 was paid to anybody who denounced a Catholic teacher.

But the Penal Laws did not work, of course; a minority colony in an alien, hostile, lawless land could never produce enough spies and policemen, official or unofficial, to enforce such a set of prohibitions, even if there ever was a serious intention to use them other than, as Sir George Clark suggests, as a reserve of power. In fact, they had precisely the opposite effect. Catholics, educated in the first instance in the 'hedge' schools which immediately sprang up when the formal schools were closed down (so-called because classes were sometimes quite literally held in the shelter of a hedge or in a ditch), escaped to the Continent where they continued their education and were eventually ordained as priests. They then returned to disseminate the Faith, living on the run, sharing the lives of the poorest peasants, celebrating Mass in caves, in clearings in the woods, and secretly in the homes of Catholic families. These circumstances drew the priests and their congregations together in an intimacy which could never have been achieved within the formal parochial framework, and must be partly responsible for the privileged role the priest has enjoyed in Irish life ever since. Throughout the century, there were about one thousand priests regularly administering the rites of the Roman Catholic Church up and down the country, and despite the 'expulsion' of religious orders, roughly about four thousand monks and nuns lived through the period unmolested.

Nevertheless, the overall effect of the Penal Laws was to turn the Irish into a downtrodden subject race, without sufficient self-respect to rebel. Edmund Burke, whose mother had been a Catholic, wrote: 'All the Penal Laws of that unparalleled code of repression were manifestly the effects of national hatred and scorn towards a conquered people whom the victors delighted to trample upon and were not at all afraid to provoke. They were not the effect of their fears, but of their security.'

But it would be altogether inaccurate to give the impression, as some Irish histories do, that the Irish Catholics were ignored by the remainder of the world and utterly abandoned to their fate. Again and again throughout William III's reign, attempts were made by the ambassadors from Spain, the Holy Roman Empire and even Holland, and by the Papal Curia to persuade the English King to alleviate the lot of the Irish Catholics. Shortly after the Treaty of Limerick had been signed, there was a complaint from the Papal Curia that it was being disregarded, and William promised that nobody who obeyed the law would suffer on account of his religion. In 1692, at the request of the ambassadors from Spain and the Holy Roman Empire, he refused his consent to a bill of the Irish Parliament which would, in effect, have proscribed Irish Catholics. Again in 1696 the ambassador of the Holy Roman Empire protested against the Acts passed by the Irish Parliament which sought to expel the religious orders, and again the King refused his consent. An Act for the Security of the King's Person passed in the Irish Parliament, as a consequence of an assassination plot in England, condemned to imprisonment for life anybody who refused to take the Oath of Supremacy. No Catholic could take this oath. In this instance the King would not refuse his consent but included an amendment to the effect that the Act would only be enforced at the King's pleasure. This was fine so long as William remained on the throne, but he could not legislate for his successors. And, in fact, many of the more severe penal statutes were enacted – and far more of them enforced – during the reign of Queen

Anne, who also proved less susceptible to protests from the ambassadors.

The English Parliament had the power, in effect, to make laws, for Ireland. An Act known as Poynings' Law (passed at the end of the fifteenth century, during the reign of Henry VII) had stipulated that no Irish parliament could initiate legislation without first securing the consent of king and council in England; and in 1719 it was reinforced by the Declaratory Act, which reaffirmed the right of the British Parliament to make laws for Ireland.

In passing legislation excluding members of certain religions from public posts and directing or limiting the trade of her colonies for the convenience of the mother country, England was not alone. But the big difference was that in Ireland, Catholicism was not a minority faith, but the religion of the vast mass of the people; and the laws which the English Parliament introduced to eliminate Irish competition in certain trades were particularly unfair since Ireland, unlike Britain's colonies across the ocean, produced – with the single exception of coal – exactly the same commodities as England.

As early as the reign of Charles II the English Parliament had forbidden Ireland to export goods to British possessions or import goods from them, unless these goods were sent through English ports. This naturally increased the cost of transport and hampered the development of an Irish shipping industry. Then it was enacted that no Irish livestock could be shipped to England for fear of interfering with the English farmers' profits. And when, as a result of this law, Irish farmers started sheep-farming for wool instead of exporting the sheep, and there were signs that a competitive wool trade was developing in Ireland, Ireland was suddenly forbidden to export wool anywhere other than to England and a heavy duty was clapped on wool sold there.

Another Irish industry – small, but promising – was glass manufacture; suddenly Ireland was forbidden by Act of Parliament to export glass. Ireland was thus thrown back on agriculture as her sole industry and even that was crippled by the exaction of tithes – to the value of one-tenth of all the land's produce – payable to the Established (Protestant) Church of Ireland. The Irish Parliament decreed that only land used for sheep-farming or dry cattle would be free of these tithes. Since it takes only one boy with a stick to look after a whole herd of dry cattle, and sheep-farming offers little more in the way of employment, this amendment had two effects. It increased unemployment and tended to throw the main burden of the tithes on to the small farmers, and to exempt the richer ones who could afford ranches.

The net effect of the Penal Laws and the laws affecting Irish trade was to introduce among the Irish, north and south, a contempt for the law which they have never since lost. Any law that is so demonstrably unfair that it cannot be enforced must bring the whole concept of law into disrepute; and this is what now happened in Ireland. The country was full of wool for which there was no legal market; so smuggling began on a very big scale. Irish wool was much in demand in France and the Low Countries and the smugglers' ships travelled one way carrying wool and exiles and returned carrying duty-free wine and tobacco. This illicit trade also had the side-effect of enabling the Irish to establish useful contacts on the Continent, particularly in France.

One industry was encouraged in Ireland. England was not greatly interested in the manufacture of linen, and in return for the damage done to Ireland's wool trade, William III agreed to encourage the setting up of a linen trade in Ireland. Plain Irish linen was admitted to England free of duty, and William encouraged skilled workers from the Continent, mostly exiled Huguenots, to come to Ireland to teach the Irish improved methods of linen manufacture. The linen industry, largely confined to Ulster, succeeded because the climate was suitable, there were adequate water supplies for bleaching, and spinning and weaving could be carried on in the homesteads and cottages as subsidiary occupations. But it was the one success story in a long, dark century during which the Irish had not even the heart to rise once in revolt.

There were other things the Irish resented. As we have seen, the Irish Parliament, manned by the Anglo-Irish gentry and landowners and exclusively Protestant in composition, had in any event to take orders from the English Parliament. The Lord-Lieutenant and his Chief Secretary were members of the English Government and were always sent over from England. The Lord Chancellor was also always an Englishman, as was the Primate.

The system of taxation, too, was desperately unfair, though this did not bother the native Irish very much as they were too poor to have to pay much in the way of taxes. A separate Irish army, larger in proportion than the standing army in England, was financed out of taxes collected in Ireland, though it was used wherever else it was needed.

Inevitably these measures led to protests – not at first from the native Irish, who were too cowed to protest, but from the Protestant middle-class merchants and traders who objected to being governed by laws in which they had little or no say. The first expression of this irritation appeared as early as 1698 in the form of a pamphlet by William Molyneux entitled *The Case of Ireland's being bound by Acts of Parliament in England stated.* A more articulate champion appeared twenty-five years later when Jonathan Swift, Dean of St Patrick's Cathedral in Dublin, opened a long series of blasts of defiance against the authorities with an attack on the scandal of 'Wood's halfpence'. A man called Wood had been given a contract to mint coin for Ireland, and in a document known as *Drapier's Letters*, Swift revealed that half of the very substantial profits on this shady deal were going to a mistress of the English King George I. Although he never had anything except profound contempt for the Irish Catholics, Swift's dislike of hypocrisy and injustice led him to a kind of patriotism; 'Burn everything English except their coal' was one of his slogans.

Gradually, within the Irish Parliament, the nucleus of a patriot party began to form around men like Henry Flood and Henry Grattan, and the American War of Independence provided them with an opportunity to assert their cause. Troops were sent from Ireland to fight the rebel North American colonists; and in their place, to preserve law and order and defend the country against a possible French invasion – for the French, still smarting at the loss of Canada, were secretly aiding the colonists and were only waiting for an American victory to declare war on England – the Protestant middle classes were encouraged to form their own volunteer force. No sooner had the force been formed and trained than they realized that it could also be used to redress some of the wrongs from which they suffered. They demanded free trade from a British government weakened and humiliated by the loss of the American colonies – and got it. Grattan was now determined to seek an entire new constitution for Ireland. In 1782 the Declaratory Act was repealed and the right of the English Parliament to alter Irish laws was abolished; only the King's consent was required to legislation passed by the Irish Parliament. Unfortunately, the Irish Parliament was not to remain in existence long enough to effect any major changes; in any event, it was still very largely controlled by the executive through patronage and bribery in the form of peerages and titles.

## 2

At this point, having helped the Americans to win their independence, the French decided that they wanted independence for themselves, and in 1789 rose in revolution in a shattering convulsion of liberty and equality which had repercussions all over Europe and nowhere more strongly than in Ireland.

A young Protestant lawyer called Theobald Wolfe Tone formed in Belfast a society of United Irishmen, pledged to abolish religious distinctions and to unite all Irishmen against the unjust influence of Britain. This seemed possible at the time because the Ulster Nonconformists had recently been suffering both from the sacramental test and the trade restrictions, and were no more kindly disposed towards the English Parliament than were the Catholic peasants.

In 1793, when Britain went to war with France, Tone travelled to America and thence to France where he persuaded the French to send a force of 150,000 to augment his own estimated 150,000 United Irishmen in a projected insurrection. But the weather was bad, fog scattered the French ships, General Hoche was separated from the remainder of his fleet, and the entire force sailed back to France taking Tone with them, without ever making an attempt at a landing.

Two years later, in May 1798, the United Irishmen under Lord Edward Fitzgerald decided to go it alone and stage their own uprising. But like so many of Ireland's attempts at armed resistance, the rebellion went off at half-cock. As always, the secrets were badly kept and on the eve of the rising most of the leaders were arrested. Having captured the ringleaders, the British authorities tried to prevent the rising by using collective punishment to disarm the peasants. This was done with so much cruelty and injustice that the militia merely augmented the rebellion they were attempting to quell. Loyal peasants, tortured to force them to give information about the local leaders and concealed arms which they did not even possess, threw in their lot with the rebels; others, disgusted at the behaviour of the militia, joined the United Irishmen.

In the south-east initially, and in other isolated pockets all over the country, the peasants, ill-clad, untrained and armed only with pikes and pitchforks, rose against the British and Anglo-Irish gentry and were ruthlessly cut down or blown to pieces as they charged up to the very mouth of the cannon. In the course of a few weeks, 30,000 people – many of them defenceless women and children – had been slaughtered, often with horrible cruelty. Collective punishment was used to force the surrender of arms, and troops were quartered on the towns and villages in the disturbed areas where they were encouraged to use punishment 'to excite terror'. One of these punishments involved a large triangular piece of wooden scaffolding: the triangle, as the apparatus was called, was designed for securing a man while he was being flogged with a cat o' nine tails. Flogging was a common enough punishment in Europe in the eighteenth century, but the British authorities in Ireland now planned to put it to a different purpose: as an instrument of torture to discover concealed arms. In his book, *The Year of Liberty*, Thomas Pakenham quotes the diary of a Mrs Leadbeater of Ballitore, Co. Kildare:

> They set fire to some cabins near the village – took P. Murphy the father of the family, who kept a shop of spirits in the house where B. Wills had lived – apparently an inoffensive man – tied him to a car opposite his own door, and these above-mentioned officers degraded themselves so far as to scourge him with their own hands. James Carney, tied to a tree, underwent a similar punishment – the torture was excessive – they did not recover soon. Guards were placed to prevent anyone coming into, or leaving, the village. The village, so peaceful, exhibited a scene of tumult and dismay – the air rang with the shrieks of the sufferers, and the lamentations of those who beheld them suffer. These violent measures caused a great many pikes to be brought in – the street was lined with the numbers who came to deliver up these instruments of death.

Pakenham goes on:

> In Athy the blacksmiths [suspected of manufacturing the pikes] were now tied to the triangle and, with the full authority of martial law, flogged to extort confessions. A local man called Thomas Rawson was one of the Athy interrogators. He acted on 'speculation' to make men 'whistle' as he termed it. 'He would seat himself,' we are told by one of the arrested men, 'in a chair in the centre of a ring formed round the triangles, the miserable victims kneeling under the triangle until they would be spotted over with the blood of others. Two of his victims were father and son. Another received 500 lashes and was then found to be innocent.'

Under this treatment, the huge citizen army, painfully built up through the years around the country forge and city tavern, as Pakenham puts it, was melting away before their very eyes. Even the name United Irishmen was a contradiction in terms: in the nature of things Irishmen never have been and never will be united. 'The Irish are a fairminded people,' Dr Johnson remarked: 'They never speak well of one another.' The movement which had been started in Dublin, Belfast and Cork among the middle class by Protestant intellectuals was now turning, throughout the country, into a peasant revolt aimed against all men of property, whatever their political views.

In Dublin, where the outbreak of the rebellion was heralded by the display of three mutilated rebel bodies in the yard of the Castle – one subsequently returned to life was taken into the guard-room and duly pardoned by the viceroy after making a full confession – stories began to circulate of the terrible atrocities being committed throughout the country. Many were mere stories, but some were true. For example, at Dunshaughlin, the rebels had killed the local schoolmaster and a gardener and had mangled their bodies, and put a third man into a cauldron of boiling pitch. All these victims were Protestants and the whole affair began to take on something of the horrific atmosphere of 1641. In Kildare, the rebels had piked to death an old Protestant gate-keeper, his fourteen-year-old granddaughter and even the faithful dog which had attempted to defend them.

When Wexford rose in revolt, the authorities began to clean up along the borders of Wicklow and Wexford. Eleven men were ordered out of their houses in Tinahely, accused of being sworn into the United Irishmen and were well flogged with others looking on, after which their homes were burned as a warning to the onlookers. In County Wexford itself, the 'pitch-cap', a frightful form of torture, was employed. This was a system in which pitch was rubbed into the victim's hair, gunpowder added and the mixture set on fire. Tales of atrocities multiplied. Hunter Gowan, it was said, entered Gorey with the amputated finger of one of his victims on the end of his sword and used it to stir his punch. A hermit in New Ross had been tortured in the backyard of the barracks, half-hanged three times, and flogged four times – merely because he had been found to be carrying Catholic prayer-books.

Typical of many encounters during this terrible rebellion was the Curragh affair. The Limerick commander, General Sir James Duff, determined to make an example of the rebels, marched on the

Curragh. Meanwhile the rebels, unknown to Duff, had started to make terms with the British forces, through the agency of the Protestant rector of Kildare, who was in their hands. An enormous gathering, perhaps six thousand strong, had assembled at an old fort called Gibbet Rath. Let Pakenham take up the story from this point:

> What exactly happened next in the tragedy remains disputed. Duff claimed that he sent on some yeomen to tell the people they would not be hurt if they laid down their arms. Unfortunately the rebels fired on this party, and from that moment were attacked on all sides. 'Nothing could stop,' Duff admitted rather lamely, 'the rage of the troops.'
>
> A ghastly scene followed. Several thousand people, many unarmed, and huddled together on a great plain without a scrap of cover were set upon by an infuriated pack of militia and dragoons. Three hundred and fifty were cut down in the massacre, with virtually no loss to the army. In their enthusiasm for this task, the Dublin militia even mistook Kildare's Protestant clergyman for a Catholic priest and were preparing to hang him with a chain from one of the cannons when the colonel, who happened to be his brother-in-law, pointed out the mistake. The ordinary peasantry were less fortunate in their relatives. Their bodies lay on the hillside gashed with sabres and piled up where they had fallen That night the women came out from Kildare and turned over the bodies one by one to find their sons and husbands.

Ballitore was again attacked by troops from Athy. Most of the houses were burnt to the ground and those left standing were ransacked and looted. Many of the inhabitants were shot without trial or hacked to death. 'Having made an example of the town,' Pakenham writes, 'the troops returned cheerfully to Athy, wrecking two more villages on the way. That night the pigs, snuffling blood, wandered through the streets of Ballitore strewn with broken glass and earthenware and the mangled bodies of the inhabitants.'

Once again, as in 1641, the war had very largely devolved into a religious one. In Rathangan a squadron of dragoons got the worst of an encounter with the rebels, who, after the engagement, mutilated the bodies of the dead and even, it is said, hacked up the corpse of one of the horses, screaming 'Take that, Protestant!'

Wexford and Enniscorthy fell to the rebels, and in Wexford a huge leaderless army of some fifteen thousand peasants, some wearing white bands around their hats, or green cockades, but otherwise still dressed as labourers, milled about in the narrow streets uncertain how to celebrate the first Irish Republic or what to do next. All Protestants were held to deserve the fate which, it was believed, they had been planning for the Catholics: extermination. During the attack on New Ross, some 135 loyalist prisoners – the majority of them Protestant but including some Catholics who had refused to quit their masters or had fallen foul of the rebels in other ways – were murdered as a reprisal for the way in which the King's soldiers were reported to have been butchering the rebels. Thirty-five men were shot on the lawn at Scullabogue; the remainder, their families, locked in a barn, were burnt to death. To quote Pakenham again:

> In their terror of being burnt or suffocated the wretched people inside apparently tried to push open the heavy door at the back. The guards rushed to the door, hacking at their hands and fingers; the door was jammed shut again. By weight of numbers, the prisoners again forced the door open – to be thrust back by pikes. One two-year-old child actually crept under the door and lay unobserved by the house till someone spotted the wretched creature and ran it through with his pike.
>
> At last the business was over, the screams faded into silence and the flames died away. In the ruins of the barn they found over a hundred charred bodies, families huddled together and still standing upright for want of space. For several days the guards were occupied turning over the bodies to look for coins or other valuables.

In New Ross, after the rebels had occupied and abandoned it, parties of drunken soldiers of the King went roaring through the streets, shooting at anything that caught their attention, even dead bodies, and the pigs that had started to feed on them. One witness claims that sixty-two cartloads of rebel bodies were tipped into the river to be carried out to sea, and 3,400 were buried in a gravel pit. Other estimates are more conservative. But the savagery on both sides was intense and terrible, and I have quoted Pakenham's book in detail in this chapter because the events of the rebellion of 1798 – like the events of 1641 – have left a mark on the minds of Irishmen, Protestant and Catholic alike, which the intervening years have never effaced. Nothing like the Rebellion of 1798 ever happened in England: the Civil Wars were gentlemanly affairs by comparison. And it is impossible to understand the deep and bitter gulf that lies between the Protestant and the Catholic in Ireland except in the light of these fearful and savage reprisals and counter-reprisals.

Encouraged by the success of the rebels in Wicklow and Wexford, an army of three thousand United Irishmen under Henry Joy McCracken staged a rebellion in Antrim which collapsed after a couple of days with the usual savage aftermath. A horrifying story is told of a cart-load of dead arriving at a sandpit for burial. When a yeoman officer inquired where the devil these rascals had come from, a 'corpse' in the cart raised a blood-stained head and feebly answered: 'I come from Ballyboley.' He was buried along with the rest.

But support for the United Irishmen was beginning to wane in Ulster with reports of the religious war in Kildare and Wexford. A predominantly Protestant middle-class population, many of them property-owners, could hardly be expected to look with favour on the killing and looting by Catholic peasant mobs, led in some instances by their priests. If this was what liberty resulted in, then it was wiser to support the establishment, however unjust its laws. When Antrim fell there was a brief rising in Down which was quickly extinguished and thereafter Ulster remained staunchly loyal to the Crown.

As the Crown forces mustered to put an end to the Wexford Republic, a 'Protestant plot' was uncovered and a tribunal set up in Wexford in a billiard-room on Custom House Quay, near the bridge across the estuary. In the space of two hours, ninety-seven prisoners were condemned and summarily executed, their backs and stomachs ripped open by the pikes of the executioners and their bodies left on the bridge or tossed into the Slaney. In the middle of the massacre, news arrived that the main rebel camp at Vinegar Hill was being assailed by the Crown forces.

Attacked by an army of ten thousand with artillery and muskets, the pikemen's stand on Vinegar Hill soon caved in, and before long the town of Enniscorthy was recaptured by the British forces, who celebrated their victory by setting fire to a house which had been turned into a hospital for the rebel wounded; the next morning the bodies were still hissing in the embers. A couple of days later Wexford fell and the short-lived Republic was over.

Father Roche, the effective commander-in-chief, rode back to Wexford on the day of the triumphal British entry to try to negotiate terms for his rebel troops. He was dragged off his horse, beaten about the face until he was barely recognizable and hanged after a court martial.

All over the country, retaliations began. The Anglo-Irish and the

English talked openly of exterminating the Catholics as the only real answer to the problem, and imprisonment was no solution for the simple reason that there were not enough gaols in the country to contain the defeated remnants of the United Irishmen. 'With the best will in the world, you can't imprison half a nation' complained a British loyalist. In Dublin the insurgents were very leniently treated, but throughout the country the fate of the rebel leaders depended more or less on the temper of the local military authorities. The records give a total of 106 death sentences passed on United Irishmen and 268 sentences of transportation. Flogging and torture were used as a means of extracting names of leaders of the revolutionary movement, and there is no doubt that many people, coerced by circumstances into throwing in their lot with the rebels, suffered equally with those who would have been regarded by the British as the real culprits.

A terrible injustice permeated the immediate aftermath of the 1798 rebellion. To take only one example – again from Pakenham's *The Year of Liberty* – the High Sheriff of Tipperary, Thomas Judkin Fitzgerald, was called upon to deal with one of the prisoners – a French professor at Clonmel accused of being an officer of the United Irishmen. In point of fact he was a Protestant of unimpeachable loyalty. Fitzgerald seized him by the hair, flung him to the ground, kicked him and cut him across the forehead with his sword, then had him stripped to the waist, tied to a ladder and lashed. He then ordered a further fifty lashes, during which part of the unfortunate man's bowels could be seen protruding from his wounds, after which his waistband was cut and yet another fifty lashes ordered. Leaving the poor wretch languishing from the ladder, the sheriff went away to find a firing squad to finish him off. He failed to find a firing squad, and the professor eventually recovered from his injuries in the town gaol.

Two months after the rebellion had petered out, about one thousand French troops landed in Mayo but there was no longer any insurrection for them to support and so they had to surrender; and finally Tone himself arrived back in Ireland, two months after that again, with a further French force which was overpowered almost immediately. He cut his throat in order to avoid the dishonour of being hanged. Yet the memory of Wolfe Tone, the first true republican, came to be revered, and all the separatist movements of the following generations gained inspiration from his example. The United

Irishmen – disunited as they proved to be in practice – had pointed the way to a new sort of society in which all religion, would have equal rights.

But the rebellion had one other very profound effect on Irish politics. It has been argued that William Pitt, the British Prime Minister, had been contemplating running Ireland from Westminster long before the Revolution of 1798 – indeed there are people who suggest that he was instrumental in fomenting it in order to provide himself with an excuse for the union of the Irish and English Parliaments – but there is no doubt that as soon as the 1798 Revolution had been contained, Pitt pressed for control of Ireland from Westminster. There was widespread opposition to this idea in Ireland, but peerages were scattered around freely, borough owners were bought out, bribes of every conceivable kind were offered – even the Irish Catholics were promised a measure of emancipation – and in 1800 the Act of Union was carried.

Ireland, still smarting from the events of the last two centuries, was now to be administered from Westminster. Years later, Augustine Birrell, who was Chief Secretary at the time of the 1916 Rising, was to comment: 'Nobody can govern Ireland from England save in a state of siege.'

CHAPTER THIRTEEN

# Catholic Emancipation, the Famine and the Fenians

## 1

In deciding that Ireland could be more conveniently managed from England, Pitt was probably partly motivated by a desire to strengthen the British Isles for the coming struggle against Napoleon, and partly by nervousness of the growing independence of the Irish Parliament which had succeeded in getting free trade and, without waiting for permission from Westminster – no longer necessary in any event, due to the repeal of the Declaratory Act – had been gradually undermining the effects of the Penal Laws. There was a precedent, too: the successful Union of the Scottish and English Parliaments about a century earlier. Under the Act of Union, Ireland would be represented by 100 – later 105 – members sitting at Westminster, plus four spiritual and twenty-eight temporal lords sitting in the Upper House. The whole territory of the British Isles was henceforth to be known as the United Kingdom of Great Britain and Ireland.

The cost of bringing about this 'reform' amounted to about £1,260,000 in straight cash payments of one sort or another, as well as the creation of twenty-eight new peerages and twenty-six promotions among the Irish peerage – bribery on a vast and cynical scale, the cost of which, as a final gratuitous insult, was added to the Irish National Debt.

The arrangements also included a promise that Catholics would be allowed to sit at Westminster. Pitt probably felt that he could now safely make this offer, since any Catholics in the Irish Party would be hopelessly outnumbered by Protestants in a House of Commons which represented the whole of the British Isles. In any event it didn't arise, because King George III refused to give his assent. Due largely to the work of what was called 'Grattan's Parliament' – Grattan himself had been in opposition – Catholics could now enter the professions, as well as vote.

One reason why the Act of Union was bitterly resented, particularly among the merchant middle classes in the capital, was that there had been a marked and very noticeable improvement in Ireland's circumstances towards the end of the eighteenth century. The freeing of trade from Westminster's restrictions had produced a sudden surge of prosperity which was reflected in the atmosphere of Dublin and in the many fine buildings which were erected around this time, notably Gandon's elegant Custom House and the Four Courts, both on the River Liffey.

From the moment the Act of Union was passed, however, a sort of apathy descended on Ireland. It could have been partly the effect of moving the seat of Parliament out of the city of Dublin, which reduced it once more from the status of a capital to a mere provincial city, like Manchester or Glasgow. The office of the Lord-Lieutenant was retained and although legislation for Ireland was now all framed in Westminster, executive power rested in Dublin, and Dublin Castle continued to be the effective centre of the British administration in Ireland. And the Parliament at Westminster, when it was not trying to curb Irish trade to reduce competition with England's, or ignoring Ireland altogether, was legislating for the country as if it were a province of England. The provision of work-houses on the English pattern, designed for increasingly industrialized areas and utterly unsuited to the needs of a scattered agricultural population, was a case in point.

Three years after the Act of Union, Dublin's apathy was briefly shattered by the bold Robert Emmet, a Protestant patriot who with a tiny band of fanatical followers tried to seize Dublin Castle. The only concrete result of the affair was the killing, in the confusion, of an elderly and well-intentioned judge called Kilwarden. But although it turned out to be little more than a street riot, owing to a series of typical mishaps, it might have been more serious because for once the authorities were unprepared. Emmet was hanged in the street where Kilwarden had been killed, but not before he had made from the dock a speech which was to keep the faint flame of rebellion smouldering for yet another generation. 'When my country takes her place among the nations of the earth,' he said, 'then, and not till then, let my epitaph be written.' With this speech he joined the illustrious ranks of Tone and Lord Edward Fitzgerald in the innermost circle of political martyrs, and probably advanced the ultimate cause of Irish liberty far more effectively than anything he might have achieved by a small measure of military success.

But at the time, public opinion in Ireland was against Emmet. Grattan was opposed to the rising: so was Daniel O'Connell, a Catholic lawyer soon to emerge as the chief protagonist of total Catholic emancipation. They both were convinced that the liberation of Ireland could be achieved without shedding any more blood.

After the dissolution, by bribery, of Grattan's Parliament – and there is a certain irony in the fact that the old Parliament House now became the headquarters of the Bank of Ireland – the middle-class merchants and traders, who regarded themselves purely as Englishmen living in Ireland, became the dominant element in the community. It was from this class that members of Parliament for Westminster – and juries – were largely elected; in general they were bigoted anti-Catholics.

Although Catholics now enjoyed freedom of worship, and the government had even endowed a seminary at Maynooth in 1795 to stop the practice of candidates for the priesthood studying abroad where they might find themselves exposed to dangerously revolutionary ideas, there was considerable resentment at the fact that everybody still had to pay tithes to the Established Protestant Church, which represented the religious views of far less than a quarter of the total population. Another Catholic grievance was over land: Catholics officially held no land except as tenants, and (outside Ulster, where a system known as the 'Ulster Custom' gave tenants certain rights of tenure and sale) only on very insecure and often unfavourable terms.

Daniel O'Connell was born in 1775 in County Kerry, educated abroad and in London, and practised as a barrister at the Irish Bar. He was extremely popular and won many verdicts in favour of his Catholic clients. Eventually, in 1828, he stood as a candidate for Parliament in the County Clare constituency. He won such a resounding victory at the polls, and his success was greeted with such wild scenes of enthusiasm, that although he was technically disqualified from taking his seat, King George IV was advised to give way on the issue. O'Connell took his seat at Westminster and began to campaign for the redress of all the Irish Catholic grievances. He was convinced that Ireland's only real chance of solving her problems was to get back the right to manage her own affairs, and so he started to agitate for the repeal of the Act of Union, which would have revived the

Irish Parliament – with the enormous difference that its ranks would now include Catholic members.

But although O'Connell and other Catholics could now take seats in the English Parliament, they were not able to achieve much in the face of English Protestant opposition, and the Irish peasants began to get impatient. In 1831 a fierce agitation against the payment of tithes began. O'Connell was in favour of abolishing tithes altogether and dis-establishing the Church of Ireland, but the British Parliament wouldn't hear of this. The Irish people began to resist the seizure of their cattle and other stock as punishment for non-payment of tithes and there were a number of ugly incidents in which several lives were lost. Eventually a solution was found by which the landlords paid all the tithes, passing the extra cost on to the tenants in the form of rent increases; curiously, this system was less bitterly resented than the straight collection of tithes direct from the tenant farmers.

O'Connell got nowhere with his attempts to gain the repeal of the Act of Union, but a Whig Parliament – less unfriendly to Ireland than the Tories had been – set up a police force, and provided a free popular educational system, which was theoretically undenominational. But, in practice, as every school was under a local manager who was almost invariably the Protestant clergyman, the schools were strictly denominational; they taught the Protestant religion and no Irish history was included in the curriculum.

O'Connell still stoutly maintained that the only answer to Ireland's problems was Repeal, and he began to hold a series of Repeal meetings which attracted enormous crowds. In 1843 the British Government banned a monster rally scheduled to take place on the site of Brian Boru's great victory over the Danes at Clontarf, calling out the troops to enforce the ban. O'Connell wavered, cancelled the meeting, was arrested, tried for treason by a 'packed', all-Protestant jury and found guilty. When he was released from prison about three months later, after a successful appeal to the Lords, he had lost a lot of his old fire, and the task of carrying on the struggle for a separate Irish Parliament was left to other, younger men.

But his long struggle for Catholic emancipation had produced a break with the predominantly Protestant, Anglo-Irish nationalism that had been such a feature of the end of the eighteenth century. O'Connell's fiery and extravagant speeches alarmed many Protestants who might otherwise have been favourably disposed towards his Repeal Movement, and the word 'Ascendancy' began to take on a new dimension: it now embraced the whole Protestant population of the island, as well as what were known as the 'Castle Catholics' (that is, Catholics who supported the Union and the establishment represented in the public mind by Dublin Castle, the seat of the administration).

The Catholic Emancipation and Repeal movements also had the effect of further estranging Protestant Ulster from the remainder of Ireland. The Ulster Dissenters, long since relieved of the restrictions they had suffered during the period when the Penal Laws were enforced against them, and further softened by Pitt's offer of a direct payment by the State to Presbyterian ministers loyal to the British connection, as an equivalent to the Church of Ireland tithes, had lost the resentment which had led them to support Wolfe Tone, and all of Protestant Ulster was now firmly behind the Union. Also, Ulster, unlike the remainder of Ireland, was developing a new prosperity. The industrial revolution, which missed out the remainder of Ireland for the very simple reason that there were virtually no industries to revolutionize, had come to Ulster towards the end of the eighteenth century, when factories began to replace the old workshops and steam-power was used for mass production of goods. The cotton industry was mechanized; and it was the development of the cotton industry which was largely responsible for the increase in Belfast's population which had reached thirty thousand at the time of the Union and continued to grow through the century. Belfast had now replaced Carrickfergus as the principal town in east Ulster; by 1900 it had a population of nearly 350,000.

But there had been what is now known as a 'population explosion' all over Ireland in the early nineteenth century. The population of the whole island in 1801 was between four and five millions; by 1821 it had risen to seven millions, and by 1840 to about eight millions. The bulk of these people – outside Ulster and the Pale – had no source of livelihood except the land, which naturally could not bear the ever-increasing pressure on it. The result, inevitably, was unemployment on a massive scale. Unemployment was a permanent problem in Ireland throughout the nineteenth century. A commission set up in 1836 to examine the situation reported that the number of persons simultaneously requiring relief in Ireland during thirty weeks of that year was not less than 2,385,000 out of a total population of eight million. Of these, 585,000 were actually out of work and in distress and the other 1,800,000 were dependent on them.

A change in the system of farming had aggravated the situation. So long as England was at war with Napoleon, there had been a constant demand for corn and other food. Labour was very cheap in Ireland and one easy way of getting it was to let out the land to a multiplicity of small tenant farmers who would work it for the landlord. This system had another advantage from the landlords' point of view. Since everyone with a holding worth 40 shillings a year had a vote, and these votes had to be given openly and not in any form of secret ballot, this meant that a landlord with a number of small holdings could make his influence felt in Parliament.

But when the war ended, prices fell and the return the tenant farmers got for their corn was not always adequate to cover the rents they paid. Also, many of the men who had been employed in Britain's army now came home looking for work, adding to the total of unemployed. Soon the evictions started. In the new circumstances it paid the landlords far better to let off their land in large packages to sheep and cattle ranchers; and this meant evicting the small farmers who had to look for uncultivated land elsewhere which could be broken in by clearing away the stones, and digging up the hard, infertile earth. Whenever the quality of the land was marginally improved by this back-breaking labour, the rent was immediately racked up, and many of the Irish labourers and small farmers suffered terrible hardships. But worse was to come. There had already been a partial failure of the potato crop in 1821 and 1822, a serious matter in a country in which the staple diet was potatoes and milk – when they were available.

In 1845 the potato crop failed completely, and the Irish starved to death in thousands in their hovels or fields – their mouths green-stained from trying to live on grass – or they travelled, battened down in the holds of cargo ships, to the United States of America where, as soon as they had settled in, they began to organize themselves into societies pledged to do something to get the British out of Ireland.

One curious feature of the famine was that throughout the entire period, while the Catholic peasants were starving to death, Irish food was being exported to England and elsewhere. The Irish grew corn, but they could not afford to buy it; still less could they afford to buy meat. Some well-meaning but ill-organized attempts to provide relief for the starving Irish were attempted, but in general the English were quite incapable of understanding that the failure of such a relatively unimportant crop as potatoes could cause any great hardship.

The following year, thc potato crop failed again, and things went from bad to worse. For the moment, the political struggle was swamped by the miseries of a starving people. As Brian Inglis remarks in *The Story of Ireland*, 'a hungry peasant may make a dangerous rebel; a starving peasant thinks only of his next meal'. Also the essentially divisive nature of the Irish political movements had already led to a rupture between O'Connell (and his sons) on the one hand and the Young Irelanders, on the other. The Young Ireland movement had been started in 1842 by three young men – Thomas Davis, John Blake Dillon and Charles Gavan Duffy – who founded a newspaper called *The Nation* and originally had worked with O'Connell for Repeal. Basically, the new quarrel was on the question of whether physical force was ever justified; to the end, O'Connell was against shedding blood. Even the Young Ireland movement was divided against itself: John Mitchell, one of the few Ulster Protestants in the movement, went too far for most of the Young Irelanders in his open advocacy of revolution. O'Connell left Ireland in 1847 on a pilgrimage to Rome, sick and broken-hearted both at the famine and at the way in which the forces of Irish resistance were crumbling.

In the meantime, England continued to mismanage Ireland in a way that can only be described as spectacular. This was a period when private enterprise was regarded as sacrosanct and not to be upset by Government relief schemes, however well-intentioned. So instead of using the vast unemployed labour force to drain the land or build railways, the starving men were set to digging holes and filling them up again, or, at the instigation of some well-meaning landed gentry, into building high walls around their estates, many of which still block the best views in Ireland today. Worse still, no man who had a farm was allowed to take relief work unless he gave up his holding. And throughout all the time that the famine raged, the evictions continued. Troops and police were used to evict tenants who had been deprived by the famine of the only means they had of paying their rent, and the holdings were turned into large farms and cattle ranches.

The potato blight lasted for five years from 1845 to 1850, during which time the population dropped by about two million. Since, in the main, it was the people from the poorer, Gaelic-speaking parts of Ireland who died or emigrated, the Irish language suffered a blow during the famine from which it never recovered, and the population went into a steady decline which has only been slowed within the last couple of decades.

## 2

This period did not pass without one small, insignificant attempt at rebellion. The Year 1848 was a year of revolution throughout Europe and the success of the French attempt to re-establish the Republic swung even the moderates in the Young Ireland movement over in favour of the use of force. Once again, information leaked out to the Government forces; Mitchell was captured and sentenced to deportation. Duffy and others were also arrested and Smith O'Brien, who had been the most moderate of them all, staged a short-lived stand for freedom at Ballingarry, where 3,000 members of the Young Ireland party laid siege to a party of police, barricaded in a cottage surrounded by a cabbage-patch. The police managed to hold out until reinforcements arrived from Cashel and peace was again restored by the Irish Constabulary. This latter was an armed militia force, mainly Irish in composition, but so deployed that men never served in their own home counties – county loyalties were dangerously strong – and as far as possible men from the same county were never placed together in the same barracks. They wore dark bottle-green, almost black, uniforms and by the middle of the century were 9,000 strong. O'Brien was condemned to death but had his sentence commuted to transportation for life.

The failure of this attempt at rebellion produced a reversion to O'Connell's 'constitutional' approach, and, as the next step in improving the lot of the Irish tenant farmers and labourers, a tenants' protective league was formed. Gavan Duffy, who had escaped the fate of the other leaders of 1848 by virtue of the fact that the various juries who tried him could not agree, became one of its leading figures. But again, internal dissensions wrecked the League, which sought the support of Irish M.P.s at Westminster to redress the wrongs of the tenants. The conservatives in the movement tended to look for guidance to the Catholic Primate, Cardinal Cullen (and thereby earned for themselves the derisory title of 'The Pope's Brass Band'), and when Tenant League M.P.s were returned in sufficient numbers in 1852 to make their influence felt at Westminster, some of them allowed themselves to be bought off by offers of ministerial posts.

The Tenant League collapsed in disgrace; and Gavan Duffy left the country in disgust.

The next attempt to organize the Irish to rise in revolt originated in the United States. By the latter part of the nineteenth century it has been estimated that there were five or six million Irishmen living outside Ireland, three-quarters of them in the United States and the remainder in Canada and Australia, in addition to about a million in England, Wales and Scotland. And wherever they went, they settled in the towns rather than in the country, for farming had brought them nothing but hardships at home.

The new rebel movement was known as Fenianism and it quickly spread from the United States to Ireland and England; its central organization was the Irish Republican Brotherhood, a secret, oath-bound society in the Wolfe Tone tradition, though with a much smaller proportion of Protestants. John O'Leary was one of the leaders of this movement; he believed in the use of armed force, and thought that any attempt to involve the movement with the agitation for tenant rights was an irrelevant side-issue.

But, in the event, the American conspiracy proved every bit as fissiparous as all its predecessors; on the eve of a rising, a split in the American Brotherhood prevented a shipment of arms, and informers in Dublin, as usual, spread rumours of the proposed rebellion in time to enable the Government to arrest all the ringleaders so that the Rising of 1867 was even more ineffectual than that of 1848. For their part in aborting this insurrection the Irish Constabulary were rewarded with the prefix 'Royal' and a gift of £2,000 to be shared between them.

The Fenians were the first to carry the struggle for Irish independence to England. Attempting to rescue some Fenian prisoners from Clerkenwell Gaol, a wall was blown up killing and injuring several people, and another attempt to rescue Fenian prisoners in Manchester led to the shooting of a police officer for which three Fenians – Allen, Larkin and O'Brien, the 'Manchester Martyrs', as they were known – were hanged.

In the meantime, the constitutional struggle for the repeal of the Act of Union continued at Westminster – now under the far more forceful slogan, 'Home Rule'. Two new Irish leaders emerged: Isaac Butt, a Protestant barrister, who advocated a 'federal' solution under which an Irish Parliament would legislate for all internal affairs, leaving external matters to the Imperial Parliament; and Charles

Stewart Parnell, a wealthy Anglo-Irish landowner with radical ideas, whose latent nationalism had been awakened by the fate of the Manchester Martyrs, and who succeeded Butt when his federal Home Rule ideas were laughed out of court, although it was on exactly this basis that the Dominions were administered not so very long afterwards.

Parnell – like O'Connell before him – spent a proportion of his time in English gaols on various charges of sedition and treason but he did eventually succeed in getting the Liberal Party to adopt Home Rule officially as part of its political platform and Gladstone, the Liberal leader, made the first of many attempts to win Ireland over by kindness when he succeeded in disestablishing the Protestant Church of Ireland. This finally removed what had been one of the big grievances, the payment of tithes.

Parnell's chief accomplishment, however, was the destruction of the power of the landlords in Ireland. This he achieved by two means. First, by continuously obstructing the business of the British Parliament, he succeeded in drawing a great deal of attention to the Irish Question; and, second, he worked with Michael Davitt – whose family had been evicted during the famine and who himself had been imprisoned as a Fenian – to make Davitt's new Land League effective in its struggle with the landlords.

The Land League tactics were simple and straightforward. League members would offer a reduced rent to a landlord whose demands seemed unreasonable; and if the landlord refused to accept the reduced rent, all the members of the Land League in that area would withhold all rent payments. Naturally the landlord would reply with eviction; whereupon the League would turn to their second weapon, the boycott. This got its name from the first man against whom it was effectively employed, a Captain Boycott, agent for an absentee landlord with big estates in the west.

The boycott was easily operated and very effective; it carried a faint echo of the ancient papal weapon of excommunication. When a man was boycotted, nobody in the neighbourhood would have anything to do with him, or his agent, or his family or servants, or any tenant who took land from which another had been evicted. Nobody would work for a man who was boycotted, or serve him, or feed his animals, or transport his farm produce, or even bury his dead.

It worked. A series of Land Acts were passed which transferred the power to fix rents from the landlords to the courts and gave the tenants security of tenure so long as they paid what the court decided was a fair rent for the property. In time, these Acts and subsequent legislation replaced the absentee, alien landlords with a race of peasant proprietors.

Parnell and Davitt had been gaoled for their part in the Land League disturbances – this was one of the periods in Ireland when habeas corpus was suspended – and it was most unfortunate that on the very day of their release in 1882, when it seemed as if Home Rule was at last becoming a feasible policy, a gang of revolutionaries calling themselves 'The Invincibles' fell upon Lord Frederick Cavendish, the new Liberal Chief Secretary and his Under-Secretary, Burke, as they walked in Phoenix Park, and stabbed them to death. The gang did not even know who Lord Frederick Cavendish was: their sole purpose had been to kill Burke. And it was doubly unfortunate in that Cavendish was exactly the type of liberal-minded Englishman who was beginning to realize that Ireland had a just case.

The effect in England – and throughout most of Ulster – was to rule out any immediate possibility of Home Rule and there was introduced another, even more drastic Coercion Act. This resulted in consolidating Irish opinion behind Parnell, so that in the elections of 1885, Irish nationalists won every seat in Ireland outside of Ulster and, surprisingly, a great many in Ulster. Parnell now held the balance of power between Liberals and Conservatives in the British Parliament.

It was at this stage that Gladstone, despite the Phoenix Park murders, decided to press for a measure of Home Rule, along the 'federal' lines that Butt had suggested, rather than run the risk of provoking further violence by continued repressive measures. The Tories, who had been considering something along the same lines and for the same reasons, now came out strongly in favour of maintaining the Union. At another General Election, Gladstone's party was outnumbered and Home Rule was shelved for the moment.

It was during this election campaign that Lord Randolph Churchill went to northern Ireland to play, as he put it, 'the Orange card'. For over a century, Ulster had been growing farther and farther away from the remainder of Ireland in outlook, character and even prosperity. The famine had affected Ulster far less than the rest of Ireland, if only for the reason that most of the people in Ulster had some money with which to buy food. Between the famine and the land revolution, industrialization made further great strides. Between 1851 and 1881 the population of Belfast doubled, and Belfast produce – linen above all – was regarded as the best in the world. This industry and the cotton industry employed principally women, but in 1862 a shipyard was set up in Belfast which, under Edward Harland and his chief draughtsman, Wolff, was soon turning out some of the world's greatest liners and employing vast armies of Ulstermen. This new-found prosperity increased Ulster's self-confidence and enhanced the contempt of the Protestants for the feckless Catholic peasants in the south who could boast no industry other than brewing. At the same time despite the growing industrialization of Ulster, it remained a predominantly agricultural area, with the prosperity, and the Protestants, largely confined to four counties, Derry, Antrim, Down and Armagh. Donegal, Cavan and Monaghan were overwhelmingly Catholic, and there were slight Catholic majorities in Fermanagh and Tyrone as well as in the city of Derry. But all the power and privilege in the north of Ireland was now firmly clutched in the hands of the rich Protestant merchants and farmers, and they had no intention of letting it out of their grasp. In 1795 the Orange Order had been formed to prevent Catholic infiltration into Protestant lands and uphold the Protestant Ascendancy in Ulster. This Orange Order – which in time permeated, and to an extent controlled, the whole establishment in Northern Ireland – held frequent provocative parades through the streets to commemorate the Battle of the Boyne, which often resulted in sectarian riots. In 1864, for example, seven people were killed in Belfast and 150 injured in riots arising out of an Orange Order demonstration.

It was this powerful, intransigent, anti-nationalist, anti-Catholic strain that Lord Randolph Churchill now decided to tap on behalf of the short-term partisan political interests of the Tory party. In a series of speeches he left the northern Protestants with the idea firmly implanted in their minds that it was in their best interests to resist Home Rule, by force if necessary, and that if they did so, Parliament would not leave the Ulster Protestants in the lurch. In all conscience, the Ulster Protestants were not difficult to convince on this score, and two slogans 'Ulster will fight and Ulster will be right' and 'Home Rule means Rome Rule' were born out of this mischievous political manœuvre which has since had such tragic results.

Parnell was hoping that in time Gladstone would return with a sufficiently strong majority to bring in the Home Rule issue again, but in the meantime, he himself was overtaken and destroyed by events. First a series of letters was published in *The Times* attempting to establish that he had connived in the Phoenix Park murders, and although they were later proved to be forgeries, some of the stigma remained. Then in 1889 a divorce case was filed citing Parnell by one of his followers, Captain William O'Shea. Parnell did not attempt to defend the suit and, after her divorce, married Kitty O'Shea – a pretty flagrant piece of improbity in Victorian Ireland. For a time Parnell's party stood by their leader, but when Gladstone threatened to withdraw his support for Home Rule unless Parnell resigned, the Party split, the cause of Home Rule was dealt another shattering blow, and the bitterness between the two factions endured long after Parnell's death in 1891.

Gladstone, influenced partly by American pressure and partly by the fact that the Irish members again held the balance of power in Parliament, did manage to get a Home Rule bill through the Commons in 1892, but it was defeated by the Lords. And when the Liberals returned to power in 1906, it was with a large enough majority to manage without the Irish vote. It was not until yet another General Election in 1910 had again given the Irish M.P.s control of the balance of power in the House of Commons that Home Rule once more became a vital issue.

And in the meantime, the Irish Republican Brotherhood, still convinced that the only way to achieve independence was through force, were making their own secret plans for another armed insurrection as soon as a suitable opportunity arose. They were not to have very long to wait.

CHAPTER FOURTEEN

# The Troubles—and the Treaty

## 1

Although religion and its effect on history has been the prime concern throughout this book, it will have been noticed that for the last chapter – from the moment when Catholic Emancipation was achieved, in fact – religion became less and less of an issue, and nationalism or patriotism took its place as the chief concern of the politically-minded Irish. The vast bulk of the Irish peasantry were not in any way politically-minded; and once the worst of their grievances had been removed they settled down to cultivate their plots of land. Most of the leading revolutionaries until now had been Protestants, and although the Catholic priests had in some areas supported the people in their struggle against the landlords during the Land League disturbances, in general, as soon as the Protestant Church of Ireland was disestablished, the Catholic Church remained firmly on the side of the establishment against any attempts to unseat it by force of arms. Ireland – at any rate outside of Ulster's industrial area – was a poor country with a low standard of living as compared with its rich next-door neighbour, though not as compared with any other small peasant community without a vast empire. This is something which is still often overlooked in Ireland, where a comparable standard of living with England's has always been regarded as a minimal requirement, even at a time when England was living off the plunder of the greatest empire the world has ever known. But the Irish people were not in general discontent with their lot, and Patrick Pearse was probably right in his theory that it needed the blood sacrifice of Easter Week to shake them out of their complacency.

During the early years of the present century, various attempts were made to 'kill Home Rule with kindness', and the reaction which these moves instantly provoked in Ulster ought to have been an indication of things to come. An innocent and sensible proposal for the co-ordination of all the various boards in Ireland under one central authority – a system known as 'devolution' – caused a furious agitation among the Unionists in the North. It was described as fatuous, ridiculous, unworkable and impractical and the Under-Secretary for Ireland, Sir Anthony McDonnell, the man who suggested it, was represented, according to Leon OBroin's *The Chief Secretary*, 'as a criminally unscrupulous conspirator whose aim was to destroy the Empire and, under instruction from the Catholic bishops, to force Protestants and Protestantism out of Ireland'. There was another equally innocent and well-intentioned proposal to reorganize the existing University of Dublin so as to include, besides Trinity College in Dublin, the Queen's Colleges in Belfast and Cork, and the recently formed Catholic National University in Dublin, with the Seminary at Maynooth and Galway and Magee Colleges as affiliated institutions. Queen's College in Belfast immediately protested against the scheme; they did not want to have any connection with Dublin, and the Ulster Unionists made it clear that they would have nothing to do with any arrangement which included the Seminary at Maynooth.

## 2

The events of Easter Week 1916, and the Troubles which followed have been so often and so fully described by so many writers – including myself (in an anatomy of Ireland called *The Irish Answer*) – that it may seem tedious to reiterate them here. And yet there may be people who will read this book who are unaware of these events, and since they have a direct bearing on the present situation in Ulster, they cannot, for that reason, be omitted. I will, however, deal with them as briefly as possible.

It is significant, perhaps, that the first faint spark which flared up into the war of independence which marked the beginning of the end of the British Empire came not from the Nationalist Catholics of the south, but from the fiercely loyal northern Protestants.

In 1913, Asquith, the Prime Minister, made yet another attempt to keep faith with the Irish Nationalist Parliamentary Party at Westminster by bringing in a Home Rule Bill which would have set up a parliament in Dublin to deal with purely Irish affairs. This time there was a fair chance that the Bill would get through: under a new Act, the Lords could no longer veto a Bill, but merely delay it.

But even before the Bill was introduced Sir Edward Carson,* the leader of the Ulster Unionists, had drawn up a 'solemn league and covenant', based on the old Scottish one. It was signed by half a million people† and declared that if such a parliament should ever be convened Ulster would refuse to recognize it. So strongly did the Ulster Protestants feel about the matter that many of them signed the covenant with their own blood.

Carson had also founded the Ulster Volunteers to resist Home Rule by force if necessary, and made arrangements to set up a provisional government which would take over the moment the Bill came into effect.

Carson spoke for Ulster as a whole though in fact he was supported by only a narrow majority in Ulster; during the reading of the Home Rule Bill, the province was represented in Westminster by seventeen Unionists and sixteen Home Rulers. On the other hand, Carson's Unionist supporters were made of very stern stuff indeed. Carson himself had said that if necessary the men of Ulster would march from Belfast to Cork, even if not one of them ever returned; and Sir James Craig, another prominent Ulster Unionist, told a newspaper reporter that Germany and the German Emperor would be preferred in Ulster to rule from Dublin. There was something almost Gilbertian in the whole situation: Carson, a Dublin man, arming Ulster to fight the forces of Britain in order to remain within the United Kingdom. But it was no joke, and he had the support of the Conservative Party under its new leader, Bonar Law, a dour Presbyterian Scot with Ulster connections, as well as of such rugged imperialists as Rudyard Kipling. Bonar Law had once declared that Ireland was not a nation 'but two peoples, separated by a deeper gulf than that dividing Ireland from Great Britain'. During the years 1911–13, there were endless discussions, many of them in secret, between representatives of the various political parties in Ireland and England to discuss all sorts of proposals for the exclusion of Ulster, or part of it, for a time at any rate, from the provisions of the Home Rule Bill. So the partition of Ireland, even if only on a temporary

* Interestingly, Carson was directly descended from one of Cromwell's generals, Lambert.

† To be precise, in a province with approximately 500,000 adult Protestants, the Covenant was signed by 471,414.

basis, was a very real issue long before there was any question of an independent Irish republic. And, even as early as this, Carson refused to entertain any idea of a temporary partition: 'We don't want a sentence of death with a stay of execution for six years' was the way he put it as he proceeded to organize and drill his Ulster Volunteers.

The formation of the Ulster Volunteers made it inevitable that a similar volunteer force would be formed in the south, to support Home Rule, and in fact not one but two volunteer forces were set up in Ireland inside a year.

The first was the Irish Citizen Army, formed in 1913 by the Irish Labour Party, not to fight Carson's volunteers, nor even, initially, to fight for Irish freedom, but simply to protect Irish workers from police attacks. There had been a great deal of labour unrest in Dublin, and during street riots on Sunday, 30 August 1913, the police ran amok, killing two workers and injuring several hundred. The Irish Citizen Army were a small, well-trained force under James Connolly.

The second force was the Irish Volunteers, set up by the Irish Republican Brotherhood operating as usual in and through other societies. At a meeting in Dublin, all the parties in Ireland likely to be sympathetic towards such a proposal were brought together. Eoin MacNeill, Vice-President of the Gaelic League (a movement set up a few years earlier primarily to revive the now rapidly dying Irish language) was invited; so was Arthur Griffith, a political journalist who had been expounding a new doctrine of separatism, based on Hungary's resistance to Austria and known as 'Sinn Fein' (pronounced Shin Fayn) – the words are Gaelic for 'Ourselves' with a slightly emphatic overtone, like *nous-mêmes* in French. Sinn Fein did not go as far in its aims as the Irish Republican Brotherhood, which was now headed by Tom Clarke, an old Fenian who had spent many years in British gaols. Clarke stood for an all-Ireland independent republic; Griffith would have been quite satisfied with a separate Dublin parliament under the English king. Among the first recruits to the Irish Volunteer force was a tall, gangling mathematics master with a fanatical interest in the Irish language and an odd, Spanish name – de Valera.

The Volunteer movement spread like wildfire. Before long there were 250,000 men meeting in drill halls, or in the fields, or among the mountains, training to be soldiers, and using an out-of-date British War Office Manual as their textbook.

At this stage, they had no arms; within ten days of the formation of the Volunteers, an edict was issued prohibiting the importation of arms into Ireland. But once again the answer came from Ulster.

Ignoring the ban, Carson's Ulster Volunteers imported 35,000 rifles and three million rounds of ammunition from Germany. No attempt was made to interfere with this shipment; indeed, the generals had already warned the British Government that they would not attempt to suppress a revolt in Ulster, and at the British Army camp on the Curragh in County Kildare, over fifty officers had threatened to mutiny rather than be involved in any attempt to force Ulster to accept Home Rule.

Naturally, the Volunteers in the south attempted to follow suit, and a small consignment of second-hand German Mauser rifles was landed at Howth, Co. Dublin from Erskine Childers's yacht *Asgard* in July 1914. A party of Irish Volunteers collected the 1,500 rifles and 50,000 rounds of ammunition and were carrying them back into Dublin when they were intercepted by a body of about two hundred policemen and a company of the King's Own Scottish Borderers. Most of the Volunteers got away over the fields with the weapons but the fact that this had happened after the Ulster Volunteers had been allowed to import a much greater quantity of weapons unmolested caused a great deal of resentment. And later that day, when the British troops, marching back through the city, were jeered and stoned by crowds angered at the unfairness of it, the troops halted and fired on the mob, killing two men and injuring thirty-two people. It was perhaps not surprising that the Irish felt that there was now one law for the Protestant Ulstermen and another for the Catholic Irish.

Ten days later war broke out between England and Germany, the Home Rule Bill was rushed through the House with the proviso that it would not become law until after the war, and thousands of Irishmen, Protestant and Catholic, joined the British Army. The bulk of the Irish Volunteers – there had been, needless to say, a split in its ranks soon after it was formed – left to fight for England; but about ten to twelve thousand of them stayed on in Ireland, convinced that Ireland at the very least should remain neutral. Sir Roger Casement, an Irishman who had been knighted for his work for the British Foreign Office and who had been involved in the gun-running at Howth, said: 'Ireland has no blood to give to any land or any cause, save Ireland.'

The Irish Republican Brotherhood reaffirmed the view they had always held – that England's difficulty was Ireland's opportunity – and made plans to get in touch with Germany to try to arrange an armed insurrection.

Casement went to Germany to talk Irish prisoners of war in German prison camps into forming an Irish Brigade, and to persuade the German government to supply Ireland with arms. He was not markedly successful in either endeavour, though he did eventually succeed in getting a consignment of 20,000 obsolete Russian rifles dispatched to Ireland in a ship called the *Aud.* Casement himself travelled back to Ireland in a German submarine. The *Aud* found no one waiting to take delivery of the arms when she arrived off Tralee on the appointed day and had to put to sea again. She was challenged by a British ship, the H.M.S. *Bluebell,* whereupon the crew took to the boats and scuttled the *Aud,* arms and all. Casement was arrested a few hours after he landed – with a Berlin sleeper ticket still in his pocket – taken to London, tried for treason and hanged a couple of months later.

A rising had been planned for Easter Sunday – ostensibly it was to be disguised as a nation-wide series of manœuvres of the Irish Volunteers – but when the news of the scuttling of the *Aud* and the arrest of Casement reached Eoin MacNeill, the Chief of Staff of the Irish Volunteers, he put an advertisement in the *Sunday Independent* cancelling the 'manœuvres'. In the meantime, however, there had been yet another split in the Volunteers and a more militant group, which did not even take their own Chief of Staff into their confidence, planned to go ahead with the rising in any event, with the assistance of the Irish Citizen Army. The leaders of this military council within the Volunteer force decided to prevent isolated actions on the part of small units by confirming MacNeill's cancellation order, but warned officers at the same time to be ready for a fresh mobilization. Those in the know in Dublin were told of the new plan, but the main body of Volunteers in Dublin heard about it only when they received a surprise mobilization order on Easter Monday morning.

At eleven o'clock, small parties of men, some in uniforms of one sort or another, some armed, started to form up at various prearranged points in the city, and as noon approached began to move on to the buildings which had been picked out for occupation.

The main body, with Patrick Pearse, a poet and a schoolmaster, and James Connolly, the Labour leader, at their head – 150 men armed with rifles, sledge-hammers, pickaxes, pikes and homemade bombs – occupied the General Post Office in what is now O'Connell Street, bundled the staff outside, sandbagged the windows, hauled down the Union Jack from the roof of the building and replaced it with two flags: the green, white and orange tricolour and the ancient flag of Ireland, green with a golden harp. Pearse next read the now famous Proclamation from the steps of the Post Office. It began with the stirring words, 'Irishmen and Irishwomen: In the name of God and of the dead generations from which she receives her old tradition of nationhood, Ireland, through us, summons her children to her flag and strikes for her freedom.'

Pearse and the other six signatories to the Proclamation knew that they were signing their own death warrants but they were convinced that the gesture they were making was necessary to shake the Irish nation out of the apathy into which it had lapsed. British military forces outnumbered the rebels right from the start by three or four to one – and later in the week, when reinforcements arrived in Dublin, by about twenty to one. Within two days, the British also had a gunboat, the *Helga*, in the Liffey to shell the strongholds of the rebels.

By Friday the centre of the city was in ruins and fires in the G.P.O. forced Pearse and Connolly to withdraw their headquarters to a row of shops in nearby Moore Street. Both issued proclamations. Pearse wrote: 'If they [the Volunteers] do not win this fight, they will at least deserve to win it. But win it they will, though they may win it in death. Already they have done a great thing. They have redeemed Dublin from many shames and made her name splendid among the names of cities.' Connolly was more matter-of-fact and prosaic: 'For the first time in 700 years, the flag of a free Ireland floats triumphantly over Dublin city. The British Army . . . behind their artillery and machine guns, are afraid to advance to the attack or storm any position held by our forces.'

De Valera was still holding out in Boland's Mill, which controlled the southern approaches to the city and the railway line from Dun Laoghaire (then called Kingstown) harbour; and MacDonagh in Jacob's biscuit factory could probably have held out for another week; but on the Saturday, to prevent further bloodshed, Pearse offered to surrender. The tricolour was hauled down from Jacob's factory and the other rebel strongholds, and from behind the barricades and out of the battered houses the Volunteers emerged, dazed and weary, into the shattered streets to lay down their arms at the foot of the Parnell monument. As they were marched through the city streets to gaol or internment in England, they were mocked and jeered by Dublin women whose husbands and sons were away fighting in Flanders and the Near East. There was no general sympathy with the rebels at this stage; even ardent Home Rulers felt that demonstrations of this sort must inevitably persuade the English that the Irish were not yet ready for Home Rule.

Sir John Maxwell, who had been given unlimited powers to quell the revolt, soon changed all that by court-martialling the signatories of the Proclamation and the commanding officers of the Volunteers and executing them, in twos and threes, over a period of a week. James Connolly, so badly wounded that he had to be carried to the execution yard on a stretcher and propped up in a chair to be shot, was the last man to be executed. De Valera had his death sentence commuted to one of life imprisonment; it is likely that his American birth was a contributory factor to this leniency. In any event, he did not come up for trial until twelve of the fifteen executions had been carried out and already liberal opinion in Britain was beginning to swing against Maxwell. 'The executions are becoming an atrocity,' warned the *Manchester Guardian*. 'These men were prisoners of war,' wrote George Bernard Shaw, 'and therefore it was entirely incorrect to slaughter them. I cannot regard as a traitor any Irishman taken in a fight for Irish independence against the British Government, which was a fair fight in everything except the enormous odds my countrymen had to face.'

## 3

Most of the Volunteers were taken by cattle boat to England and interned without trial under the 'Defence of the Realm Act' – over 1,600 of them in one camp at Frongoch where they spent their time discussing what had gone wrong and how much better they would organize things next time.

After a grim period during which General Maxwell was installed as military dictator and all public meetings were banned, things in Ireland returned to normal except in one respect: by executing the rebel leaders, the British had made martyrs of them and the very limited concept of Home Rule which would have been perfectly acceptable to the bulk of the Irish people before Easter 1916 was no longer good enough. They now wanted a complete break with England.

Agitations soon began for the release of the political prisoners, and the British, anxious to placate Irish-American opinion, released most of the internees by Christmas 1916. To their surprise, they were welcomed home with bonfires and bands and torchlight processions, and cheered resoundingly by the very people who had jeered and spat at them nine months earlier. Arthur Griffith was released and so was Michael Collins, now a key man in the still all-powerful Irish Republican Brotherhood. De Valera was still in gaol.

Griffith and Collins now began to put up Sinn Fein candidates for all by-elections: their plan was to win the seats and then abstain from attending Westminster. De Valera, who was selected as Sinn Fein candidate for West Clare in one of these by-elections, was released in June 1917 and was welcomed back to a city thronged with cheering crowds singing 'The Soldier's Song', the new national anthem of the Irish Republic, which, in the eyes of the Sinn Fein supporters, still existed.

Lloyd George, who had now become Prime Minister, called a convention representing all shades of opinion in Ireland to see whether a solution to the problem of the North could be found, but because its terms of reference excluded any possibility of declaring Ireland a republic, Sinn Fein boycotted it, and it achieved nothing. Sinn Fein was now irrevocably committed to securing international recognition of Ireland as an independent republic, and with de Valera back in Ireland, now had a forceful leader: in October 1917 de Valera was elected President of Sinn Fein and leader of the Irish Volunteers.

The war ended in November 1918, and a General Election was held the next month. Collins and Griffith now decided to put forward as many Sinn Fein candidates as possible, who, if elected, would not take their seats at Westminster but instead would set up an independent parliament in Dublin and attempt to govern the country. Sinn Fein fought 80 out of the 105 seats (there was no point in putting up Sinn Fein candidates in most constituencies in Unionist Ulster) and won 73 of them. The old Nationalist Parliamentary Party, which would have settled for a limited form of Home Rule, had previously held 80 seats; they were now reduced to 7.

Sinn Fein next set about implementing its pre-election promise to set up an independent parliament in Dublin. All 105 M.P.s who had been elected to the Irish seats at Westminster – Unionists, Independents and the 7 Nationalist M.P.s as well as the 73 Sinn Fein members – were invited to a meeting in Dublin in January 1919. Only Sinn Fein members turned up; and they formally declared Ireland an independent republic and made arrangements to float a national loan to finance their activities. In the absence of de Valera (he had been arrested again and was in a British prison) Cathal Brugha was elected acting President and opened the proceedings with the fighting words: 'We are now done with England; let the world know it.' Michael Collins was not present either; he was over in England arranging de Valera's escape from Lincoln gaol.

De Valera went to America to raise funds for the new Republic, which began setting up government departments as if British rule did not exist any longer. The Irish Parliament, known as Dail Eireann (pronounced Dawl Erin, approximately) was prohibited and suppressed so that ministers could not openly meet and in any event they could only legislate for Sinn Fein supporters, which by no means included the whole population at this or any other period. However, the existence of the Dail, even if it could not govern, made it increasingly difficult, and eventually impossible, for the British administration to govern either. In time, Sinn Fein even set up its own courts and police force.

Meanwhile, the first armed attack on the Royal Irish Constabulary was carried out. Dan Breen and Sean Treacy, with six members of the Irish Republican Army – as the Volunteers were now called – captured a supply of gelignite at Soloheadbeg in County Tipperary, killing two constables in the process.

This raid set the pattern for hundreds of similar attacks on the R.I.C. all over the country; in the first instance the I.R.A. were after explosives, guns and ammunition, but later other motives entered the picture.

Under the direction of Michael Collins – now Head of Intelligence of the I.R.A., guiding light of the Irish Republican Brotherhood and Minister for Finance – the 11,000 members of the Royal Irish Constabulary were subjected to a long and bitter guerrilla war. They were everywhere ambushed and harassed, fired on from behind hedges, raided by flying columns, sniped at in the streets, and their barracks were blown up or set on fire.

A curfew was imposed and all civilians were confined to their homes from ten o'clock, or in some places even earlier, while the police and military patrolled the country, raiding houses for arms, looting and ravaging, carrying away prisoners and murdering suspects in front of their families.

The R.I.C. were soon augmented by two specially enlisted forces. The Black and Tans – recruited so hurriedly that they had to wear makeshift uniforms, part British Army khaki, part the near-black bottle-green of the R.I.C., hence the nickname – were tough ex-soldiers unable to find work in post-war Britain. They soon became demoralized in a strange country where they couldn't understand the accent, and didn't know what the fuss was all about, a country, moreover, in which every man in a macintosh was a potential terrorist with a hand-grenade in his pocket. The other force was known as the Auxiliaries; they were all ex-officers and were twice as well paid (£1 a day) as the Black and Tans. Both of these outfits were supplied with armoured cars in which they tore around the countryside, drunk much of the time, pillaging, looting and terrorizing the civilian population.

Month after month the atrocities on both sides continued. Thomas MacCurtain, the Lord Mayor of Cork, was awakened from his sleep and murdered by policemen in front of his wife and children. A British civil servant was hauled from a tram in Ballsbridge in Dublin and murdered by the I.R.A. in broad daylight. MacCurtain's successor, Terence MacSwiney, was arrested for his revolutionary activities and went on hunger strike in protest. The world watched with interest and horror as MacSwiney, after seventy days of resolute fasting, began to weaken. And when on the seventy-fourth day of his self-imposed sentence he died in Brixton Prison, a lot of people began to wonder if there wasn't something more to the Irish Question than they had suspected. The execution of Kevin Barry, a boy of eighteen, captured in a street fight in which a British soldier had been killed, also caused considerable controversy. His revolver had jammed and had not been fired, and the bullet taken from the body was of a different calibre in any event; there was also a suggestion that he had been tortured or at any rate roughly manhandled to make him reveal the names of his comrades. Despite many appeals for clemency, he was hanged.

The Anglo-Irish war reached its culmination on Bloody Sunday, 21 November 1920. Collins, in an all-out effort to liquidate the key members of the British Secret Service in Dublin, sent members of his execution squad around to their lodgings and hotels. Fourteen men were murdered in their beds, in front of their wives and families, or wherever they happened to be that Sunday morning, shortly after 9 a.m.

The same afternoon, the police and military retaliated by firing on the crowd at a football match in Croke Park, Dublin, killing fourteen people and wounding sixty.

There was trouble, too, in the North. On 21 July, Carson made a speech linking Catholics, Sinn Fein and Labour; the result was an outbreak of riots during which eighteen people were killed and two hundred injured. Between June and December, twenty-eight people were killed in riots in Derry and sixty-two in Belfast. There had also been tremendous damage to property all over the country; barracks and court-houses had also been burnt down. It was clear that this could not go on.

By now de Valera was back in Ireland, and the first, tentative peace feelers were made. Lord Derby, General Smuts and Arthur Cope, Assistant Under-Secretary at Dublin Castle, all made guarded approaches but de Valera held his hand and awaited an official move.

The Home Rule Bill now came out of the cold storage in which it had been placed at the outbreak of war, and in May 1941, Lloyd George's 'Government of Ireland' Act came into force. It provided for two Parliaments, one representing the six counties of Antrim, Armagh, Down, Fermanagh, Derry and Tyrone, and the other for the remaining twenty-six counties. The Parliaments were limited in their power: matters excluded from their jurisdiction included the Crown, the making of war, treaties and foreign relations, the Navy, Army and Air Force. The Act also provided for a Council of Ireland to co-ordinate the administration of the two Parliaments which could proclaim a United Ireland and set up one Parliament for the whole country, provided that both Parliaments were agreeable. Lord Fitzalan, a new viceroy and the first Catholic one for centuries, was sent to Ireland, but this sop did not have its desired effect; 'We would as soon have a Catholic hangman' was one comment.

This Act also called for another General Election, to provide M.P.s for the two Parliaments, and Sinn Fein decided once again to use the British electoral machinery to make another appeal to the country. Sinn Fein's candidates were returned unopposed in every single constituency save the four Trinity College seats.

When he went to Belfast to open the Northern Parliament in June

1921, King George V made an appeal to Irishmen to forgive and forget, and a few days later de Valera had a letter from Lloyd George inviting him and any colleague he might choose to a conference in London to seek a settlement.

De Valera and Lloyd George were at cross purposes right from the start of the talks. In effect, Lloyd George was offering Ireland a measure of self-government which roughly corresponded with that of the Dominion of Canada. If it had been made before the Easter Week Rising and all that had happened since, there is little doubt that it would have been welcomed; it certainly would have seemed a generous offer to Wolfe Tone, or Lord Edward Fitzgerald, or Robert Emmet, or Dan O'Connell.

The two key issues were Partition and the Oath of Allegiance. De Valera saw Ireland as an island entity with the sea as its frontier and he was determined on full freedom, including freedom from any Oath of Allegiance, not merely for the twenty-six counties but for the six partitioned counties of Northern Ireland as well. 'We cannot admit the right of the British Government,' he said, 'to mutilate our country.' He was not concerned at the fact that the mutilation was necessitated by the certainty of civil war in Ulster if it were placed under a Dublin parliament. The problem was insoluble then – and it has remained insoluble ever since.

In my book, *The Irish Answer*, I attempted to synthetize the two opposing arguments on partition, and since the underlying problem has not altered one whit since it was written, it would probably be useful to reiterate the arguments here.

De Valera and the Irish nationalists argue that Ireland is an island, whole and indivisible, and that the majority of the people living in that island want to be independent of Britain. They admit that a majority of the people in one particular part of the island are passionately anxious to maintain the link with Britain, but contend that these people represent a small minority of the whole and that the wishes of these people should not be allowed to block the prospect of a United Ireland. To support this view they quote, among others, Winston Churchill, who once said: 'Whatever Ulster's right may be, she cannot stand in the way of the whole of the rest of Ireland. Half a province cannot impose a permanent veto on the nation.' If there is any logic in partitioning off the area in which this minority lives, they argue, it would be only logical to partition off other areas inside that again, where there are pockets of Nationalists who fervently want to be ruled from Dublin. And smaller Unionist pockets inside them again, and so on, *ad absurdum*.

The Ulstermen argue that the fact that Ireland happens to be an island is irrelevant and does not necessarily make it a homogeneous whole. They believe that the basic unit, if you could put it that way, is the British Isles, and within that unit all their ties are with Britain. They admit the right of the Republic to break away from the United Kingdom, but they believe that in the areas where people of their own persuasion are in a majority, they have an equal right to maintain the British association.

It was, above all, a religious problem, at any rate so far as the Ulster Protestants were concerned. At this period there were about 820,000 Protestants and 430,000 Catholics in the six Ulster counties partitioned off, as against 327,000 Protestants and 2,800,000 Catholics in the south.

In a way, it was the choice of these six counties rather than the whole of Ulster which caused so much bitterness then and since. There might have been some sort of a case for partitioning off the whole province of Ulster; but the Ulster Unionists didn't want this because it would have included an uncomfortably high proportion of Catholics. Equally, there might have been some sort of a case for partitioning off the predominantly Protestant counties of Armagh, Antrim, Down and the borderline case of Derry, but the Unionists didn't want this either as it wouldn't have given them an area large enough to be viable as a separate state. So what they had already talked Lloyd George into accepting was a completely arbitrary and gerrymandered sub-province which included two counties where the Catholics were in the majority, Fermanagh and Tyrone. There were also a number of Catholics in Derry and Belfast. In Derry city, the population was 54 per cent Catholic, though in the county as a whole the Protestants had a slight majority.

There is no doubt that the Ulster Protestants had followed events during the Anglo-Irish War with horror and interest, and equally no doubt that they regarded de Valera, Michael Collins and the other prominent Republican freedom fighters as the natural heirs and successors to the Catholic desperadoes of 1641 and 1798, who would, if they ever gained power, turn the Protestants out of their homes and murder them in droves. Rather than submit to this, they would fight to the last man. On the other hand, by accepting partition, de

Valera knew that he was abandoning nearly half a million Catholics – at worst to pogroms and persecutions, at best to reduction to second-class citizens, deprived for all practical purposes of their civil rights.

But at this stage of the talks, the border was not really in dispute. The offer Lloyd George was making was on the basis of a 26 county state. The machinery was there for the removal of the border, if at any time both Parliaments desired it; in the meantime de Valera could take the British offer or prepare for a furious onslaught.

Lloyd George's proposals were put to the second Dail on 16 August and, despite threats in the British newspapers of the terrible repercussions which would ensue if negotiations broke down, it was unanimously rejected. Instead of the terrible onslaught which had been threatened, de Valera received a letter from Lloyd George reopening the negotiations.

In October a delegation from Dail Eireann left for England with a draft treaty which had been drawn up by the Cabinet. To everybody's surprise de Valera, instead of heading the delegation himself, stayed on in Dublin; his absence could always be advanced by the delegates as a good reason for not allowing themselves to be stampeded into making any hasty decisions in London, he argued, though that is exactly what did happen, with tragic results. He also claimed that his presence might be needed in Dublin to persuade Cathal Brugha and some of the more hot-headed Republicans into accepting something less than they believed they had been fighting for. The delegation had plenipotentiary powers but were not to sign anything final without consulting de Valera.

The delegation returned to Dublin more than once during the talks, and eventually on 6 December 1921 signed a treaty, without consulting de Valera, by which Britain gave the twenty-six counties Dominion status, but retained certain ports, as a precaution in the event of any future war. The Treaty also included the unacceptable Oath of Allegiance and accepted Partition. It was immediately repudiated by de Valera; and the Cabinet, the Dail and the Irish Republican Army immediately split on the issue. De Valera's opposition to the treaty was out-voted in the Dail, and Arthur Griffith succeeded him as President of the Executive Council.

A provisional Government under Michael Collins ran the country until a constitution could be drafted and a General Election arranged. At the election, de Valera's anti-Treaty candidates received only 36 seats out of 128. In these circumstances, various remarks made by Mr de Valera – who never took kindly to defeat – began to acquire a slightly sinister connotation. 'A majority has no right to do wrong,' he had once said, and again, 'There are rights which a minority may justly uphold, even by arms, against a majority.' The rabidly Republican element in the I.R.A. had already set up an independent military council which did not recognize either the Provisional Government or Mr de Valera. They had seized a number of strongholds in the city and country, including the Four Courts, and had started a new series of raids for arms and money. Collins, feeling that he had forsaken his co-religionists and fellow nationalists in the North, was keeping in touch with this military council, giving them guns and encouraging them in armed intervention in the North, where in a new series of pogroms, Catholics were being burnt out of their houses in thousands – a double game wich was bound to recoil on him.

The British authorities, keeping their part of the bargain, had started to withdraw their forces from the barracks and army camps throughout the country, and their places in many instances were being taken, not by the soldiers of the new Irish Free State, but by the breakaway Republican arm of the I.R.A. It needed only a spark to start a civil war. That came when Field-Marshal Sir Henry Wilson was murdered outside his London home in Eaton Square by two Irishmen. Wilson, as Military Adviser to the Northern Ireland Government, was largely responsible for the way things had been going in Ulster. Ironically, the order to shoot him had probably come from Collins himself, before the Treaty; now Collins was ordered to get Rory O'Connor and his Republican 'Irregulars' out of the Four Courts without delay. Borrowing field guns from the British, Collins opened fire on the Four Courts.

The Civil War which followed was like a ghastly parody of the Anglo-Irish War as the Irregulars formed up once again into flying columns and resumed the so-familiar guerrilla tactics, except that now it was their former comrades and friends – sometimes even their relatives – that they were attacking. Griffith, worn out and disillusioned, died on 13 August and was succeeded by William Cosgrave. Michael Collins was shot in an ambush on 22 August. During the winter and spring of 1922–23, seventy-seven 'Irregulars' were shot and about 12,000 gaoled. The British reprisals after Easter Week, 1916, were trivial by comparison.

In April, Liam Lynch, the I.R.A. Chief of Staff, was killed. Frank

Aiken took over and on 30 April ordered a cease-fire. On 24 May came another order: dump arms. For the moment, Ireland's troubles were over.

It is perhaps not surprising that the Ulster Protestants, watching these events from their side of the border, rejoiced in the fact that they had succeeded in remaining a part of the United Kingdom if this was the way in which a free independent Catholic state conducted its affairs.

CHAPTER FIFTEEN

# No Surrender——Not an Inch!

## 1

When the shooting stopped, and the smoke clouds started to drift away, and those charged with the administration of the two segments of the now dismembered and badly-battered island began to look around them at the job to be done, they cannot have felt too cheerful at the prospect that faced them.

Neither the Protestants concentrated in the North, nor the Catholics who dominated the rest of the country had ever wanted Partition. It was purely an English compromise to avert civil war in Ulster. The Ulster Protestants accepted it as a tolerable alternative to Home Rule, which would have placed them in the position of a small minority in a predominantly Catholic state rather than part – as they were under the Union – of an overwhelmingly Protestant United Kingdom. Griffith, Collins and their pro-Treaty colleagues accepted Partition because they didn't believe, at that moment, that there was any alternative, other than an immediate renewal of hostilities for which they were unprepared. Collins talked openly about the Treaty as a stepping stone to further concessions later, and although he felt to the day of his death that he had betrayed his fellow countrymen and co-religionists in the North by signing it, he also genuinely believed that the Boundary Commission which had been promised during the talks would readjust the area of Northern Ireland to include in the Free State many thousands of Catholics living along the fringes of the partitioned area.

After the Treaty, the Irish Free State found itself in the position that England had reached after the bloodless revolution of 1688; from that year onwards the proportion of Catholics in England was never more than 10 per cent of the population and was often nearer to 5 per cent. Consequently the Catholics represented no menace to the realm and could be treated with complete leniency. In 1922, about 11 per cent of the population of the new Free State were

Protestants, but almost immediately, as members of the military and civil administration moved out, and many Protestant members of the civil service elected to move to England, the figure dropped to around 8 per cent and then, within another ten years or so, to about 5 per cent, a proportion which has remained more or less constant ever since. This 5 per cent represented no more serious threat to the Free State than England's 5 per cent of Catholics, and they were not in any way molested, despite the fears of Ulster Protestants for their co-religionists in the South: on the contrary, they were treated with utter impartiality.

The Ulster Protestants were still convinced that the driving force behind the Republican movement which had produced the Irish Free State was the Catholic Church, despite the fact that the Catholic hierarchy had openly condemned the Rising and had even excommunicated many of the leading republicans. In point of fact, the Catholic Church had always been every bit as strongly opposed to Home Rule as the Ulster Protestants, though for a very different reason: so long as the Union was maintained, Rome could count on a solid bloc of Catholic votes at Westminster. But to the Ulster Protestant, and particularly to the Orangeman, the memories of 1641 and 1798 were stronger than logic. Home Rule was Rome Rule, and that was the end of it.

Long before Partition was even discussed, a division had already arisen between the Protestants in the North who, as Brian Inglis points out in *The Story of Ireland*, 'formed a homogeneous society, and the Protestants of the South, who had no particular sympathy with their Northern co-religionists (they did not even like them). Although to the last the Northerners objected to Partition (it was imposed on Ireland by English votes alone) on the ground, among others, that it would leave the Southern Unionists at the mercy of Rome, the fact was that so strong an emotional partition already existed, long before 1920, between the Protestant North and the Catholic South, that the Southern Protestants were certain to be regarded as expendable in any settlement that could be reached.'

But, in fact, partly because they represented so small a percentage of the population that they could not constitute any kind of menace, and partly because the Irish Free State wanted to demonstrate to the Ulster Protestants how fair and broad-minded a Catholic administration could be, not merely were the Protestants not in any way molested, but successive governments went out of their way to give them more than a fair crack of the whip. Multi-seat constituencies with members elected on a system of proportional representation gave minorities of all sorts a disproportionate voice in the Dail and Senate. (This latter is an Upper House, partly elected by the Dail on a vocational basis and partly nominated by the President to represent minority interests which could not be adequately represented in the Dail. There were Protestants in the Dail, the Cabinet and the Diplomatic Corps.)

In Northern Ireland, the situation was completely different. The partitioned area contained slightly under one million fervently loyal Ulster Protestants and about half a million Catholics who considered themselves cut off by an arbitrary and unfair border from the remainder of their fellow countrymen. With one-third of the population of the new state either openly or covertly dedicated to its overthrow, and with the distinct possibility of losing two of the Six Counties when the Boundary Commission sat to reconsider the question, not to mention the fact that Catholics, being more prolific, could be expected to increase their numbers more rapidly, the Ulster Protestants could not afford to be complacent.

There was also the disturbing fact that Northern Ireland itself was a bit of an anomaly: it was neither a nation nor a state, but merely a subordinate part of the United Kingdom which could be suspended or abolished at the drop of a White Paper from Westminster. Even its very title raised all kinds of problems. You couldn't really call it Ulster because it did not include the whole of the old province of Ulster, though most of the more militant Ulstermen always did – and still do – refer to their territory as Ulster. Equally, you couldn't really call it Northern Ireland because the most northerly county in the country, Donegal, was in the Free State – though Northern Ireland did become the official title of the area. In the South, it has always been contemptuously referred to as 'the Six Counties'.

All over Ireland, and particularly in Ulster, after 1641, there had been a strong tradition of relying on localized 'amateur' armed forces to redress wrongs and enforce laws which those armed forces thought to be right, regardless of the actual laws of the land. In the seventeenth century, there had been the Rapparees: peasants armed with pikes and scythes and occasionally muskets. In the eighteenth century, violence took the form of attacks by agrarian Whiteboys on landlords and agents exacting tithes. Through the years, various unofficial armies waxed and waned; there were the Hearts of Steel, the Peep o' Day Boys and the Ribbonmen. It was a clash between a party of Protestant Peep o' Day Boys and a Catholic 'amateur' army, the Defenders, in 1795, at the battle of the Diamond, where about twenty Defenders were killed, which led to the formation of the Orange Order, a movement sworn to protect Protestant tenants from Catholic infiltration upon their lands and to uphold the King and his heirs *'so long as he or they support the Protestant ascendancy'*. One of their first exploits was to intimidate Catholics to make them leave their homes in Protestant areas, and about seven hundred families fled from Armagh to Connaught as a result. I mention this here because, both in the early 1920s and more recently, events in Ulster are easier to understand in the light of this long tradition of private armies with hidden caches of weapons of one sort or another which they were always ready to use to enforce their own version of the law.

'In Belfast, in 1922, there were 97 cases of murder and 96 reported attacks upon life; the city was under curfew, except for two brief intervals, until Christmas 1924,' writes Richard Rose in his book, *Governing Without Consensus*. 'During these troubles in the North, 232 people were killed, including two Unionist Members of Parliament, and nearly 1,000 men injured and property valued at £3,000,000 was destroyed. Granted the difference in population, the casualty list was the equivalent of 40,000 injuries from political violence in Britain, or 160,000 injuries in modern America. By the standards of Irish history, casualties were substantial, but not unprecedented.'

Elsewhere in the same book, Richard Rose writes:

> The intensity and dispersion of civil war during the Troubles from 1916 to the middle 1920s made popular resort to arms a necessary condition for the maintenance of the British connection and the Protestant rule in Northern Ireland. So widespread was the arming of Protestants by the regime that the official statistics report that the strength of the police in Northern Ireland for each year from 1921 to 1926 'cannot be stated'. Protestant farmers fearing an attack in the countryside armed themselves and fought the enemy. For example, in Desertmartin, County Londonderry, in revenge for R.U.C. [Royal Ulster Constabulary] men killed in ambush and mills burned, a group of Protestants took four Catholics from their beds one night and shot them a short distance from the village.

In 1920 some of the unofficial vigilantes were organized to form the core of the Ulster Special B Constabularies, or B Specials as they were commonly called, a spare-time armed force – who kept their guns in their homes – and could be called upon at any time to assist the R.U.C. in their task of maintaining order. They were exclusively a Protestant force, the assumption being that only Catholics would be likely to do anything to disrupt order.

## 2

Because de Valera and his followers refused to take the Oath of Allegiance, they 'abstained' from the Free State Parliament, just as they had previously abstained from the Parliament at Westminster, and for some years carried on the pretence that the remnants of the anti-Treaty element of the old second Dail represented the only true Parliament of the Irish Republic.

In the North, a somewhat similar situation prevailed. When the Northern Parliament met for the first time in June 1920, only the forty Unionist members took their seats; neither the six Nationalists nor the six Sinn Fein members appeared and it was not until 1927 that the full complement of Nationalists began to turn up regularly at Stormont.

But right from the outset of its existence, Lord Craigavon (formerly Sir James Craig), the first Northern Ireland Prime Minister, made no bones about the way he was going to run the Six Counties. The Ulstermen had watched the terrible aftermath of the War of Independence and the executions and murders during the Civil War in the South, and had asked themselves, if the Irish Catholics were prepared to treat one another in such a brutal fashion, what would they not do to the Ulster Protestants, given the chance. The Boundary Commission which had been promised under the terms of the Anglo-Irish Treaty was soon to start its deliberations. Craigavon would have none of it. 'No surrender' had been the cry of the Ulster Protestants of the seventeenth century; 'Not an inch' became the new Ulster motto. Craigavon warned the British Government that if the Commission recommended any alteration in the border, he would resign as Prime Minister and place himself at the head of an Ulster Volunteer Force which would maintain the Protestant ascendancy in Ulster against all comers. In the face of such intransigence, the Cosgrave Free State Government caved in and accepted the Border as it existed – on a *de facto* if not a *de jure* basis – in return for certain financial considerations including the writing off of Ireland's share in the National Debt, a sum of £160 million.

Having secured the Six Counties, Craigavon was equally adamant about the nature of the community with which he was charged. He spoke of the regime as 'a Protestant Parliament for a Protestant people'. Only the Protestants had been loyal to the Crown; therefore only Protestants could be trusted to have any say in the running of the country. The constitution originally provided for proportional representation, as in the Free State, a system which ensures the minorities have a voice in the community; but Craigavon abolished it because he believed that third and fourth preferences clouded the issue and there was a danger that the voters might make a mistake and wake up one morning to find Northern Ireland subordinated to a Dublin parliament. Election was on a single seat, one vote system, but there was an additional vote based on ratable valuation in local government elections. The 'property' or 'company' vote was a system by which additional votes were allocated to occupiers of business premises above a certain valuation and of course it tended to favour the Unionists since most business premises in Ulster were in their hands. Also some of the constituency boundaries were shamelessly gerrymandered to ensure Unionist majorities even in predominantly Catholic Nationalist areas.

As a result, from the first election in 1921 until the present day, the pro-Union M.P.s have always remained around the 40 mark while the anti-Partitionists have stuck around the 10–12 mark. Also, until a few years back, the twelve M.P.s elected to Westminster were all solidly Unionist; since then such diverse elements as Gerry Fitt, Bernadette Devlin and the Rev. Ian Paisley have managed to fight their way into the House of Commons. But since the opposition in Northern Ireland has always stood for the overthrow of the constitution, the issue at every election has always been the retention or the destruction of the link with Britain, a situation which does not create a healthy, democratic parliament. And one result of this has been that in Northern Ireland, the Labour Party – which should enjoy a fairly substantial support in an area with a great many industries and a permanent unemployment problem – has never been able to emerge as an effective opposition.

# 3

It is not surprising that the first governments of the Irish Free State were a bit slow getting under way. Continued outbreaks of violence provided one of the biggest headaches. For although de Valera had authorized a cease-fire in 1923, he had no power to enforce it – the rabidly republican element in the I.R.A. merely added his name to the long list of authorities which they already refused to recognize – and it was far too much to expect a generation of men who had grown up with guns in their hands to change their tactics overnight.

During the first years of its existence the new Free State Government had its hands full coping with what might loosely be called political crimes: the settling of old scores, continued attacks by the militant wing of the I.R.A. irregulars on houses of the Anglo-Irish Ascendancy and on Cabinet ministers, outbreaks of violence at political meetings, and one extremely ugly incident in 1924. A party of unarmed soldiers on shore leave from the garrison at Cork Harbour – one of the three naval bases retained by the British under the Treaty – were machine-gunned, from a car; one soldier was killed, an officer and seventeen soldiers were wounded and there were five civilian casualties.

Events of this kind did not go unnoticed in Northern Ireland – nor did certain other 'unsavoury' features of life in the Catholic Free State. The fact that there was no provision for divorce in Ireland, even for non-Catholics, incurred the wrath of the Protestant poet W. B. Yeats, who had been made a senator, and provoked from him a splendid outburst of indignation: 'We against whom you have done this thing are not a petty people. We are one of the great stocks of Europe. We are the people of Burke; we are the people of Grattan; we are the people of Swift, the people of Emmet, the people of Parnell.' The Ulster Protestants, most of whom basically disapproved of divorce themselves, read such speeches and rejoiced in the fact that they did not have to suffer under such restrictions.

The prohibition of the sale of contraceptives was probably far less important an issue in the 1920s than it has since become, but the fact that people from the Irish Free State who wished to use contraceptives had to buy them in Belfast and smuggle them back over the border was yet another evidence of a hypocritical, priest-ridden state.

And the censorship laws probably did more damage than all the other 'un-English' features of life south of the border put together. Not that the average Ulster Protestant would dream of reading any of the banned books; if anything, he was even more puritanical in outlook than his Catholic counterpart in the Free State. But he would not admit the right of any man or body of men to decide what he might or might not read; and when the Censorship Board really got down to its task and started banning thousands of books written by a formidable list of authors which included most of the leading names in contemporary literature, including a great many leading Irish writers, Orangemen who had never opened a book in their lives were loud in their condemnation of this outrageous encroachment on the freedom of the citizens of the so-called 'Free' State.

Another source of disaffection was the Irish language. Attempts to revive the now almost defunct Irish language by making it compulsory for posts in the Civil Service and other semi-state bodies and by encouraging schools to teach other subjects through the medium of Irish, though well-intentioned, wasted a lot of money and caused a good deal of ridicule among the Ulster Protestants who claimed that the system would merely produce a race of people illiterate in two languages.

There were other bones of contention: a rash of badly-designed Irish souvenirs of bog oak and crude representations of round towers, thatched cottages and Celtic crosses, and a general mania for painting everything green were deservedly mocked by such Irish Protestants as remained on after the Treaty and by visitors from the North; the attempt to revive the ancient Tailteann Games and the annual review of the Free State Army, which marched past the Post Office trundling behind it a few pathetic items of mechanized weaponry, were not impressive; and the Eucharistic Congress in 1932, held to mark the 1,500th anniversary of St Patrick's arrival in Ireland, while perfectly natural in a Catholic country, was not exactly reassuring to its Northern neighbours. The presence, on Irish soil, of such a vast concourse of panoplied priests, prelates, cardinals and Papists of all sorts was another proof, if any were needed, that there should be no relaxation in the stern vigilance of the Ulster Protestants.

# 4

Despite the scorn that was heaped on it by de Valera's Irregular Republican supporters, by the Irish Protestants still living in Ireland and still, at that period, dominating the business life of the city of Dublin, and by the Ulster Protestants, Cosgrave's first Free State governments were hacking their way through a surprising amount of highly useful legislation. Acts were passed setting up various departments of State, regulating the Civil Service, establishing an unarmed police force – as opposed to the armed one, in Northern Ireland – and reorganizing the judicial system. They also passed legislation designed to raise the general standard of Irish agricultural produce, set up a factory to manufacture sugar from Irish beet instead of importing it from Britain, and embarked on a highly ambitious scheme for harnessing the longest river in the United Kingdom to produce electrical power. They succeeded in getting the Free State admitted to the League of Nations and the International Labour Office, and through their part in the discussions at the Imperial Conference, assisted in the transformation of the British Empire into a Commonwealth of free nations.

In a General Election in 1927 – while the Cosgrave Government was still suffering from its failure to achieve any alteration in the composition of the Six Counties at the Boundary Commission – de Valera won forty-four seats to Cosgrave's forty-seven, and led his party into the Dail, hoping that Cosgrave would not insist on them taking the Oath. Cosgrave, however, was determined to rub de Valera's nose in it, and not only did he insist on them taking the Oath but he also introduced a Bill which would make the Oath obligatory before a candidate could even be nominated for election. De Valera, faced with political extinction, then took the Oath, declaring that it wasn't really an oath, and he wasn't really taking it anyway. De Valera's arrival in Dail Eireann was greeted with a no-confidence vote and there was another General Election in which the de Valera's party got fifty-seven seats to Cosgrave's sixty-two, so that de Valera party remained in opposition for its first four years in the Dail.

De Valera used this period to very good effect; he made plans to get rid of the Oath of Allegiance and the Governor-General – the permanent representative of the Crown in Ireland – and he promised that Britain would be urged to restore the three naval bases. And, as a master-stroke, he raised the question of the Land Annuities.

The Land War, towards the close of the nineteenth century, had resulted in a series of Acts which controlled Irish rents and made it impossible for the landlords to increase rents except through the machinery of the courts. Ultimately the landlords had been bought out altogether by a public loan issued by the British Government. The Irish tenants thus became a race of peasant proprietors, and their rents were compounded into annuities which were paid half-yearly. This money went to the Irish Land Commission, which in turn paid it to the British Government and it was used to pay off holders of the stock, in most cases the original landlords. De Valera now argued that since the land in question was sovereign Irish territory, the British Government had no right to these Annuities. This argument held a formidable appeal for the Irish farmers who assumed that it meant they would not have to pay anything for their land in future. This was not de Valera's intention: he had it in mind that the Annuities – worth about £3 million a year – would continue to be paid, but into the Irish Treasury. The farmers didn't find this out until too late, and in the meantime they had given de Valera a majority of seventy-two as against Cosgrave's fifty-seven in the 1932 elections. The inability of Cosgrave's Government to control the continuing outbreaks of violence – as recently as 1927 Cosgrave's Minister for Justice was murdered outside his own house on his way to Mass – and its use of strong-arm methods in an effort to deal with the still frequent I.R.A. raids were other factors contributing to Cosgrave's defeat.

De Valera's accession to power was viewed with great anxiety in Ulster. Although in point of fact de Valera and his followers were far less priest-ridden than the Cosgrave pro-Treaty Party – men who have suffered the extreme penalty of excommunication and have survived it need never walk in quite the same fear of Mother Church again – de Valera was regarded in the North as a dark, Rasputin-like figure, the very epitome of evil, and a Spaniard to boot. It was known that he was deeply committed to the dream of a 32-county Gaelic-speaking republic and it was thought that he would stop at nothing to achieve it. The Orangemen girded their loins for battle and, in the meantime, tightened the reins on the one-third Catholic Nationalist minority in their midst, with the assistance of the three thousand armed members of the R.U.C. and the eight thousand armed B Specials.

Within a fortnight of taking over, de Valera had abolished the Oath of Allegiance; he claimed that it was not mandatory in the Treaty, that it was a relic of medievalism and that its removal was purely a domestic matter for the Irish people to decide for themselves. At the same time he announced that he was going to withhold the Land Annuities.

The British were not over-concerned about the Oath of Allegiance, but the dispute over the Land Annuities led to a long and bitter economic war between Britain and the Free State during which Britain imposed punitive tariffs on Irish imports and de Valera retaliated in the same way.

At this period of history, Ireland's *per capita* wealth was only about 20 per cent that of Britain and there is no doubt that there was a good deal of poverty in the Free State in the early 'thirties and would have been far more except for emigration. Such Ulster Protestants as ventured south of the border brought back tales of barefoot boys selling newspapers in the rain; old ladies in shawls begging at street-corners; well-fed, red-faced priests drinking large whiskies in the lounge bars of Grade A hotels; street-names and other signs in weird Gaelic hieroglyphics; badly-stocked shops selling shoddy Irish-made goods turned out in factories hastily set up and heavily protected by tariffs to replace consumer goods no longer available from Britain because of the economic war; and a general, all-pervading air of depression and decay. They were relieved to return to their own tight little Protestant community where the standard of living (for most of the Protestants anyway) was considerably higher, even if artificially maintained on a par with the British standard of living by means of a grant from what Ulstermen always refer to as 'the Imperial Parliament'. Estimates as to how much Northern Ireland costs the British Government vary considerably; I have seen various annual estimates between £78 million and £140 million.

In 1936, de Valera took advantage of the abdication of King Edward VIII to remove the Crown from the constitution except for formal diplomatic purposes and abolished the office of Governor-General. Within three short years of taking office, he had now cut most of the formal ties with Britain. The British still had control of the three naval bases and the border remained a fact which had been strengthened rather than weakened by his own accession and by his almost fanatical determination to sever all the ties with England;

otherwise, he had turned the Free State into a Republic in all but name.

His new Constitution, published in April 1937, tackled this question of the name in a manner typical of de Valera. He had always been a great man for semantics – his Treaty formula which contained the phrase 'in external association' is a magnificent example: if it meant anything at all it meant that the Free State would remain a part of the Commonwealth (in association) and yet would remain at the same time outside it (external). He now proposed that the new title of the Irish Free State should be changed to Eire (Gaelic for Ireland) and that it should be taken as referring to the whole island of Ireland, including the Six Counties in which the Constitution, for the moment, was not operative. The British Government did not regard this as fundamentally altering the position of the Free State as part of the Commonwealth, and could not accept that the adoption of the title Eire, or Ireland, involved any change in the position of Northern Ireland as an integral part of the United Kingdom.

The Constitution recognized the special position of the Catholic Church as the religion of the majority of the people in Ireland, but it did no more than that; freedom of conscience and the free profession and practice of religion were guaranteed to every citizen, subject to public order and morality. No religion could be endowed by the State and no discrimination on religious grounds would be permitted.

Throughout this period there were sporadic raids on Border posts and frequent outbreaks of violence in Belfast and Derry, usually occasioned by celebrations of the Battle of the Boyne, the Easter Week Rising, or the locking of the gates of Derry against the Jacobite army by the Apprentice Boys. In July 1935, to take just one example, eleven people were killed and five hundred injured in Ulster, and juries often refused to convict Protestants even when they were clearly guilty of incitement. The attitude of the Ulster Protestants at this period was quite literally shameless; they did not make any secret of the fact that the Catholics were discriminated against because they felt that the Catholics, whose aim – as Nationalists, not as Catholics – was the overthrow of their Protestant state, did not deserve any consideration.

The depression of the 'thirties led to a fierce unemployment problem in Ulster which at one period reached the level of three in ten. Sir Basil Brooke (later Lord Brookeborough), then Prime Minister of Northern Ireland, supported the campaign of the Ulster Protestant

League against employing Catholics at a time when jobs were scarce. In 1933 he said: 'Many in the audience employ Catholics but I have not one about my place. Catholics are out to destroy Ulster with all their might and power. They want to nullify the Protestant vote, take all they can out of Ulster and see it go to Hell.' In 1933, when the unemployment level was 28 per cent for the Six Counties work-force as a whole, it was over 40 per cent among the Catholics.

By 1938, de Valera had ended the economic war and brought the two countries, Great Britain and Eire, closer than they had ever been. The ports were handed back to the Irish on the understanding that they would never be allowed to be used by Britain's enemies, and Northern Ireland was excluded from compulsory military service as a result of pressure put on the British Government by de Valera who argued that the Catholic Nationalists – who now numbered more than one in three of the entire population – could not be expected to take kindly to the idea of being forced to fight for a regime which had placed a border between them and the remainder of their fellow countrymen. This exclusion of Ulster from conscription was bitterly resented by the Ulster Protestants, who disliked being treated in any way differently from the remainder of the United Kingdom – though in point of fact more Irishmen from the Republican South fought in the war than Ulstermen and it was one of the stock jokes of the war that in a bomber, over Berlin, at the height of one of the heaviest air raids, with flak coming up on all sides, the pilot and chief navigator, both Southern Irishmen, were arguing about politics. 'Well you've got to say one thing for Dev,' shouted the chief navigator as a shell exploded uncomfortably close to the plane, 'at least he's kept us out of this bloody war.'

## 5

De Valera's failure, in his talks with Britain, to secure any more concrete concessions on the Partition question than had been achieved by the earlier Cosgrave governments, led to an outbreak of I.R.A. outrages in Britain.

The outrages took the form of time-bombs left in letter-boxes, warehouses, railway-station left-luggage departments and cinemas in England. Plans to disrupt English life by blowing up public utilities like gas and electricity power stations fell through largely due to the inefficiency and inexperience of the terrorists, many of them no more than boys. The amount of damage to life and property was not excessive (though there was one nasty explosion in Coventry which killed five people, wounded more than fifty and did thousands of pounds worth of damage), but the publicity which these exploits received in the British – and Northern Ireland – Press did the Irish image an incalculable amount of harm.

Ireland's neutrality in the war which broke out the following September also did considerable damage to the Irish image, despite the large numbers of Irishmen who joined the forces. And yet neutrality was a natural and obvious outcome of the separatist policy Ireland had been pursuing all along, and it also served as a clear and unequivocal demonstration to the world at large that the Southern Irish really were in complete control of their own affairs at last. In any event, it would not have been possible to go into the war on the British side without, at the very least, fresh outbreaks of violence or, at worst, another civil war. Whether, having demonstrated her independence to the world, and when the full horror of the Nazi regime came to be revealed, it might not then have been wiser to throw in her lot with Britain and America is another matter; but the naval bases, the loss of which had seriously weakened British defences during the Battle of the Atlantic, grew less important as time passed and the majority of the Irish people never wavered in their support of the policy of neutrality.

Nevertheless, there were features of life in neutral Ireland during 'the emergency' – in an effort to pretend to themselves that there wasn't really a war on, the Irish always referred to the war as 'the emergency' – which must have been pretty galling to the Ulster Protestants and members of the British Armed Forces stationed in Ulster. The bright lights of Dublin in blacked-out Europe, the relative abundance of food, the strict newspaper censorship which tried to conceal the fact that there were Irishmen fighting in Britain's war, and above all Mr de Valera's fastidious observance of the correct rules of diplomatic procedure in relation to the German and Japanese legations in Dublin, even to the extent of calling on the Germans to express his condolence at the news of Hitler's death – all were irritants not likely to appease Northern Ireland opinion. When Belfast was blitzed, fire brigades from the south were rushed across the border to help fight the flames. 'After all, they are our own people,' Mr de Valera said, a point of view which would not be shared by two-thirds of the people he had sent the fire brigades to assist; for a loyal Ulster Protestant would as soon see his house burned down as have the flames put out by Fenian Catholic firehoses.

The period of austerity which followed the return to peace in Britain was reflected in Ireland – as indeed are all fluctuations in the British economy – and delayed de Valera's plans for the continuing industrialization of Ireland. At a general election in 1948 he was returned without a clear, overall majority, and a shaky coalition of the other parties under a Dublin lawyer called John Costello formed a Government.

De Valera had always gone to great pains to avoid declaring the country an independent republic, partly because he felt that such a declaration would render even more permanent the division between North and South, and partly because he wanted to hold on to whatever slight advantages might be squeezed out of the very loose connection with the Commonwealth which had been maintained. Now, without any warning, Costello – a member of the pro-Treaty Party which had always stood for the link with the Commonwealth – suddenly announced that he was going to break the final tie with Britain and declare the twenty-six counties a Republic. It is difficult to understand what on earth possessed him to reach this decision. Perhaps he wanted to go down in history as the man who finally declared Ireland (or a part of it) a Republic; certainly he is not likely to go down in history on any other score. Some say he did it in a fit of pique, because he had been snubbed at a dinner in Canada by Field-Marshal Earl Alexander of Tunis, a die-hard Ulster Protestant from County Tyrone who had no time for any Catholic Irish Republican, even if he happened to be Prime Minister.

The declaration of the Republic, marked by a military parade through the streets of Dublin and fireworks in the Phoenix Park, made no dramatic change in the pattern of Irish life. Citizens of the Republic could still live and work and vote in the United Kingdom, and British citizens could do the same in the Republic. Questions relating to Ireland continued to be dealt with by the Commonwealth Office, and Irish travellers arriving at British ports found that they were still treated as British subjects.

On the other hand, the declaration of the Republic was greeted in Westminster – and by a Labour government, which was surprising because the Labour Party had always previously favoured Irish unity – with the Ireland Act, 1949, a new and explicit guarantee to the

North which declared that 'Northern Ireland remains a part of His Majesty's Dominions and of the United Kingdom and it is hereby affirmed that in no event will Northern Ireland or any part thereof cease to be a part of His Majesty's Dominions without the consent of the Parliament of Northern Ireland'.

'Not an Inch' had been enshrined in the Statute Book at Westminster.

CHAPTER SIXTEEN

# Too Little—and Too Late

## 1

When I was doing the research for *The Irish Answer*, I spent some time in Ireland talking to Captain Terence O'Neill, who was then premier, talking to M.P.s, to taxi-drivers, to barmen, to members of the R.U.C., to journalists, to shopkeepers and farm labourers and factory workers, and all sorts of people; and the thing that struck me most forcibly was the fact that most of the Ulster Protestants I talked to were utterly and openly shameless in their distrust and dislike of Catholics. A Belfast journalist who has lived and worked in London told me that when he went back to Ulster he had to be very careful not to bring his free-and-easy London ways with him. He could not, for example, risk upsetting his parents by having Catholic friends stay in his house. 'They're broadminded enough to their own way of thinking,' he said; 'they understand that I'm obliged to meet Catholics in the way of business once in a while, and even have them back to the house sometimes. But they wouldn't want them sleeping under one roof with me.'

In practice, except in intellectual and university circles, until recently, Catholics and Protestants never met much socially and if 'one of the other sort' was expected at a Protestant gathering, the remainder of the guests were discreetly warned in advance, partly to avoid the risk of any inadvertent offence but also partly to allow the other guests to stand down, in case they felt sufficiently strongly about it. I found it difficult to persuade the Ulstermen that there was anything odd or unusual about this. If you point out that it is possible to work alongside a man in London for five years without ever discovering his religion, he will politely point out that it is quite different in England, 'because the constitution is in no danger from the Roman Catholics over there.' If you argue that there is no discrimination against Protestants in the Republic he will say: 'What's the need for discrimination down there when the R.C.s have control of everything anyway.' And if you raise the question of discrimination against Catholics in handing out jobs, you will find the Ulster employers just as unabashed about this as they are about the gerrymandering of the constituencies. 'Why shouldn't we look after our own kind?' one businessman said to me, arguing with irrefutable logic that if his own experience had taught him that Catholics are not to be trusted, he couldn't see why he should not be entitled to choose his own employees from among people he feels that he *can* trust. Because discrimination has always been accepted as a way of life since the formation of the state, it is very difficult to convince an Ulsterman that Protestants would not be similarly treated if they ever went into a United Ireland under a Republican government. Nor can they appreciate the fact that the militant Ulster Catholic Nationalists fighting this discrimination in what they genuinely believe to be a part of their own country held under alien rule by force of arms are no more typical of Catholic thought in the Republic than they themselves are typical of Protestant thought in Britain.

The consolidation of Unionism by force – with the connivance of the armed R.U.C. and the B Specials, which were formed expressly to protect Protestantism from 'the enemy within' and were not a police force in the normal sense – was fully supported by Britain until the Second World War. Imperial opinion at this period, when Britain still controlled a vast empire, was not very kindly disposed towards Southern Ireland, and in 1922, 1931, 1933 and 1935, British troops were used to assist the R.U.C. in putting down outbreaks of sectarian rioting in Ulster.

The Special Powers Act was passed in 1922 as a temporary measure. It was made permanent in 1933 and sections of it have been invoked from time to time whenever the Stormont Government felt the need. Under the Act, the civil authority has power to 'take such steps and issue such orders as may be necessary for the preserving of peace and maintaining order', and in effect permits the authorities to arrest suspects without warrant, breaking into their homes at dead of night to do so: deny claims to trial by jury; imprison suspects without charge or trial; prevent access of relatives or legal advisers; prohibit the holding of an inquest after a prisoner's death; prohibit the circulation of any newspaper; and authorize the total or partial stopping up or diversion of any road by means of barricades and road blocks. Under the Act, crimes involving explosives are punishable by death.

Over the years, the power behind the Unionist Party has been the Orange Order. Unionist M.P.s do not have to be members of the Orange Order, but it helps; in fact it would be very difficult to be accepted as a Unionist Party candidate without the backing of an Orange lodge. The Orange Order was as strong in 1965 when I was in Ulster as it was in 1922, and, what is even more significant, had more young people than ever in its ranks. 'I'll give you an example,' a Unionist M.P. said to me at Stormont. 'Take my son. He's got long hair on him, like one of the Rolling Stones. Nothing I can do will make him get it cut. He's a rebel, d'you see? But he's a member of the Orange Order for all that.' Since 1965, I think the picture has changed a bit, and a lot of the young people in Northern Ireland, as everywhere else, are against the establishment in all its manifestations, but the Orange Order is still a very powerful voice in the province.

During the depression of the 1930s, the organization of working-class militancy which would have destroyed the Unionist establishment (and could still, as Bernadette Devlin and Ian Paisley have both realized) was averted by what amounted to the destruction of the Trade Union movement in Ulster. In 1924 the Stormont Government made it illegal for trade unions to finance political organizations, and Westminster legislation on trade unions has never been accepted by Stormont.

After the war the North, like the Republic, went through a period of economic depression. However, the benefits of the socialist welfare state were accepted by the Conservative Unionists who controlled Stormont and became an important plank in the Unionist propaganda in favour of retaining the link with Britain; 'the benefits' probably also explain why there was very little Catholic emigration from Northern Ireland to the Republic after the war, despite the continued refusal of the Ulster Protestants to give the Catholics anything like a fair deal.

Just how much discrimination was there against the Catholics in, say, the middle or late sixties? In an issue of an Irish news magazine *Nusight*, dated September 1969, and devoted to the troubles in the North, there is an article listing examples of discrimination. In the Civil Service Professional and Technical Grades, the Catholics, who by this time amounted to more than 35 per cent of the population, only accounted for 6 per cent of the staff; at administrative levels the proportion was 7 per cent and on Public Boards Catholics held 15 per cent of the seats.

In the case of local authorities, discrimination was more marked. In Tyrone, where the population is largely Catholic, the County Hall had a staff of one hundred of whom only four were Catholics. In an area where housing has always been scarce, it was never any secret that Catholics were blatantly discriminated against. Dungannon, Co. Tyrone, is 50 per cent Catholic. The post-war allocation of new houses was 45 for Catholics and 207 for Protestants.

The gerrymandering of constituencies to enable Unionists to pick up a disproportionate number of votes in predominantly Catholic districts was another form of discrimination. In the County of Armagh for example, which is about 50 per cent Catholic, the Unionists held all three Stormont seats in 1969.

## 2

Violence again threatened the regime in 1954 when the I.R.A. began another series of armed raids. In December 1956, the I.R.A. issued a formal declaration of war on the Stormont regime, calling for the unity of Protestants and Catholics to remove British political control in the North, and British economic control in the South. As a result of armed attacks on police, military installations and other targets, nineteen people were killed between 1956 and 1961, and about two hundred men were interned in the North and another 100 in the South where the I.R.A. has been an illegal organization since the 1920s. The campaign formally ended in February 1962 with an announcement from the I.R.A. that arms had been dumped.

By this time both Northern and Southern Ireland were undergoing a change in their economic policies. They had both decided to go for tourism and industrial expansion by attracting foreign capital and know-how, and in the South this had the effect of changing the Republic's attitude to Britain; political energy was now being more and more directed to attracting British capital and British tourists, and less and less to beefing about the border. It is possible that the general improvement in the standard of living and the rise in employment may also have been partly responsible for the I.R.A.'s suspension of its activities in 1962; for its principal source of recruitment had always been from among the unemployed urban youths who were now finding jobs in the new factories.

Lord Brookeborough's retirement from the post of Prime Minister in 1963, after twenty consecutive years in office, was another step towards what then appeared to promise a lasting peace.

When Captain Terence O'Neill – a descendant of the O'Neills of Tyrone – succeeded Lord Brookeborough, it began to look as if a new era of peace and co-operation was at hand. O'Neill, in common with the younger generation of politicians then becoming prominent in the Republic, was too young to remember the Troubles, and since a great deal of his life had been spent at school in England, abroad and in the Army, he had a broader, more enlightened outlook than the average Ulster politician. He introduced an entirely new form of Unionism supported by the prosperous middle class, which stressed economic prosperity more strongly than the purely constitutional issue; he hoped to create a healthy, democratic state in which the Catholics would want to play a normal part and support the Constitution for economic reasons, because, as he told a meeting of Ulster associations, 'there was never a better time for an Ulsterman to be alive'.

O'Neill's attitude to the Republic represented an even more radical break with the past. Until then, the Stormont Parliament had never had any official dealings with the Parliament in Dublin and a meeting between the two Prime Ministers would have been unthinkable; Brookeborough openly boasted that he had never been south of the border. In 1965, O'Neill – without even consulting Stormont – invited Sean Lemass (who had been a rebel in the Post Office in Dublin during the 1916 Rising, and was now Irish Prime Minister) to Stormont; their meeting was followed by another in Dublin, some time later. O'Neill never saw the slightest prospect of abolishing the border, but he felt that the economic development of the country was being hampered by keeping it as a major issue in Ulster politics. The Nationalist Party, led by Eddie McAteer, agreed in 1965 to accept the title of official Opposition at Stormont.

On the religious front, too, things were looking brighter. The indignation among Northern Protestants at the Noel Browne affair was beginning to be forgotten. This was an attempt by Dr Noel Browne, Minister for Health in Costello's Coalition Government, to bring in a comprehensive mother-and-child welfare scheme for the Republic in 1951, which met with the disapproval of the bishops and was promptly squashed. Dr David Thornley, lecturer in Political Science at Trinity College, Dublin, described it as 'perhaps the last of the head-on confrontations between a politician and the Church . . .

the Church offering an absolute *non-fiat* to a political proposal; a layman remaining obdurate and suffering dismissal from power; *The Irish Times* speaking up for secular liberalism and the Ulster Unionists drawing the moral that Carson was right.'

Now Pope John XXIII – a humble, simple man who did and said irresistibly endearing things – was on the throne at St Peter's and a powerful ecumenical movement was sweeping through the corridors of the Vatican and the World Council of Churches. As a friendly gesture towards the Catholics, O'Neill visited many Catholic organizations and institutions. But, as Richard Rose points out in *Governing Without Consensus*, 'at no time did the Prime Minister encourage the appointment of Catholics to prominent positions in the regime, let alone within the Unionist Party. While he was able to increase Catholic representation on statutory committees and Boards, a survey in 1966 found that out of 102 members, nine were Catholics.'

O'Neill's policies were favourably received by the well-to-do middle class, Catholic and Protestant, but they contained potential dangers. To some, these new policies offered a glimmer of hope where formerly there had been none; and an oppressed man who sees a glimmer of hope is far more likely to fight for his rights than one who sees none at all. To others they seemed like a threat: economic integration of the Catholic 35 per cent of the community would mean an end to discrimination, which would make it far harder for Protestants to get the few jobs and houses that were going and would probably mean that the small shopkeepers and factory owners would have to pay Catholics a fair wage.

The Rev. Ian Paisley, of the Free Presbyterian Church in Ulster, became the chief spokesman for the two groups most bitterly opposed to O'Neill's new liberal Unionism: the Protestant working-class youth and the petty bourgeoisie. The young Protestants feared Catholic integration because there were still not enough jobs to go round; if they had jobs it was simply because their Catholic counterparts were out of work and they naturally wanted that situation to continue. The small shopkeepers and factory owners survived by keeping their wage bills low, which they could do because of the high Catholic rate of unemployment; they also got preferential building grants, rate reductions, government contracts and so on from Unionist councils, and these perquisites now seemed threatened by O'Neill's projected reforms.

Paisley used the traditional Orange methods to protest against the growing tolerance of Romish trends and the new friendly relations with the Republicans in the South – organizing marches, protests, services and demonstrations. He stood for a return to the ancient intransigence towards the South and the continued repression of Catholics in the North. In 1966, he was arrested and convicted of unlawful assembly. When he and two of his fellow clergymen refused to be bound over to keep the peace, they went to jail for three months.

To quote Richard Rose again: 'During this summer, three people were killed in Belfast in incidents to intimidate Catholics. Terence O'Neill denounced Paisley and his followers for using the tactics of a Fascist movement. The issue raised was simple: "Who is to rule in Northern Ireland?" Dr Paisley answered the question by declaring, "My voice will not be silenced by all the police at the command of the Prime Minister." Apropos the efforts of the Prime Minister to build bridges to the Catholic community, he commented, ". . . a traitor and a bridge are very much alike, for they both go over to the other side".'

Paisley's quarrel with the O'Neill administration meant that militant Ulster Protestantism was now ranged against the Unionist Government as well as against Rome and the Republicans in the South. It was the first crack in the monolithic Unionist Protestant alignment since the foundation of the State.

## 3

The situation was further complicated at this period by the emergence of a civil rights movement in Northern Ireland. The protest that sparked off the first civil rights demonstrations was a successful squatting protest organized by Austin Currie, Nationalist M.P. for County Tyrone. He had been trying to get a council house at Caledon, Co. Tyrone, for a Catholic family in bad need of accommodation; the local council were planning to let it instead to an unmarried nineteen-year-old Protestant secretary of a Unionist politician. The Stormont Unionists claimed that they could not intervene in what was purely a local matter. It was a perfect case to fight. Currie organized a 'squat-in' at the house in June 1968, and the publicity which the affair received in the press and on television led to a civil rights march at Dungannon in August. It was peaceful, and the police did not attempt to intervene. This in turn led to the planning of another, bigger march in October 1968, in Derry, the second largest city in Northern

Ireland and the one most blatantly gerrymandered to ensure that the predominantly Catholic population was quite inadequately represented both at Stormont and on the local Corporation and Council.

William Craig, Minister of Home Affairs in O'Neill's Cabinet, banned the march. The Civil Rights Association decided to go ahead with their protest anyway. When the 3,000 unarmed marchers reached the 'Loyalist' area of Derry, they found the road blocked by R.U.C. men armed with batons and shields and supported by water cannons. The marchers appealed to be allowed through the police lines to continue their march. Without warning, the police baton-charged the marchers and turned the water cannons on them. An official inquiry afterwards admitted that the police had 'used their batons indiscriminately' and with 'needless violence'. Ninety-six people, including two Labour M.P.s, received injuries which required hospital treatment.

Over the following weeks, several further civil rights demonstrations took place, and provoked the Paisleyites into more violent and outspoken militancy. Right from the outset, the newspaper and television coverage of the civil rights marches in Ulster overwhelmingly favoured the cause of the marchers, and this perhaps made the militant Protestants feel that their privileged position in regard to houses, jobs and votes was in jeopardy. In Armagh, in November 1968, Dr Paisley led 15,000 supporters in a day-and-night vigil to prevent about 6,000 civil rights marchers from passing along a route approved by the police. Richard Rose adds: 'Searches of Protestant counter-demonstrators at the scene found two revolvers and 220 weapons such as scythes and cudgels studded with nails. No weapons were found on the civil rights marchers. Paisley was later sentenced to a three-month prison term in consequence of the Armagh disorder.'

The Stormont Parliament was now subjected to a bit of pressure from Westminster to introduce reforms which would satisfy some of the demands of the civil rights protesters. At a meeting between Harold Wilson, then Prime Minister, and Terence O'Neill with two members of his Cabinet, Wilson expressed embarrassment at the frequent use of the Special Powers Act, which was in contravention of the Human Rights Convention that Britain had signed. The system of local government voting, the whole question of the allocation of houses and the position of Derry were also discussed at this meeting, which was followed by the announcement from Stormont of the first batch of reforms.

Derry was given priority with a promise of 1,200 new jobs and 960 new houses – by 1981. The Civil Rights Association didn't regard this as much cop, but it was altogether too much for the rabid Unionist backbenchers who declared that the Government had no mandate for introducing such reforms and called for a General Election. Further reforms announced later in November included the abolition of the 'company' vote in local government elections, the appointment of an Ombudsman at some future date to look into minority grievances, and the setting up of a Commission to administer Derry in place of the Derry Corporation and County Council.

A split within the Unionist Party at Stormont now seemed inevitable. A few days after these reforms were announced, William Craig, Minister of Home Affairs, made a militant speech which included the sentence: 'We must face reality: where you have a Catholic majority you have a lower standard of democracy.'

O'Neill went on television and appealed for an end to the violence, hinting that if the Ulster people did not face up to their own problems, the Westminster Parliament might well decide to act over their heads. Craig replied by declaring that Northern Ireland would resist any attempts at British intervention and the following day was dismissed from office. O'Neill faced his own Parliamentary Party and won a resounding vote of confidence, but it was a very temporary respite.

The civil rights demonstrators regarded the O'Neill concessions quite simply as 'too little . . . and too late', but this reaction to the fact that two months of demonstrations had won more concessions for the Catholic Nationalists than they had been able to achieve in forty-one years' attendance or non-attendance in opposition at Stormont merely proved to the diehard Ulster Unionists that they were a collection of ingrates who did not merit any further consideration. In this, the Unionists were missing a vital point. If a minority feels that its case has no chance whatever of a sympathetic hearing, it will accept its fate and soldier on in silence. If, however, there are signs that demonstrations will result in reforms, the minority will not be content until all its rights are ensured. So, to this extent, Ulster's current troubles are partly due to O'Neill's new liberal Unionism which demonstrated to the oppressed 35 per cent of the community that protest could result in reforms which would ameliorate their lot.

Most of the civil rights demonstrators, relatively satisfied with the way things were going, decided to call a truce over Christmas 1968, but one group of young socialists, known as the People's Democracy, was determined to break the truce by holding a protest march from Belfast to Derry on 1 January 1969. This demonstration was harassed shortly after it left Belfast. The R.U.C. made no attempt to protect what was a perfectly legitimate march from attacks by militant Protestants who intercepted it at various points along the route. The worst incidents occurred at Burntollet Bridge, outside Derry, where marchers, deserted by their police 'escort', were set upon by a mob of militant Protestants armed with stones and cudgels. Nobody was killed but many were injured, including a number of girls, ten of whom were driven into the River Faughan and pelted with stones. When the marchers arrived in Derry they were again attacked by Protestants lying in wait for them.

During the week-end that followed, R.U.C. men invaded the Catholic Bogside area of Derry, batoning men, women and children in the streets and even in their homes. Again there was a Commission of Inquiry which coldly reported that 'a number of policemen were guilty of misconduct which involved assault and battery, malicious damage to property in streets in the Catholic Bogside area, giving reasonable cause for apprehension of personal injury among the other innocent inhabitants and the use of provocative sectarian and political slogans (e.g. "Come out you Fenian bastards and we'll give you one for the Pope").'

In despair, O'Neill called a General Election. The Unionist Party was now irrevocably split and in his own constituency of Bannside he was re-elected on a minority vote: he took only 47 per cent of the poll, against 39 per cent for the Rev. Ian Paisley and 14 per cent for Michael Farrell, one of the People's Democracy leaders. Bernadette Devlin, an undergraduate at Queen's University and another prominent member of the People's Democracy movement, was elected to one of the Westminster seats at a by-election in mid-Ulster and her militant maiden speech in the House of Commons made headlines all over the world. When in April an electricity plant at Castlereagh was blown up and the provisions of the Special Powers Act were reintroduced, it became clear that O'Neill no longer was able to maintain order in the province, and on 28 April he resigned as Prime Minister and leader of the Unionist Party, and was succeeded by Major James Chichester-Clark.

# 4

The next potential flash-point was the annual march of the Derry Apprentice Boys on 12 August, and the Catholics feared another Protestant invasion of the Bogside with the connivance of the R.U.C. To prevent a recurrence of the events of January, the residents of the Bogside began to erect barricades and manufacture petrol bombs from milk bottles and petrol drained from parked cars, and when the R.U.C. approached the area, bombarded them with stones and petrol bombs. The R.U.C. replied with C.S. gas.

A 'Free Derry' was proclaimed and various flags including the green, white and orange tricolour (banned in Northern Ireland since 1921), the Plough and the Stars of James Connolly's Workers' Republic, and the Stars and Stripes of America flew from the tallest buildings in the area. Bernadette Devlin was later singled out and sentenced to gaol for her part in the Bogside Rising.

In Derry it was possible for the Catholics to hold out against the R.U.C. because they were concentrated in one area; in Belfast the Catholic ghetto area of the Falls Road and the poor Protestant quarter of the Shankill Road run parallel to one another, with a narrow 'no-man's-land' between them. Catholics in Belfast now began to build barricades to protect themselves against the reprisals they knew would follow, even commandeering double-decked buses for the purpose. By Thursday, 14 August, street fighting had broken out and before it could be contained, six people were killed and eighty-seven injured in the shooting.

These incidents were followed by the arrival of the first reinforcement of British troops in the province (in addition, of course, to the token Ulster standing garrison of 2,500), who set up a Berlin Wall type 'peace line' of corrugated iron and barbed wire between the Protestant and Catholic areas in Belfast and patrolled it, carrying automatic weapons. Initially the British soldiers were welcomed by the Catholics, particularly in Derry, but the British public, knowing little and caring less about affairs in Ireland, were increasingly puzzled at pictures in their newspapers and on their television screens more reminiscent of Budapest or Prague than a city in the U.K. less than one hour's flying time from London.

After Major Chichester-Clark had hurriedly visited the Prime Minister and the Home Secretary, Mr James Callaghan, in London, a further series of reforms were announced including a revision of the system of franchise, anti-discrimination legislation in public employment, and a central housing authority to be responsible for the allocation of houses; at the same time it was announced that the British Army would now be responsible for security in Ulster. Two committees, one under Lord Hunt and the other headed by Lord Cameron, deliberated the problem. Hunt's committee proposed that the R.U.C. should be disarmed and the B Specials disbanded and replaced by a new defence force (Ulster Defence Regiment – U.D.R.) with a proportion of Catholics in its ranks, responsible to the British Ministry of Defence, while Lord Cameron's commission blamed the regime for the riots and reached the conclusion that the civil rights grievances had a substantial foundation in fact.

Now that the grievances of the civil rights demonstrators seemed about to be redressed, the British people confidently expected that Ulster's troubles would be at an end. They assumed that the Stormont Government could be trusted to put the reforms into effect as rapidly as possible. The Catholics in Ulster knew better; not only could the Stormont Parliament not be trusted to put the reforms into effect, but if they attempted to, they would meet with immediate and bitter opposition from the militant Ulster Protestants. When the disbanding of the B Specials was announced in October 1969, there was rioting in the Protestant Shankill Road area in which Protestant gunfire wounded sixteen of the soldiers of the Queen, sent there to protect the regime the Ulster Protestants were so fanatically determined to maintain.

The Paisleyite movement continued to grow in strength and in popularity. In a by-election in April 1970, Paisley won the seat at Stormont formerly held by Captain Terence O'Neill. Two months later he was elected to the House of Commons, unseating a Unionist relative of O'Neill's. The disbanded B Specials were encouraged to form amateur shooting clubs so that they could keep their marksmanship up to scratch in case they were ever needed.

In order to protect themselves from attacks by Protestants and the Protestant police, the Catholic Nationalists in Ulster began to equip themselves with arms supplied by the I.R.A. and, presumably, by well-wishers in the Republic. There had recently been yet another split in the ranks of the I.R.A.: one section, the so-called 'official' I.R.A., was against armed intervention in Ulster at this stage; the other section, known as the I.R.A. 'Provisionals', was in favour of this and had already started to send snipers and explosives experts into Northern Ireland. In these circumstances it was inevitable that the friendly terms which had existed between the Catholic Nationalists and the British troops could not be maintained, and the first open battle between Catholics and British troops occurred in April 1970, during riots in the Ballymurphy area. It was at this stage that Lieutenant-General Sir Ian Freeland, G.O.C. in Northern Ireland, announced a new 'get tough' policy, and threatened to shoot anyone seen throwing petrol bombs.

In a raid on the Catholic Falls Road area, a house-to-house search unearthed a formidable armoury of weapons – fifty pistols, twenty-six rifles, five machine guns and 25,000 rounds of ammunition – and continued Army activity in the area led to incidents in which the troops were stoned, and replied with tear gas. When the real shooting started, the Army imposed a curfew and, as the months passed, the troubles escalated into those scenes which became all too familiar on our television screens, night after night after night: British armoured cars and personnel carriers prowling around the seedy back streets; soldiers and police in riot gear with shields and batons and C.S. gas guns; gangs of Belfast and Derry citizens, many of them no more than schoolboys, hurling stones and petrol bombs at the troops; homes and pubs and shops and factories in flames.

It would be tedious to give a detailed, week-by-week account of all the riots and pitched battles and burnings and stonings and murders which have occurred since the British troops were moved in to keep the peace. But perhaps this account of what happened in one microcosm of the area, a district in Belfast known as Ardoyne and always referred to on British television and in British newspapers as 'the Ardoyne', will serve to remind readers – if they need any reminder – of the horrors of sectarian urban warfare. It is taken from an article by Michael McKeown, Belfast correspondent of the Irish review, *Hibernia*, published in January 1972:

> Two things distinguish Ardoyne from the other areas of violence. It is more than a Catholic ghetto. It is an enclave, and within that enclave the level of death and destruction has been of an order unequalled in any other area of comparable size . . . The perimeter is marked by elevated watch towers, barbed-wire barricades, street ramps and the eight-foot-high corrugated fencing, euphemistically called a 'Peace Line' which seals off the district from the Protestant areas on the western side of the Crumlin Road.

The violence began in mid-August 1969, when a combined R.U.C./Protestant invasion of the southern area of Ardoyne resulted in two dead and forty houses destroyed, and culminated in August 1971 when on the northern side of the district one hundred and eighty houses were destroyed when in their evacuation Protestant residents fired their own houses and in the ensuing conflagration the best part of three streets were destroyed.

The killing which started in August 1969 has not stopped yet. Catholics and Protestants, British Army and R.U.C., I.R.A. and non-combatants: all have died within this one square mile of death and horror. For some it has been the hazard of the job, such as the six soldiers cut down by snipers or the four R.U.C. men or the two I.R.A. captains, McAdorey and McDade. For most, however, it has just been the hazard of living in Ardoyne at this point in time. Joe Parker was dancing in a local social hall with his sister when he was shot dead by a soldier. His sister had been widowed at the beginning of the year when her husband Barney Watt had been shot dead in a riot situation by an Army rifleman . . . Sammy McLarnon was shot dead as he sat in his own kitchen by shells fired from an R.U.C. Shorland armoured car. Margaret McCorry was killed as she was doing a message, by bullets fired by an I.R.A. unit attempting to ambush a British Army patrol. In all, twenty-three people have been killed in Ardoyne in the past two years – a frightening statistic for a district with an adult population of just over six thousand people.

## 5

In 1971, there were disturbing signs of the trouble escalating over the border and involving the Republic. Millions of words were written in the newspapers and spoken on television about the situation. *The Sunday Times* and *The Observer* devoted article after article to the Ulster question and usually came out heavily on the side of the civil rights demonstrators and against Stormont and the British troops; the Tory imperialist press tended to jump to conclusions and use emotive terms like 'terrorist' long before it was firmly established who was responsible for the outrage in question. Bernadette Devlin made it clear that what she was interested in was an international socialist workers' republic and that she cared as little for the Lynch administration and the Catholic hierarchy as she did for the Stormont Government or Westminster.

Jack Lynch, the Prime Minister of the Republic, found himself in an impossible position. The whole economy of Southern Ireland is to a large extent dependent on British tourism, exports to Britain, and British investments in Ireland, so he could not altogether ignore British pressure to get tougher with known members of the I.R.A. who were carrying out raids in Northern Ireland and then escaping to safety over the border where they often openly gave press and T.V. conferences; equally, he was not sufficiently strong within his own party to ignore those members of it who were patently in favour of intervention, so he had to content himself with intermittent threatening and soothing noises aimed in the direction of Westminster. He did call several times for the abolition of the Stormont regime, which the British Parliament could easily dissolve or suspend under the terms of the Government of Ireland Act.

Throughout the years, things went from bad to worse. There were even clashes between the rival factions of the I.R.A., and when in March, Lord Carrington, the British Defence Secretary and the British Army Chief of Staff, flew to Belfast to explain a new British Army Security policy to Stormont, Major Chichester-Clark in turn resigned and was succeeded by Mr Brian Faulkner.

A British naval launch was blown up in Cork, explosions wrecked the homes of two senior R.U.C. men in Belfast, and some indication of the growing concern south of the border for the Nationalists in the North could be gained from the fact that ten thousand people joined a march of the I.R.A. 'Provisionals' to Wolfe Tone's grave at Bodenstown, near Dublin. Although the I.R.A. is an illegal organization in the Republic, its supporters openly collected funds for it in the Dublin streets and were not prevented from doing so by the police.

In a series of dawn raids on alleged I.R.A. members in Northern Ireland in July 1971, forty-eight were taken into custody. In August, James Callaghan called for immediate tripartite talks between the London, Dublin and Stormont Governments with a view to setting up a Council of Ireland. Lynch appealed to the British Government to ban the Apprentice Boys March in Derry, and more troops arrived in the North, bringing the total up to 11,900.

On 7 August a van driver was shot dead when his van backfired, and at dawn two days later, three hundred men were arrested by the Army who broke into their homes, with their faces blackened, and hauled them out of their beds and into custody. Faulkner announced the introduction of internment without trial under the provisions of the Special Powers Act. In the violent protests that followed, twenty-three people were killed and 6,000 refugees crossed the border where army camps were hurriedly converted to house them.

The nine Stormont Opposition M.P.s – who had formed themselves into a united Opposition under the title of the Social Democratic and Labour Party – announced a campaign of civil disobedience, including the non-payment of rents and rates, and refused to be party to any official discussions of the problem until all the internees were released.

The I.R.A. 'Provisionals' and the 'official' I.R.A. replied to internment without trial by stepping up their activities in the North and a new horror was introduced when bombs began to be planted in public buildings and offices during the day. On 25 August one man was killed and thirty-five injured when a bomb exploded in the offices of the Electricity Board of Northern Ireland in Belfast. A few days later thirty-nine people were injured when four bombs exploded in the city centre of Belfast at noon. The 'official' I.R.A. had by now resumed hostilities in Northern Ireland.

Jack Lynch, the Prime Minister of the Republic, had talks with Mr Heath at Chequers; Mr Wilson, the Labour leader, put up his own twelve-point peace plan for a settlement to the crisis which included an all-Ireland council, and towards the end of the month there were tripartite talks between Lynch, Faulkner and Heath at Chequers which seemed to achieve very little. In Belfast a bomb exploded in a public house killing two people and injuring twenty-five, and young girls were tied to lamp-posts and tarred and feathered because they were known to be 'courting' British soldiers.

Another increase in the armed forces came in October when three battalions – about 1,500 men – were added to the 11,900 already billeted in Ulster. A large cargo of arms, allegedly for the I.R.A. 'Provisionals', was intercepted in Amsterdam and a few days later six suitcases of arms and ammunition were found in a cabin on board the *Q.E.2* when she arrived in Cobh, near Cork. Earlier in the year there had been a spectacular trial in Dublin of three men – two of them former Government ministers – who were accused, but found not guilty, of implication in an attempt to run guns into Ireland for use in the North. By November the death toll for the year had reached 133, and the total of arrests since internment was introduced stood at 882. The Compton Inquiry into allegations of torture and brutality against the interned men reported that a number of the detainees had been 'ill-treated' but not actually tortured. Mr William Craig had formed his hard-line, ultra-Protestant supporters into a Vanguard movement, dominated by militant Orangemen and dedicated to maintaining the Constitution and the link with the United Kingdom, and was making threatening noises which sounded very close to those made by Carson when he was opposing Home Rule back in 1913. There was talk of appeals to the United Nations and the Council of Europe, further meetings between Lynch and Heath, and a bomb explosion in a crowded Belfast pub which killed fifteen people. A Unionist senator, John Barnhill, was shot dead and his house blown up; the 'Official' I.R.A. claimed the credit, if that is the word, for this incident. By the end of the year, the total of British troops killed in the area had reached forty-three.

The much discussed open-ended television debate, which the Government tried to ban for fear it would inflame passions further, turned out to be a very damp squib indeed; 4,700 rounds of ammunition were discharged in a cross-border clash between British forces and the I.R.A.; and on 'Bloody Sunday', 30 January 1972, thirteen people were shot dead by paratroopers during a banned civil rights march in Derry. In reprisal, there was a bomb explosion in the paratroopers' headquarters at Aldershot which killed a priest, a gardener and five women cleaners. It was clear that this couldn't go on. Wilson had already produced his own plan for solving the Ulster question; now Heath began to talk about a political 'initiative' which his cabinet was preparing. While Heath worked out the details of this 'initiative', there were more random explosions in the streets of Belfast and other Ulster cities, and more innocent people were killed.

Mr William Craig called for dossiers on 'enemies of Ulster' who would be 'liquidated' if the politicians failed. Whatever he may have meant by that phrase it could only be taken as an encouragement or an incitement to his militant Orange supporters to go out and murder Catholics.

Any further hesitation was increasingly dangerous, and on Wednesday, 22 March, Mr Heath revealed the details of his 'initiative' to Mr Brian Faulkner, the Northern Ireland Premier. From the fact that the talks went on all day and late into the evening – and on a day when Mr Heath should have been at the House for the debate on the Budget – it was clear that things were not going too smoothly. That night, Faulkner returned to Belfast and was back in London a day later to tell Mr Heath that if his proposals were implemented it would mean the resignation of the Northern Ireland Government.

Mr Heath's initiative had included three points: periodic plebiscites on the border issue, an immediate start on phasing out internment without trial, and the transfer of all responsibility for law and order to Westminster. It was on this final point that Faulkner balked and, as a result, Heath prorogued the Stormont Parliament for a year and appointed Mr William Whitelaw as Secretary-of-State for Northern Ireland to administer the Six Counties under direct rule from Westminster.

The strongest reaction came, predictably, from Craig's Vanguard movement which immediately announced a two-day token general strike in protest. The strike paralysed Belfast and most of Ulster for two days and there was some evidence that intimidation was used to ensure that it would spread even among those who did not want anything to do with it.

Just as the Southern Irish discovered, when they first gained control of their own affairs in 1921, that independence had not solved the Irish Question but had merely transferred it from England's plate to their own, so Heath and Whitelaw quickly discovered, if they did not already know, that direct rule did not provide in itself an answer to any of the many almost unanswerable problems that have bedevilled the 'State' of Northern Ireland since its inception.

And so, far from moving the troops out, the announcement of the initiative was followed by the news that Britain had additional troops standing by for service in Ulster to bring the number up to 18,500. In a television speech to the nation Mr Heath assured the people of Northern Ireland on three separate occasions that they would never be forced into an all-Ireland Republic against their will, but politicians have been known to break such solemn promises in the past, and there are cynics who argue that if a politician makes a point of repeating a promise three times in one speech it merely means that he is three times as likely to go back on his word.

Nevertheless, in spite of such misgivings, the initiative seemed, at first, to be working. Mr Whitelaw's patient, dogged determination not to be hustled into making a false move, and his obvious concern for the rights of the Catholic minority were enormously reassuring. He came across well on television; you got the impression that this was a quiet man whose word you could trust. There was a reconciliation between Craig and Faulkner; the S.D.L.P. announced that it would support the initiative; and there were pleas for peace from the Catholic hierarchy. Despite the fact that both wings of the I.R.A.

rejected the initiative and pledged themselves to continue the terrorist campaign, there was a distinct easing of tension. The ban on processions was lifted in April, and by May, 377 of the interned men had been released from Long Kesh, the prison ship *Maidstone* and the Magilligan Camp near Londonderry. The *Maidstone* was closed down as a prison ship.

But the violence continued. In the first six weeks after direct rule had been introduced, 36 people (27 civilians and 9 soldiers) were killed and there were 119 bomb incidents. One bomb in Kelly's bar in Belfast injured 47 people, and 12 people were injured when a bomb exploded in a parked car in Sandy Row in May.

The period was marked, too, by a noticeable increase in the numbers of armed Protestant vigilantes prowling around the Belfast streets. The U.D.A. (Ulster Defence Association) emerged as a new private Protestant army, its members usually dressed in para-military camouflaged uniforms, and frequently masked. At least 100,000 firearms remained lawfully in Protestant hands in Ulster, and Heaven knows how many are hidden away illegally.

But the initiative was welcomed by Jack Lynch as a step forward in Anglo-Irish relations, and as a gesture he announced that I.R.A. men arrested in the Republic would in future be tried by a tribunal of judges and not by juries, who – understandably – had proved consistently reluctant to find them guilty of anything.

There were other signs of a desire to end it all. There was a demonstration by the women of Derry calling for an end to violence, and five Derry housewives went to Belfast for talks with Mr Whitelaw.

The Provisionals offered a cease-fire from midnight on 26 May, but, to show that they were not by any means at the end of their tether, went on shooting soldiers right up to the stroke of midnight. The cease-fire was largely effective, though the executions and the sectarian killings went on. In protest against the Army's failure to remove the barricades in the 'No Go' areas of Belfast and Derry, behind which, they claimed, the I.R.A. terrorists were hiding, the U.D.A. began to erect its own 'No Go' areas, hi-jacking 27 buses for the purpose and driving steel poles into the roadway.

On Sunday 9 July the cease-fire was called off, and the bomb explosions started again. Mr Whitelaw had secret meetings with I.R.A. leaders in London, the Twelfth passed off peacefully enough (only two soldiers and two civilians killed and ten soldiers injured), then, on Friday 22 July, 11 people died and 130 were injured when

26 bombs were exploded all over Belfast – in two bus stations, a railway station, a hotel and on a bridge over the Lagan. Another 4,000 troops were sent to Ulster, bringing the total up to 21,000, and on Monday 31 July they moved in strength on the 'No Go' areas, and, unopposed, opened up the Bogside and Creggan areas. It was emphasized that this was not an attempt to seek a military solution but merely an effort to remove the capacity of the Provisionals to cause suffering, while an economic and political solution was being sought. As I write (1 August 1972) it is too early to say what will happen but it looks as if Mr Heath's political initiative may have produced an atmosphere in which what still remains of the Irish Question can at least be discussed.

What other courses were open to Heath? One possibility would have been the total integration of Northern Ireland within the United Kingdom, with presumably a larger representation at Westminster. Paisley has come out strongly in favour of this, as a safeguard against a reunified Ireland and the dangers of the Protestants becoming a minority in a state dominated by the Church of Rome, which he has referred to in writing as 'the Mother of Harlots and the Abomination of the Earth'.

But the British Government would probably be chary of this because it would almost certainly lead to problems with the Republic. And recently, until the escalation of I.R.A. violence following internment without trial, the British and Irish Governments have been getting on better than at any period in history. Economically – and more than ever, as they go into the Common Market together – they are becoming increasingly interdependent. It is true that the Republic is infinitely more dependent on Britain than vice versa, but nevertheless, Britain has tremendous investment interests in Ireland. Many of the new chains of hotels and supermarkets as well as the factories are owned by British groups. Ireland is a natural and attractive tourist playground, with miles of good, empty roads where browned-off British motorists can enjoy driving again, in the sterling area, within easy reach, and English-speaking into the bargain. In addition, there are tens of thousands of Irishmen and women living in Britain, doing jobs that the British workers themselves would prefer not to do, and doing them well. Full integration of the Six Counties – which all Irish Republicans and most middle-of-the-road southern Irish still regard as Irish territory – would be likely to upset all this.

There were several other possibilities open to Heath. The British

Government could have pulled out altogether, leaving Stormont to solve its own problems. If that had happened, it is quite possible that Craig's militant Protestants would have fallen on the Catholic 'enemy in their midst'. And if the massacres had been sufficiently numerous or prolonged, they might have resulted in an unofficial or even an official intervention by the Republic and the end might well have been civil war. At the very least, the I.R.A. would have stepped up its operations to an extent which would have been tantamount to civil war.

If the British had pulled out and handed Northern Ireland over to the Republic, there is not much doubt that the Ulster Catholic Nationalists, sure of protection from a Republic Government, would have made life extremely uncomfortable for what would immediately have become an unpopular Protestant minority in an overwhelmingly Catholic state. Such a move would have meant, in fact, abandoning one million fervently loyal, though highly troublesome, subjects of the Queen to the sort of fate they have been imposing on the 500,000 Catholic Nationalists in their tight little Protestant state for the past fifty years. There might be some sort of poetic justice in this, but it would have been difficult for Britain to do, especially in the light of the Ireland Act of 1949, which specifically guaranteed that this would not happen without the consent of the Northern Ireland Parliament. Now, of course, for a year anyway, there is no Northern Ireland Parliament to give its consent, which wipes that guarantee out, but it has been replaced with Mr Heath's promise of periodic plebiscites.

Another possibility might have been the redrawing of the border to include, as far as possible, only the overwhelmingly Protestant areas. The Ulster Unionists wouldn't hear of this when Home Rule was first discussed, but they might have been prepared to accept it in March 1972, *faute de mieux* and in preference to direct rule from Westminster. For one thing, the old argument that the smaller, exclusively Protestant state would not be viable economically is no longer credible since the current, much larger Six County area has not proved viable either, without considerable economic aid from Britain. This might still prove to be the nearest approach to a solution of what is basically an insoluble problem.

I don't think the McCann/Devlin dream of an independent International Socialist Workers' Republic along the Cuban pattern need be very seriously considered as likely to emerge from the Northern Ireland situation in what politicians refer to as 'the foreseeable future'.

There was, of course, one cast-iron solution to most of Ulster's problems, but, sadly, it was the least likely one in the context of the events of the last three years: prosperity. If there were two cars and a boat to every household in Northern Ireland, most of the bitter sectarianism would vanish overnight. It could still happen. If the British initiative is accompanied by a massive investment programme, both to repair the damage and to get the industrial revolution initiated by Terence O'Neill under way again, and if the I.R.A. and the Protestant ultras can be persuaded, or forced, to abandon violence, it is still possible that an atmosphere may be created in Northern Ireland in which people will tend to think less and less about religion and politics and more and more about keeping up with the Faulkners. But it will be a very long time, I'm afraid, before foreign industrialists will be again tempted to put the sort of money that is needed to get Ulster under way again into industries in an area with such a bad record of violence – and you cannot blame them.

Another solution which was widely discussed was a Declaration of Rights with a supra-national, overriding body to see that these rights were everywhere observed. To be credible and acceptable to the Ulster Nationalists, this body would have had to include representatives from the Republic as well as from Stormont and Westminster. The Protestant Unionists would not have been too happy at the prospect of a supra-national tribunal which included Irish Catholic Republicans with power to impose its findings on Ulster; but under the umbrella of such a supra-national body, it would have been easier to control the I.R.A. with the active support of the Government of the Republic and if the citizens of that Republic had themselves been subject to the findings of a council which also included a fair proportion of British and Ulster Protestants, some of the sting might have been taken out of it, and it would have ensured no undue interference from the Catholic hierarchy. Such an arrangement would have entailed a certain loss of sovereignty all round, but early in 1972 both Jack Lynch and Edward Heath signed away a considerable measure of their sovereignty when they signed the Common Market papers, and such a tribunal would have given Faulkner a far larger hand in running things than he now has, under Mr Heath's temporary initiative. So a federal solution along these lines, especially if linked to the whole Common Market line-up, remains a distinct long-term policy.

But it will take months of talk to reach agreement and in the meantime, I am afraid, the Prods and the Papishes will go on killing one another in the streets of Derry and Belfast and in the border towns and villages of Ulster.

If there really is a God up there somewhere, and if he ever did incarnate himself as a Jewish Arab desert preacher whose message (if it could be condensed into one sentence) was 'Love thy neighbour', he must be utterly baffled at the way in which two equally devout factions of his followers have been interpreting that message in Northern Ireland in recent years.

# A Note on the Sources used in Compiling this Book

In the case of this book which in effect covers the impact of religion on history (if in a sketchy and perfunctory way) throughout Christendom from the birth of Christ to the Reformation, all over the British Isles from the Reformation until the Bloodless Revolution of 1688, and in Ireland since then, it would be impossible to give a conventional select bibliography, and presumptuous to suggest a comprehensive list of books for further reading, since versions of most of the matters discussed can be found in any of hundreds of books on various aspects of history available through all the ordinary channels.

So perhaps the most helpful thing which I can do is to give some indication of the books which I found most useful both in providing a general framework within which to place events and my own particular interpretation of them, and also to list books on particular aspects of problems which have not been so widely discussed and consequently are not so well known.

Three books which I have always found curiously, almost perversely, useful in putting historical and religious events in their proper context in relation to the development of mankind are H. G. Wells's *A Short History of the World* (London: Cassell, 1922); Winwood Reade's *The Martyrdom of Man* (London and Edinburgh: Trubener and Co., 1872); and Hendrik Willem Van Loon's *The Story of Mankind* (London: Harrap, 1922) which was written for children but contains many odd, quirky items of extremely adult common sense which are frequently missed by professional adult historians.

Turning to my own book, section by section, the details about Cromwell's campaign in Ireland are mostly taken from *Cromwell in Ireland* by the Rev. Denis Murphy, S.J. (Dublin: M. H. Gill and Son Ltd., 1883), until recently one of very few books devoted exclusively to Cromwell's Irish campaign. Other books on Cromwell which I consulted in writing this (and the subsequent chapters on Cromwell's attempt at a solution to the Irish Question and on his relations with Parliament in England) include D. M. R. Esson's *The Curse of Cromwell* (London: Leo Cooper, 1971); *Cromwell* by Hilaire Belloc (London: Cassell, 1934); and *Oliver Cromwell* by John Buchan (London: Hodder and Stoughton, 1934).

The section on the origin and development of the early Christian Church was based on a number of sources. Roland H. Bainton's *A History of Christianity* (American Heritage Publishing Co. Inc., 1964) is a beautifully illustrated and readable general survey. Colin Cross's excellent series on early Christianity published in *The Observer* Colour Supplement in April 1967 also proved useful, as did his study of the life of Christ, *Who Was Jesus?* (London: Hodder and Stoughton, 1970). Another useful book was C. J. Cadoux's *The Life of Jesus* (A Pelican original, London: Penguin Books, 1948). On the section dealing with early schisms and controversies I found Henry Chadwick's *The Early Church* (Pelican History of the Church, London: Penguin Books, 1967) very helpful, as well as both Bainton and Cross.

We are now getting on to more difficult ground. The period from the time of Charlemagne and the revival of the Roman Empire, through the Crusades and the struggle between the popes and the emperors to the disputes between the Papacy and the kings and parliaments about such matters as clerical courts and taxes is so well-documented that to list the handful of books which I did consult would be merely inviting people to write in and ask why I did not consult others in their opinion more reliable and authoritative. Because I happen to have them handy, I tended to check dates, names, sequence of events, etc. from such books as H. A. L. Fisher's *A History of Europe* (London: Eyre and Spottiswoode, 1935); the above mentioned H. G. Wells's *A Short History of the World*, Sidney Painter's *A History of the Middle Ages, 248–1500* (London: Macmillan, 1953) plus relevant volumes of the *New Cambridge Modern History*. To check on matters concerning papal bulls, I went to a number of specialized books on comparative religion, the most generally useful and readable of which I found to be *Religions of the World* by John A. Hardon, S.J., Associate Professor of Comparative Religion at the Western Michigan University (Maryland: The Newman Press, 1963).

Once we reach the Reformation and the events in England during which what I have described as the Pendulum Years (i.e. the years between Henry VIII's break with Rome and the defeat of James II, the last Catholic King of England, in 1690), I have used as standard works of reference the appropriate volumes of *The Oxford History of England*, edited by Sir George Clark (Vols VI–X); Macaulay's *England*, Vol. I (London: Longman Green, 1860); *The Great Rebellion* by Ivan Roots (London: Batsford, 1966); C. V. Wedgwood's *The King's Peace* (London: Collins, 1955), *The King's War* (London: Collins, 1958), and *The Trial of Charles I* (London: Collins, 1964). To fill in the general sociological background of the period, Sir Arthur Bryant's *Protestant Island* (London: Collins, 1966) is invaluable. For details of the Protestant massacres, Foxe's *Book of Martyrs* is available in variously abridged versions, some illustrated with splendidly bloodthirsty contemporary woodcuts, through the Protestant Truth Society.

Once the scene moves to Ireland, the problem becomes less difficult because the sources become more selective. For general background, Edmund Curtis's *A History of Ireland* (London: Methuen, 1936), if slightly indigestible, is accurate and comprehensive. Other general background books worth reading include *The Story of Ireland* by Brian Inglis (London: Faber, 1956); *A Short History of Ireland* by J. C. Beckett (London: Hutchinson, 1952); *The Mind and Face of Ireland* by Arland Ussher (London: Gollancz, 1949); *The Shaping of Modern Ireland* by Conor Cruise O'Brien (London: Routledge and Kegan Paul, 1960); *Ireland*, by Terence de Vere White (London: Thames and Hudson, 1968); and *A History of Modern Ireland* by Edward Norman (London: Chatto and Windus, 1969). To fill in the sociological background picture, *Life in Ireland* by L. M. Cullen (London: Batsford, 1968) is colourful and detailed. For information about the Famine, it would be impossible to improve on *The Great Hunger* by Cecil Woodham Smith (London: Hamish Hamilton, 1962), and *The Year of Liberty, 1798* by Thomas Pakenham is by far the fullest and best documented book on that rebellion and the events immediately before and after it.

Coming to more recent events, first in what is now known as the Republic of Ireland, the standard work is Dorothy Macardle's *The Irish Republic* (Dublin: Irish Press, 1951). Other, more specialized works include Max Caulfield's *The Easter Rebellion* (London: Frederick Muller, 1964); *The Orange and the Green* by Clifford King (London: Macdonald, 1965); *Peace by Ordeal* by Frank Pakenham (London: Chapman, 1962); and *De Valera* by Sean O'Faolain (A

Penguin original, London: Penguin Books, 1947). For a highly readable, very brief (and well-illustrated) run-down on events leading up to Ireland's final fight for freedom, and its immediate aftermath, you couldn't do better than Constantine Fitzgibbon's *Out of the Lion's Paw* (London: MacDonald, 1969).

Constantine Fitzgibbon has also written one of the most comprehensive and useful accounts of more recent events in Ulster, *Red Hand: The Ulster Colony* (London: Michael Joseph, 1971). Other books on this subject include *Ulster Since 1800*, edited by T. W. Moody and J. C. Beckett (Belfast: B.B.C., 1954); *Governing without Consensus* by Richard Rose (London: Faber, 1971); *Ulster* by *The Sunday Times* 'Insight Team' (A Penguin original, London: Penguin Books, 1972) and *The Battle of the Bogside* by Russell Stetler (London: Sheed and Ward, 1970). In addition, the Irish news-magazine, *Nusight* dated September 1969, devoted a whole issue to the development of the crisis in Northern Ireland, and the Irish review *Hibernia* keeps a fortnightly tally on events in Ulster, including all casualties on both sides. Finally, I consulted the infamous Special Powers Act – its full title is the Civil Authorities (Special Powers) Act (Northern Ireland) 1922 – and tried to keep abreast of the almost endless stream of newspaper, week-end review and magazine articles on the Ulster crisis and the equally voluminous television coverage, an almost impossible task in a situation that kept changing from week to week.

# Index